About this book

What happens in post-war Iraq may well be decided by what happens in Tehran. This is one message of this powerful account of the theocratic regime still in power in Iran. The author pays particular attention to the Iranian factor in the recent Iraq War (2003), and the likely impact on the future course of events in Iraq of the continuation of the Iranian regime's interference in its neighbour's affairs. He reveals startling new information about Iran's continued 'export' of Islamic fundamentalism, the pursuit of its nuclear ambitions, and its ongoing use of terrorism against its own opponents – all of which justify a high level of international concern. The author argues that, in contrast to the ruling regime, the main Iranian opposition is a democratic, nationalist movement that favours a separation of religion and state. He argues that the 'clash of Islams' between the democratic and fundamentalist versions of this religion in Iran will have far-reaching consequences for the entire Muslim world.

About the author

Mohammad Mohaddessin has been a life-long opponent of autocracy in Iran. The son of a prominent ayatollah in Qom, Mohaddessin was imprisoned under the Shah for his opposition to dictatorship and subsequently forced into exile by Ayatollah Khomeini. He is the chairman of the Foreign Affairs Committee of the National Council of Resistance of Iran, which is the main umbrella group for the diverse movements opposed to the continuance of theocratic rule in Iran.

Mohaddessin has written extensively on political and religious issues in Iran and throughout the region. In addition to many articles and essays, he has authored several books, including *Democracy Betrayed, An Unethical Policy, Appeasing Tehran's Mullahs* and *Legacy of a Misguided Policy*. His most widely known work in North America is *Islamic Fundamentalism: The New Global Threat* (Seven Locks Press, Washington DC, 2001).

MOHAMMAD MOHADDESSIN

Enemies of the Ayatollahs

**the Iranian opposition and its war on
Islamic fundamentalism**

Zed Books
LONDON · NEW YORK

Enemies of the Ayatollahs: the Iranian opposition and its war on Islamic fundamentalism was first published by Zed Books Ltd, 7 Cynthia Street, London N1 9JF, UK and Room 400, 175 Fifth Avenue, New York, NY 10010, USA in 2004.

www.zedbooks.co.uk

Cover designed by Andrew Corbett
Set in Monotype Dante and Gill Sans Heavy by Ewan Smith, London
Printed and bound in Malta by Gutenberg Press Ltd

Distributed in the USA exclusively by Palgrave Macmillan, a division of St Martin's Press, LLC, 175 Fifth Avenue, New York, NY 10010.

A catalogue record for this book is available from the British Library.
US CIP data is available from the Library of Congress.

2nd impression, 2004

ISBN 1 84277 530 8 cased
ISBN 1 84277 531 6 limp

Contents

Preface by Lord Alton of Liverpool [1]

For over a century, Iran has often been a weathervane of political trends in the Middle East. It led the way against absolute monarchy with its 1906 Constitutional Revolution. It espoused the cause of oil nationalization at the dawn of the 1950s. Its 1979 revolution brought to the surface all the grievances and anger of a Middle Eastern nation against unquestioning Western support for the Shah: an ally who remained indifferent to pluralism and democracy. It was events in Iran that portended the ominous ascent of Islamic fundamentalism in the 1980s. Today, again, it is the news from Iran that signals the closing chapter of theocratic tyranny in that country.

To speak of the demise of the Islamic fundamentalist regime in Iran is not an attempt at political clairvoyance, nor false overoptimism. It is true that if history is a guide, we would be well advised not to forecast the turn of events in the Middle East's capricious politics. Yet, having followed with great interest political developments in the Middle East, and particularly in Iran, since my early days in Westminster in 1979, I am convinced that Iran today is on the brink of change. Despite the wars, unrest, terror and fundamentalism that have plagued Iran and the broader Persian Gulf region in recent decades, this ancient cradle of civilization stands on the threshold of a seismic shift in its long history; a shift that will enable this great nation finally to shed the status of a pariah state and take the place that it truly deserves in the family of nations.

What makes the conditions ripe for such a sea-change in Iran? The basic answer is: the Iranian people. Popular discontent against the fundamentalist rulers has never run higher. The vast majority of Iranians, particularly the 20-plus million Iranians between the ages of fifteen and thirty, almost a third of the country's population, have shown their desire for an end to religious dictatorship. They are fed up with rampant corruption and chronic mismanagement of an economy which, despite huge oil revenues, produces no jobs for millions of Iranians. They are tired of the pervasive inquisition, where every minute detail of citizens' private lives can come under the punishing scrutiny of the moral police. They seek an end to the draconian suppression of dissent, to the pervasive discrimination against women, to the brutal treatment of religious and ethnic minorities.

Despite the theocratic state's crackdown, intimidation and threats, tens of thousands of students have been risking their lives at anti-government demonstrations to chant such slogans as 'down with dictatorship' and 'Khatami resign'. This demonstrates that they have no illusions about President Mohammad Khatami and that they seek the overthrow of the regime in its entirety.

While change will definitely come to Iran in the hands of the Iranian people and those who genuinely reflect their democratic yearnings and demands, the international community, and the West in particular, have a constructive role to play. They must adopt a policy towards Iran that would encourage the Iranian people in their quest for freedom and human rights and deter the ruling mullahs' export of terrorism and development of nuclear weapons and ballistic missiles. Unfortunately, this is not the case at present. Western governments are too willing to dismiss the continuing grave violation of human rights in Iran as an unfortunate aberration which should not get in the way of undertaking 'business as usual'. They have attempted to confer upon the regime a wholly undeserved aura of respectability.

How can it be business as usual with a regime that has been responsible for the deaths of an estimated 120,000 political prisoners? How can it be business as usual with a regime that continues to use stoning as a form of punishment, with a court in Mashad sentencing four persons to death by stoning as recently as 11 November 2003? How can it be business as usual with a regime that has developed Shahab missiles that can reach all Middle East capitals and many in southern Europe; that is developing weapons of mass destruction; and that has been cheating and deceiving the international community over its secret nuclear weapon project; lies that have now been catalogued in a detailed report by the International Atomic Energy Agency?

The West has a sordid memory of the folly of appeasement. The lesson of Munich 1938 was that efforts to engage and appease, rather than isolate, an outlaw regime will only whet the insatiable appetite of the aggressor. Today, we are making the same grave mistake in Iran. The British Foreign Secretary, Jack Straw, describes our current policy towards Iran as 'constructive dialogue'. We are told that soon we will be engaged in a human rights dialogue with Tehran and expand our political and trade relations. But there has been no sign of the 'constructiveness' of this engagement. The human rights situation in Iran, according to credible international organizations, has deteriorated, while Tehran remains the world's most active state sponsor of terrorism and the greatest source of instability in the region.

The European governments' policy has been based on a myth: that there is a genuine moderate faction within the regime willing and able to bring about real change. This may have been wishful thinking years ago. Now, after nearly two terms of Khatami's presidency, it is naïve to go on with this self-delusion.

Our governments should listen to the message from the millions of Iranians in Iran, and their message is loud and clear. They are determined to put an end to the religious dictatorship. When in October 2003 Mrs Maryam Rajavi, President-elect of the National Council of Resistance of Iran, called for a referendum under United Nations supervision to give the people of Iran a fair chance to determine their own destiny peacefully through the ballot-box, the reaction from the ruling ayatollahs was predictably negative. But the idea of such a referendum has struck a deep chord among Iranians of all walks of life and the pressure on the clerical rulers is rising. The West must add its voice to those who support such a referendum as the best option and perhaps a final opportunity to resolve the Iranian crisis peacefully.

For the moment, however, the same old policies persist and engagement is still viewed by some Western capitals as the preferred way of dealing with the ruling clerics in Tehran. To mollify Iran's mullahs, some governments have even branded the People's Mojahedin Organization of Iran as a terrorist organization. The PMOI is incontestably the most active opposition to the Tehran regime inside and outside of Iran. It is also indisputable that the Iranian regime considers the PMOI as its number-one enemy and a threat to its survival. The movement espouses a democratic, modern and tolerant interpretation of Islam. It thus has a unique role in combating Islamic fundamentalism.

The greatest conundrum facing the West in its dealings with the Islamic world is how to counter Islamic fundamentalism without offending the religion of Islam and Muslims. The answer is to be found in movements like the People's Mojahedin. It is tragic, therefore, to find that some governments are paying the price of their rapprochement with Iran's theocratic regime at the expense of the PMOI. This is ethically wrong and politically counterproductive. How can it ever be ethical to condemn the victims in order to appease the oppressor?

Having known this movement and studied it closely for over two decades, I have never been convinced by the Blair government's decision to place the Mojahedin on the terrorist list. After all, David Blunkett, the Home Secretary, has acknowledged that the PMOI has not engaged in any attack against UK or Western interests over the past two decades and has no plan to do so. Moreover, the PMOI's military conduct falls perfectly within the international laws governing wars of liberation. I can see little difference between them and, for instance, Nelson Mandela's African National Congress. Let us hope that Mandela's inspiration, and the peaceful transition to democracy – followed by truth and reconciliation in South Africa – will be a model for Iran.

The PMOI has been recognized as a legitimate resistance movement not only by the majority of the House of Commons and more than 120 peers, but also by the majority of the US Congress and parliaments in several European countries.

It is true that the PMOI has been the subject of a most venomous propaganda campaign to tarnish its image at home and abroad. Having failed to destroy the resistance through the sheer ferocity of repression, the Iranian regime has been levying a litany of accusations against its main opponents. For a long time, my parliamentary colleagues and I have been receiving a motley collection of anti-PMOI literature from the Iranian embassy in London. One of the allegations that I personally followed with profound interest concerned the gruesome murder of three leaders of the Anglican Church in Iran in 1994. We were told that three women publicly confessed to have received orders from the Mojahedin to murder the Christian priests. Subsequently, the women were found guilty by a religious court and the Iranian authorities even invited Western diplomats to attend the trial as observers. Several years later, however, former intelligence officials of the Iranian regime revealed that the three priests had been murdered by agents of the Ministry of Intelligence and Security and that all the allegations against the PMOI involvement in the killings were fabricated to discredit the movement.

The propaganda campaign against the PMOI has been well orchestrated, well financed and at times quite sophisticated. Anyone who has studied in detail many of the allegations against the movement can see that they bear all the hallmarks of propaganda: sinister untruths, crafted simply to distract.

The West's gravest mistake in this raging battle between the Iranian regime and its opposition would be to take the side of the clerical regime. We must remember that in this part of the world, we have been wrong before. During the time of the Shah, we did not anticipate change until it was too late, a serious miscalculation. Western governments continued their support for the Shah until the very last days of his power. We ignored the Iranian people and their genuine desires for change and we lost. We can ill afford to repeat the same mistake now; neither for the future of Iran and the Middle East, nor for our own security and prosperity.

Note

1. David Alton is a crossbench peer and professor of citizenship at Liverpool's John Moores University. For eighteen years, he was a member of the House of Commons.

Foreword by Raymond Tanter[1]

The powerful blasts that have shaken Bali, Jakarta, Casablanca, Bombay, Mombassa, Riyadh, Baghdad and Istanbul since the attacks of 11 September 2001 and claimed hundreds of innocent lives have made one thing crystal clear. The chilling attacks in New York and Washington on that fateful Tuesday morning did not represent a final magnum opus of terrorists on the fast track to oblivion in a globalized world, but the opening salvo of a more violent confrontation between radical Islam (Islamism) and the West.

After two American-led wars in Afghanistan and Iraq, no country today occupies a more central place in the debate over this confrontation than the Islamic Republic of Iran. To a large extent, the hyped-up speculation and media clamour over a secret US agenda to seek military confrontation with Iran after the overthrow of the rogue regime in Baghdad clouded the underlying issues: the threat militant Islam poses to peace and security and the prominent role of Iran at the apex of a terror coalition.

Just as a fire occurs when heat, fuel and oxygen converge, so terrorism transpires when rogue regimes, formal organizations and radical Islam come together. With the fall of Baghdad, Tehran sits unchallenged at the top of the terrorism triangle. Another point on the triangle contains formal organizations that resort to terrorism in the name of Islam; the third point includes radical Islamic movements backed up by *madrassas* that teach hatred of the West to unsuspecting youths eager to learn the Koran.

It is critical for American policy-makers to connect the dots of the terror triangle and to understand the crucial role of Iran at its apex. Indeed, the US Department of State's Patterns of Global Terrorism, an overview of state-sponsored terrorism, finds that 'Iran remained the most active state sponsor of terrorism in 2002. Its Islamic Revolutionary Guard Corps and Ministry of Intelligence and Security were involved in the planning of and support for terrorist acts and continued to exhort a variety of groups that use terrorism to pursue their goals.'[2]

In addition to terrorism, Washington recognizes Iran as a world-class proliferator of weapons of mass destruction (WMD). It is Tehran's role at the intersection of terrorism and proliferation that makes Iran such a global threat.

After repeated assertions by senior US officials, including the President, that the administration is not seeking a military solution to the Iranian problem, a more logical and in-depth debate on what to do about Iran is emerging on both sides of the Atlantic. The present book makes a major contribution to this debate. The book places diplomatic events in the context of Tehran's state-sponsorship of international terrorism and proliferation of WMD.

In this respect, the intense diplomatic jostling, posturing and bargaining behind closed doors at the Vienna headquarters of the International Atomic Energy Agency and in various Western capitals in November 2003 over the wording of the IAEA governing board's resolution on Iran marks a step in the right direction. True, the final outcome is a compromise between a US desire to take the irrefutable evidence of long-standing Iranian non-compliance with its international non-proliferation commitments to the UN Security Council and a stubborn insistence by France, Britain and Germany not to alienate Tehran. But the international community's 'ominous message' to Tehran, as IAEA chief Mohamed ElBaradei put it, was that 'failures in the future will not be tolerated'. This was a far cry from the rosy praise for Iran's 'innocuous' nuclear programme that typified past statements from Vienna.

More significantly, the discussions that culminated in the consensus resolution marked a new framework for the debate over Iran that went beyond the nuclear issue. Despite the tenacious tendency of several European governments to preserve and expand lucrative trade ties with Tehran, the more prevalent mood among Western nations is one of growing alarm and apprehension at the way the Iranian theocracy has been pursuing such nefarious activities as terrorism, political repression and acquisition of weapons of mass destruction.

The ascendancy and continuing domination of Tehran's policies by Islamist clerics means that the likelihood of a moderate state emerging from the current theocracy in Iran is as remote as that of a leopard changing its spots. Iran under clerical rule remains the world's most active state sponsor of terrorism, exporting Islamism to the world.

It is only natural that such a regime in Iran would regard Iraq in its present state as the most important battleground in its quest to dominate the Persian Gulf. Iran, four times as large and three times as populated as Iraq, has a long history of interference in Iraq's internal affairs that, in recent decades, stretches back to the Shah's support for the unsuccessful Kurdish insurgency in northern Iraq and, later, the ayatollahs' overt goal of setting up an Islamic republic in Mesopotamia. In his political will, Ayatollah Khomeini urged his disciples to uphold the goal of 'liberating Qods (Jerusalem) via Karbala'.

Even after the fall of Saddam Hussein's regime, Iran remains home to the largest Iraqi expatriate community in the world. Iraq shares its longest border with Iran. It has a majority Shiite population with strong religious and historical bonds with fellow-Shiites in Iran. Many members of the Iraqi Governing Council have spent long years of their lives in Iran or have enjoyed Tehran's political patronage.

But all these factors, however important in their own right, have today become secondary to the top priority for Iran's ayatollahs: the defeat of the United States and its allies in Iraq. They regard this goal, with some justification, as vital to their interests and critical to the survival of clerical rule in Iran. A repeat of a Lebanon or Somalia scenario, where US forces were forced to withdraw for fear of further casualties and the Islamists obligingly filled the resulting power vacuum, is no longer an ambitious agenda, but a goal Tehran's mullahs consider attainable. Since the 1980 US presidential elections, the mullahs have shown themselves to be canny manipulators, quite capable of taking advantage of election-year American politics to achieve their ominous goals.

The Iranian regime clearly sees the rising terrorism and crisis in Iraq as a necessary prelude to its objectives in Iraq, and the ultimate goal of setting up an Iranian-style theocracy in that country. As the United States faces a tougher-than-expected challenge in stabilizing Iraq and events in that country begin to resonate in American politics, the Iranian leaders grow more strident in their public pronouncements. In a speech on Eid al-Fitr to mark the end of the holy month of Ramadan, Supreme Leader Ali Khamenei said: 'The drunkard ranting of America against Middle Eastern countries is only the result of disunity among Muslims. To break out of this situation, Muslim nations and govern-ments must unite.' He added: 'The American nation should know that Iraq is America's quagmire and America is sinking deeper into it by staying longer in Iraq.

'The Americans, who entered Iraq in the name of human rights, have oppressed the Iraqis so much that they punched the Americans in the face,' Khamenei said. 'The Americans' claim about bringing democracy to the region is a disgraceful lie.'

The Iranian regime is putting its mouth where its money is. Today, evidence of Iranian meddling and pervasive presence in post-Baathist Iraq abounds, particularly in the south. Back in August 2003, the top US administrator in Iraq, Ambassador Paul Bremer, told CNN: 'The

Iranian Revolutionary Guards are present in Iraq, the Iranian Ministry of Intelligence is present here and we think that Iraqis do not appreciate interference in their affairs.' A month later, he said, 'Iranian intelligence agents have been aiding groups that have carried out violent attacks in different parts of Iraq.'

Bremer told a Senate Appropriations Committee hearing in September that sixty-two captured Iranians were the second largest group of detained saboteurs. 'Elements of the Iranian government are causing mischief in Iraq, interfering in affairs through their intelligence services and through the Revolutionary Guards. This is not helpful.'

Iran has been sending thousands of firebrand Muslim clerics into Iraq to dominate *madrassas* and take over the reins of power in villages and towns throughout the south and in many other parts of Iraq. They now dominate a major portion of southern Iraq, including Samawa, Meissan, Nasiriyah, Basra, Wassit, Karbala and Najaf provinces.

The Iranian Revolutionary Guards' Qods (Jerusalem) Force has been setting up armed underground cells across the Shiite-dominated southern regions of Iraq, while using the Iranian Red Crescent or Iranian-backed indigenous groups as a front. It has set up medical centres and local charities in Najaf, Baghdad, Hillah, Basra and Al Amarah to garner support among the local population, in much the same way as the Revolutionary Guards did in Lebanon's Bekaa Valley.

The stakes are high in Iraq. A precipitate US withdrawal would give the Islamist extremists their biggest-ever success, with unforeseeable impact on the entire Muslim world from Morocco to Indonesia. Conversely, the emergence of a prosperous, democratic Iraq would be a mortal threat to the unpopular rule of Islamist mullahs in Iran. Western governments have a shared interest in ensuring that Islamism does not succeed in Iraq. They must convince the Muslim world that their conflict with Islamists is not a war on Islam or a latter-day Christian Crusade. To do so, they must acknowledge and support those courageous Muslims who are speaking out against Islamism and fanaticism. There is a vibrant, viable and democratic alternative to the Islamism of Iran's ayatollahs, as the Iranian opposition has shown.

It is in this context that I find this book a timely addition to the critical debate over Iran, Iraq and the path that lies ahead of that region of the world. The book is a powerful exposé of the undercurrent of events in Iraq and Iran. It argues in clear terms against the appeasement of the clerical regime in Iran, noting that concessions to rogue states only embolden them without having any moderating influence on their outlaw behaviour. The prospect of a nuclear-armed government in Tehran driven by religious extremism must be a sobering reminder to the West that it can ignore this threat only at its peril.

Notes

1. Professor emeritus of political science at the University of Michigan, adjunct professor at Georgetown University, adjunct scholar of the Washington Institute for Near East Policy, a member of the Council on Foreign Relations, and a former staff member of the National Security Council at the White House. He is the author of *Rogue Regimes: Terrorism and Proliferation* (New York: St Martin's Press, 1999).

2. US Department of State, *Patterns of Global Terrorism*, 2002, released by the Office of the Coordinator for Counterterrorism, 30 April 2003, <http://www.state.gov/s/ct/rls/pgtrpt/2002/html/19988pf.htm>.

Abbreviations and acronyms

AFP	Agence France Presse
BBC	British Broadcasting Corporation
BfV	Bundesamt für Verfassungsschutz (Office for the Protection of the Constitution)
BVD	Binnenlandse Veiligheidsdienst (Netherlands National Intelligence and Security Agency)
CAR	Centre for Atomic Research (Iran)
DIO	Defence Industry Organization (Iran)
FBI	Federal Bureau of Investigation (USA)
IAEA	International Atomic Energy Agency
IAEO	Iranian Atomic Energy Organization
ICBM	inter-continental ballistic missile
ICCO	Islamic Culture and Communications Organization
ICRC	International Committee of the Red Cross
IDS	Institute for Democratic Strategies
IHL	international humanitarian law
IISS	International Institute for Strategic Studies
IRGC	Islamic Revolutionary Guards Corps (Iran)
IRNA	Islamic Republic News Agency (Iran)
LEU	low enriched uranium
MeK	Mujaheddin-e Khalq
MOIS	Ministry of Intelligence and Security (Iran)
NCRI	National Council of Resistance of Iran
NLA	National Liberation Army of Iran
NPT	Non-proliferation Treaty
PMOI	People's Mojahedin Organization of Iran
SCIRI	Supreme Council for the Islamic Revolution in Iraq
SNSC	Supreme National Security Council (Iran)
UCF	Uranium Conversion Facility
UNMOVIC	United Nations Monitoring, Verification and Inspection Commission
USCENTCOM	United States Central Command
VEVAK	Ministry for Intelligence and Security (Iran)
WMD	weapons of mass destruction

Introduction

Truth never damages a just cause. *Mahatma Gandhi*[1]

The Middle East is an area scarred by conflicts, some almost as old as civilization itself. Even by the standards of this tormented, violence-stricken region, however, the secret war waged by Tehran's ruling ayatollahs against their opponents for more than two decades has been a costly and bloody affair. Some 200 terrorist operations against Iranian dissidents outside Iran since the early 1990s, leaving more than 300 opponents of the ruling theocracy killed or wounded, form just one aspect of this ferocious secret war. The Iranian regime's use of terrorism to blackmail other countries, its back-channel deals with certain governments, its use of billion-dollar contracts to push forward its foreign policy agenda, and a vast intelligence-terrorist network stretching around the globe are other pieces of this sinister mosaic of terror, petrodollars and intrigue.

The face-off is a major part of the contemporary history of Iran and the Middle East. The resonance of numbers that sum up Iran's human rights record in the past two decades is chilling: the execution of 120,000 dissidents since 1981, the incarceration and maltreatment of hundreds of thousands of political activists, and the massacre of thousands of political prisoners in 1988 on the basis of Ayatollah Khomeini's fatwa. Indeed, as a consequence of this twenty-year confrontation and the underlying social and political tensions, Iranian society remains in a turbulent, revolutionary state.

Political observers and pundits may disagree over Iran's future course or the most likely post-clerical alternative, but few would bet on the survival of the status quo. Observers warn of 'the deepest political crisis since the 1979 Islamic revolution'.[2] The continuing anti-government demonstrations, widespread labour unrest, escalating factional infighting, the country's deteriorating economic situation and pervasive social discontent are symptoms of a terminal crisis that has beset the clerical regime. Government officials have acknowledged the arrest of more than 4,000 people during anti-government protests in Tehran and other cities in June 2003. The *Christian Science Monitor* reported that protesters not only demanded the 'execution' of the 'hard-line' Supreme Leader

Ali Khamenei, but also targeted the supposedly 'moderate' President Mohammad Khatami. It quoted 'a seasoned political analyst' in Tehran as saying: 'There is such a determination in [the demonstrators'] eyes and their behaviour. They are fearless; they are ready for combat. It's like [urban] warfare.'[3]

Simmering anger and frustration – after two decades of religious dictatorship that has imposed a most invasive repression on Iranians – have now reached boiling point. They were evident in more than a thousand demonstrations and strikes nationwide from March 2002 to March 2003. With 75 per cent of Iran's 70 million population under thirty-five and half a million joining the army of the unemployed every year, the ruling clerics know only too well that they are sitting on a time bomb.

In the area of foreign policy, optimists who thought Iran's behaviour on the regional and international scenes was mellowing as a result of domestic crises and international pressure were given a rude awakening by the clerical regime's extensive meddling in post-conflict Iraq and its continuing use of 'unconventional' means to advance its foreign policy. When Britain arrested the former Iranian ambassador to Argentina, Hadi Soleimanpour, in August 2003 after an extradition request by Argentine authorities, who suspected the former diplomat of complicity in the devastating 1994 bombing of a Jewish community centre in Buenos Aires, Tehran resorted to the old blackmail and terror tactics to have him released. Gunmen opened fire on the British embassy and diplomatic facilities in Tehran on three occasions, without being caught or even investigated. Those familiar with the stringent security measures in downtown Tehran, where the British embassy is situated, know that only gunmen on 'official' assignment could carry out such repeated attacks on this target.

The ruling ayatollahs have tried similar pressure tactics – although with less successful results, so far – when it came to their secret nuclear arms project, first revealed to the world by the Iranian opposition. In the run-up to a key meeting of the governing board of the United Nations' nuclear watchdog in September 2003, Tehran threatened to withdraw from the Non-proliferation Treaty altogether if the board adopted a harsh posture on its nuclear programme. When International Atomic Energy Agency chief Mohamed ElBaradei visited Iran in February, he was reportedly dismayed by the scale and sophistication of Tehran's nuclear facilities, particularly in the area of uranium enrichment.[4] Finally, the IAEA's governing board passed a resolution giving Tehran until the end of October to answer ElBaradei's outstanding questions. The theocratic regime's immediate reaction was to threaten a 'deep' review of co-operation with the agency. The Iranian ambassador to the IAEA, Ali Akbar Salehi, told the official news agency IRNA, 'The Western group in the (IAEA) board of governors, in line with their political goals, have made illegitimate, illegal and impractical requests from Iran.'[5] The semi-official *Jomhouri Islami* newspaper raged that Iran 'should not pay any attention to the US, the Europeans and international organizations ... and accept that the right path is the one that the North Koreans have chosen'.[6] Rhetoric aside, Tehran's favoured tactic is ambivalent procrastination, aimed at putting off international action while it buys precious time for the development of its nuclear arms programme, now at a critical stage.

As for terrorism, the mullahs' activities show no sign of abatement. A US court in September 2003 heard several experts emphasize that the Iranian regime remains the world's most active state sponsor of terrorism. They testified that Iran's Ministry of Intelligence and Security 'spends between 50 million and 100 million dollars a year sponsoring terrorist activities of various organizations'.[7]

For Iran's clerical rulers, the worst is yet to come. The sea-change in the region around Iran is making this precarious situation even more hazardous for the ruling fundamentalists. The war in Iraq and the fall of the Iraqi regime have significantly raised the stakes for the clerical regime, pushing the ruling mullahs in Iran to the brink of an inevitable choice: they must either abandon terrorism and the export of fundamentalism, policies that have been the cornerstone of clerical rule in Iran, or charge full steam ahead to exploit the instability in Iraq and the simmering conflicts in other parts of the region, tap the global potential of an Islamic fundamentalist 'front' and expand the sphere of their influence. For a regime that calls itself *Umm ol-Qora* – the mother-of-all Islamic lands – the tantalizing opportunities are hard to resist.

Dramatic geopolitical changes in the region and the unleashing of powerful forces as a result of the US-led war in Iraq have made it impossible to maintain the present balance or return to the pre-war situation. US policy-makers are now faced with a strategic choice of either withdrawing from Iraq or committing themselves to a 'must-win-whatever-it-takes' policy. The implications and ramifications of this choice for US domestic politics and foreign policy are enormous, and the debate promises to be a long and increasingly vitriolic one. Ironically, the choice facing Iran's rulers as they look on their western flanks is far more stark and unenviable. With unfriendly or hostile states almost completely surrounding the Islamic republic, the fundamentalist state's survival depends on its ability to break the noose. No one understands the urgency of this need more than the mullahs holding the reins of power in Tehran. This has prompted them to resort to even greater repression at home, terrorism and fundamentalism abroad, procurement of weapons of mass destruction and efforts to acquire nuclear arms.

An editorial in the leading pro-Khamenei daily *Kayhan* did not mince its words. It described the 12 May 2003 bombing in Riyadh, Saudi Arabia, as an indication of 'the Muslim nations' increasing and escalating opposition to America'. It characterized the welcome accorded to Iraqi Shiite cleric Mohammad Baqer Al-Hakim in southern Iraq as a sign of the 'Iraqi people's yearning for an Iranian-style government'. It wrote that Khatami's trip to Beirut confirmed that 'the Islamic Republic of Iran considered the *Intifada*, whose ultimate aim was the total annihilation of the usurper regime in Qods, as the only way to restore peace and tranquillity in the region'. The editorial branded these developments as the manifestations of 'the spread of revolutionary Islam in the region', reiterating, 'The Islamic Republic of Iran is the primary driving force' behind this revival in the Islamic world.[8]

For his part, Supreme Leader Ali Khamenei outlined the three characteristics of the 'new era': 'the revival and emergence of revolutionary Islam in Iran and the world; Iran's Islamic Revolution challenging the hegemony of the dominant system; the recognition of the Islamic Republic of Iran as the Umm ol-Qora and the focus of the global Islamic movement'. He also described 'the ubiquitous promotion of secularism, laicism and humanism' as 'the enemy's tools in its cultural aggression on Islam'.[9]

Amid these developments, the adoption of a sound policy on Iran is again being hotly debated and bitterly contested in the power centres of Western capitals, and nowhere as heatedly as in Washington, DC. In a rerun of the 1980s and 1990s, one faction in the US administration has underscored the need to support elements within the ruling theocracy and invest in the 'moderates', once aptly described by Henry Kissinger as 'extremists who have run out of ammunition'. The harsh realities of the past two decades, however, the Irangate fiasco and the failure of the Khatami experience, have undermined the position of advocates of rapprochement with the mullahs' regime, forcing the entrenched bureaucracies and change-resistant policy planners in the West to take a harder look at Iran and their own policy. The debate has led to a more profound discourse on genuine alternatives or choices that would make up a viable and sensible Iran policy, even though there remain powerful voices calling for a 'conciliatory approach' – euphemism for business as usual – to Tehran.

The debate is of paramount significance because the fate of many crises in the Islamic world, if not all of them, hinges to a great degree on the resolution of the Iranian problem. It is well understood now that the problems in the Middle East are not detached and isolated from one another. Bombs in Casablanca, instability in North Africa, explosions in Riyadh and the stalled Middle East peace process have their indigenous and unique immediate and underlying causes, but a common thread, Islamic fundamentalism, runs through all the beads of this rosary. In a sound, if belated, recognition of this truth, the *Washington Post* editorial noted on the second anniversary of the 11 September terrorist attacks, 'As the [Bush] administration has come to articulate, what was initially called a war on terrorism is a struggle against terror motivated by Islamic fundamentalism – and for democracy and modernity in the Islamic world.'

The US-led war in Iraq has thrust ancient Mesopotamia to the fore-front of the fray. Whatever the outcome of the showdown in Iraq, it would have a far-reaching effect on all the other flashpoints in the Arab and Muslim world. The clerical regime's significant investment in export-ing 'Islamic revolution' to Iraq, and its incessant efforts to build semi-overt and clandestine political and social networks across that country (the 'ballot-box and bullets' approach that it has already tested with a measure of success in Lebanon) rest on the understanding that the future of Iraq would have a decisive impact on the future of the Persian Gulf region and, more generally, the Middle East and beyond.

New York Times columnist Nicholas Kristoff made the chilling ob-servation in Basra after the war that 'America fought Saddam Hussein and the Islamic fundamentalists won'.[10] Many dismissed such warnings as too apocalyptic, but they turned out to be realistic and prudent. As *Newsweek*'s Farid Zakaria noted, 'It would be a tragedy if in the search for quick legitimacy, America ended up empowering [in Iraq] the kinds of forces it is currently battling all over the Arab world.'[11] His recom-mendation: 'In Iraq today, first establish a stable security environment and create the institutions of limited government – a constitution with a bill of rights, an independent judiciary, a sound central bank. Then and only then, move to full-fledged democracy.'[12]

In an interview with Daniel Pipes and Patrick Clawson in 1995, I pointed out,

No democratic process is possible in [Middle Eastern] countries, par-ticularly the Arab countries, so long as the Khomeini regime is in power in Iran. Fundamentalist Islam would immediately fill the void created by democratization and take advantage of it, derail it, and move it towards its own direction. Therefore, the idea of advancing democracy in the region is not realistic before fundamentalist Islam is taken care of.[13]

I added: 'Someone who truly wants to build democracy in the region must start the process in Tehran.'[14]

The need for change in Iran has drawn attention as never before to the clerical regime's principal opposition, the People's Mojahedin (PMOI) and the coalition National Council of Resistance of Iran (NCRI). Those who see Islamic fundamentalism as a global threat mostly concur that an effective and serious antidote to this dangerous phenomenon is a modern, democratic and secular interpretation of Islam. Back in 1992, a majority of members of the United States House of Representatives wrote in a joint statement in support of the PMOI and the NCRI: 'Experience has shown that this resistance's profound popular and religious roots within Iran's people are the best impediment to the Iranian regime's abuse of popular religious sentiments. Hence this resistance is the solution to the phenomenon of fanatic fundamentalism.'[15]

In the face of a suppressive, ruthless, intolerant and totalitarian 'Islam' that Iran's fundamentalist rulers symbolize, the People's Mojahedin, as the pivotal component within the broader Iranian Resistance movement, offers a liberating, compassionate, tolerant and democratic version of Islam. This Islam recognizes elections as the sole criterion for political legitimacy. The Resistance has stated unequivocally that Islam promotes freedom and people's sovereignty. It contends that, contrary to the mullahs' claim, there is no contradiction between Islam, democracy, secularism and pluralism. For its part, in the confrontation against its mortal enemy, the clerical regime has not just been content with execution, torture and terror. It has embarked on a well-financed campaign of demonization against the Resistance and the Mojahedin to stigmatize its legitimate opposition. This is a bid to justify suppression and terror at home and discredit the regime's only viable alternative, to legitimize Western countries' conciliation.

In their efforts to discredit the Resistance, the clerics share a common interest with the proponents of appeasement and their trading partners. For they, too, recognize that in this campaign, rejecting the democratic opposition is vital to expanding business and diplomatic ties with the ruling theocracy. This is, indeed, the very source of a flood of allegations against the Iranian Resistance in the years past. Allegations such as being a cult; espousing a cult of personality; believing in eclectic Marxist-Islamic views; jailing and torturing dissident members; forcing members to divorce; separating children from parents; being a pawn of the former Iraqi regime and taking part in the crackdown on Iraqi Kurds and Shiites: frivolous lies fabricated by the Iranian regime in the past two decades to undermine its legitimate opposition. The current circumstances and the serious need to search for an alternative to the clerical regime have made it all the more important, and pressing, to take a deeper look at these allegations.

At a time when the debate over Iran policy heats up around the world, it is imperative to see and understand the Iranian Resistance, the NCRI and the PMOI, as they really are. This book is an attempt to respond to this need, and to clear up the ambiguities and questions that persist in this regard. Its aim is to enable the reader to observe developments in Iran and its future in a more objective and realistic light.

Notes

1. Mohandas K. Gandhi, *Non-Violence in Peace and War* (1949), vol. 2, ch. 162, New York: Garland.

2. Agence France Presse, 11 July 2002.

3. *Christian Science Monitor*, 16 June 2003.

4. *Financial Times*, editorial, 'Iran's Nuclear Bind', 15 September 2003.

5. Islamic Republic News Agency (IRNA), 12 September 2003.

6. *Jomhouri Islami*, 13 September 2003.

7. Agence France Presse, 'U.S. Court: Iran to Pay 420 Million to U.S. Victims of Hamas Bombing', 16 September 2003.

8. Editorial, *Kayhan*, Tehran, 13 May 2003.

9. Quoted in the website of His Eminence Grand Ayatollah Khamenei's representative in the universities of the Islamic Republic <www.nahad.net>.

10. Nicholas Kristoff, *New York Times*, 25 June 2003.

11. 'How to Make Friends in Iraq', *Newsweek*, 23 June 2003.

12. 'How to Make Peace', *Newsweek*, 21 April 2003.

13. Mohammad Mohaddessin, *Middle East Quarterly*, September 1995, vol. II, no. 3.

14. Ibid.

15. Declaration, 219 members of the US House of Representatives, *New York Times*, 29 June 1992.

PART I
**Islamic Fundamentalism:
the Global Context**

1 | Terror in the name of God

And of all plagues with which mankind are curst,
Ecclesiastic tyranny's the worst. *Daniel Defoe*[1]

When it first appeared in bookshops in 1993, my book *Islamic Fundamentalism: The New Global Threat*[2] was met with scepticism in several quarters. Some in the academic world rejected the notion that Islamic fundamentalism was a threat at all, let alone a global one. Western governments, too, dismissed the call for a firm policy to confront the rising threat of radical Islamic fundamentalists and the main engine of modern-day fundamentalist-based terrorism, the theocratic regime in Iran. Most preferred, instead, to engage, rather than alienate, the ruling ayatollahs in Tehran.

Many developments on the global scene since that time have, unfortunately, served to vindicate the dire admonition to Western policymakers in that book: 'In today's world, terrorism is the other side of Islamic fundamentalism and is in fact needed for its existence ... If those countries which support peace, human rights and democracy do not target the heart of fundamentalism, world peace and the modern era will be in danger.'[3] Since then, the world has watched in horror as fundamentalist-inspired terror has struck with deadly results: eighty-five people were killed and more than 200 wounded when a powerful blast ripped apart the Jewish community centre in Buenos Aires in July 1994; nineteen American servicemen were killed and more than 500 wounded when a fuel truck bomb destroyed the Khobar Towers in Saudi Arabia in June 1996; 301 people died and more than 5,000 were injured in the twin bombings of US embassies in Kenya and Tanzania in August 1998. More than anything, however, it was the tragic events of that fateful Tuesday, 11 September 2001, that shocked, horrified and awakened the world, particularly the United States, to the global threat posed by Islamic fundamentalism. Nine days later, on 20 September, US President George W. Bush described the perpetrators of the attacks in New York and Washington as radical Muslims and extremists who 'by abandoning every value except the will to power, follow in the path of fascism, and Nazism, and totalitarianism'.[4]

The events of 11 September aroused much debate about the identities of the perpetrators and the various shades of fundamentalist-based terrorism, but few scholars or analysts have since then doubted the notion that Islamic fundamentalism is indeed a threat, and a global one at that. This, as I mentioned at the outset, was not the case prior to 11 September. Some, in fact, saw Islamic fundamentalism as a benign force and one that would pose no threat to the non-Muslim world: 'While fundamentalism is an expansive force within the Islamic world, it neither seeks jihad with nor domination of the non-Muslim world. In this respect, Islamic fundamentalism ought to matter no more to the non-Muslim world than Québécois nationalism matters to Thailand.'[5] The same analysts rejected the notion that Islamic fundamentalists sought world domination:

> Like communism, Islamic fundamentalism is an ideology. Where communism rejected capitalist rules of engagement in international affairs, Islamic fundamentalism rejects the notion that the state is an inviolable unit. But unlike communism, Islamic fundamentalism confines its aspirations to one portion of the world – the Muslim world. Thus, when fundamentalists challenge the state, it is within the Muslim world that is the target of their animus. Communism sought, and free market capitalism still seeks, world domination. Islamic fundamentalism does not and never will.[6]

Certain commentators were keen to ridicule the idea of 'a new global threat', cautioning Western governments against taking a firm position that would jeopardize political and economic ties with Tehran: 'From home and abroad voices have begun to counsel the Clinton administration that with communism's death, America must prepare for a new global threat – radical Islam. This spectre is symbolized by the Middle Eastern Muslim fundamentalist, a Khomeini-like creature armed with a radical ideology and nuclear weapons, intent on launching a jihad against Western civilization.'[7]

While the 'appeasers' – advocates of rapprochement with Iran as the primogenitor of latter-day Islamic fundamentalism in the Muslim world – clearly got it wrong, those who equated fundamentalism and terrorism with Islam were equally misguided. As we shall see in subsequent chapters of this book, there is nothing innately anti-democratic in Islam, nor is there an inherent disposition to mindless violence in this religion. Neither the Quran nor the teachings of Prophet Muhammad support these notions. It is my profound conviction that if the grave threat of Khomeini-style Islamic fundamentalism is to be defeated, the temptation to equate this deviation of Islam with the religion itself must be avoided, particularly in the West. Bernard Lewis, the American scholar on Islam, in an article in *Atlantic Monthly* (September 1990) noted:

There is something in the religious culture of Islam which inspired, in even the humblest peasant or peddler, a dignity and a courtesy toward others never exceeded and rarely equalled in other civilizations. And yet, in moments of upheaval and disruption, when the deeper passions are stirred, this dignity and courtesy toward others can give way to an explosive mixture of rage and hatred which impels even the government of an ancient and civilized country – even the spokesman of a great spiritual and ethical religion – to espouse kidnapping and assassination, and try to find, in the life of their prophet, approval and indeed precedent for such actions.

Others compare Quranic verses or Prophet Muhammad's sayings with those of Jesus and Christianity only to conclude, again, that Islam somehow inherently breeds violence and intolerance:

> Most interpreters of the Koran find no arguments in it for the murder of innocents. But it would be naive to ignore in Islam a deep thread of intolerance toward unbelievers, especially if those unbelievers are believed to be a threat to the Islamic world. There are many passages in the Koran urging mercy toward others, tolerance, respect for life and so on. But there are also passages as violent as this: 'And when the sacred months are passed, kill those who join other gods with God wherever ye shall find them; and seize them, besiege them, and lay wait for them with every kind of ambush.' (Andrew Sullivan in *New York Times* Magazine, 7 October 2001)

These interpretations fail to see the context in which violence was sanctioned by Islam and, more importantly, the fact that the overwhelming message of the religion, one that is repeated at the beginning of 113 of the Quran's 114 chapters (*surahs*), is compassion and mercy, and by consequence peace, tolerance and salvation. The entire message of a great religion cannot be extracted from a single verse, just as it would be misleading to summarize the message of the Old Testament by its praise for David, who killed 'tens of thousands' and aroused the jealousy of Saul, who only killed 'thousands', or by Moses' harsh rebuke of his army for sparing the women and children of the vanquished Midianites. As one US scholar noted:

> To compare Muhammad to Moses or Jesus, or against some contemporary standard, is meaningless and anachronistic. The world that Moses and Muhammad lived in was lawless and violent, different from even the Roman dominated world in which Jesus lived. Strong vested interests opposed the monotheism each preached, genocide was commonplace,

slavery was taken for granted. Women had few rights, and might was the only law. In this context Muhammad and Moses and all the other Biblical figures sought to create a new society based on justice and on the belief in a compassionate God. Their achievements in accomplishing this in lasting ways form the only relevant contemporary standard by which they can be truly judged.[8]

While the complacency and indulgence that characterized the attitude of a broad range of Western policy-makers and scholars towards Islamic fundamentalism throughout the 1990s had extremely serious ramifications, it is equally true, in my view, that those who have portrayed the conflict as being one of Islam versus Christianity and Judaism, rather than a deviated, fundamentalist strain declaring war on civilization and faiths of all kinds that are at peace with freedom and modernity, have played into the hands of the extremists and hate-mongers. Samuel Huntington's perception that Islam and the West, as irreconcilable civilizations, are on an inevitable collision course is, I believe, a profound misreading of the real issue. Huntington says: 'The underlying problem for the West is not Islamic fundamentalism. It is Islam, a different civilisation whose people are convinced of the superiority of their culture and are obsessed with the inferiority of their power.'[9] Huntington's theory does not hold up under inspection. To identify Islam as the threat to world peace and global security is to misunderstand the nature of the menace, with disastrous consequences. The conflict that has dominated world events since 11 September, but which actually had its turning point in Khomeini's rise to power in 1979, is not a clash between religions or cultures, but one that reflects a far more profound struggle inside the Muslim world between fundamentalists and democrats; between obscurantists and progressives, between fanatics and genuine reformers. As one commentator has rightly pointed out: 'If wars are cultural and religious, they have no solutions. They are unnegotiable and unresolvable. If the Muslim is an enemy of America and Europe because he is a Muslim, and Westerners are his mortal enemies because of who they are, all have lost control over their futures.'[10]

The search for causes
While the events of 11 September have obliterated earlier doubts and questions about the global nature of the threat posed by Islamic fundamentalism, there has been much controversy and ambivalence in the search for the causes of the rise of fundamentalism in Islamic society and attacks such as those on 11 September. Many academics

see this phenomenon as a Muslim backlash to globalization and the domination of Western culture, coupled with the failure of Muslim states in socio-economic and political development. Ankie Hoogvelt, who describes the modernization theory and development theory in the context of neo-colonialism, writes: 'It is the failure of national developmental strategies in the neo-colonial period, coupled with the present episode of globalisation that drives the contemporary Islamic crescent. Islamic resurgence is best understood as a politics of identity in response to exclusion, rather than as a subordinated incorporation.'[11] On the other side of the Atlantic, the University of Virginia's Hilal Khashan has argued that 'Islamic fundamentalism is the product of cultural and intellectual stagnation, Western colonialism, and the failure of the secular nationalist model of government.'[12] He maintains that 'the failure of Arab ruling elites to modernize their countries created an institutional vacuum and enabled the radicals to present themselves as serious contenders for political authority'.

Some see demography as the most important reason for the spread of fanatical Islam, citing the fact that 'well over half the populations of Egypt, Syria, Saudi Arabia, Iran and Iraq are under 25 years old, according to the International Programmes Centre at the Census Bureau. In Pakistan, the number is 61 percent; in Afghanistan, 62 percent.'[13] The same New York Times article noted that this 'youth bulge' was an important factor in providing a fertile ground for fundamentalism: 'The boom in young people coming of age in a broad swath of territory where terrorists recruit might seem to pose one of the United States' most daunting national security threats.'[14] Huntington, too, has underlined the demographic factor, contending that the large number of unemployed males between the ages of fifteen and thirty is 'a natural source of instability and violence'[15] throughout the Muslim world. The case of Iran, however, clearly demonstrates that the 'youth bulge' is not simply a taken-for-granted advantage for fundamentalists in Muslim societies. A French observer noted in Le Monde Diplomatique: 'The younger generation in Iran – 70% of the population is under 35 – focuses on the national and Western features of Iran's Indo-European identity, rather than Islamic values.'[16]

Others have cited education in certain Muslim societies as the seedbed of fundamentalism. This view in the journal U.S. Foreign Policy Association is typical of such thinking:

One of the world's centres of Islamic education outside of Saudi Arabia is Peshawar, Pakistan, near the once porous border with Afghanistan.

'This dusty city of intrigue just east of the Khyber Pass is where many of today's Muslims came to pick up both the Koran and the Kalashnikov,' writes the *Christian Science Monitor*. Run by religious clerics known as mullahs, the schools' curriculums are one-dimensional. 'They are providing an education which is basically unchanged from the eleventh century. There is no science, very little arithmetic – instead all the emphasis is on Koranic studies,' said Pakistani university lecturer Pervez Hoodboy, in a BBC report. 'It produces a student with a particular mindset. One who does not question, and who can be easily motivated into fighting to death.' Anti-Western seeds, as well as dreams of martyrdom, are allowed to blossom at such institutions 'when it is necessary for the safety of the country or for the protection of Islam', said Mullah Syed Chirauddin to the BBC in a 1999 report.[17]

Many of the arguments since 11 September have invoked the economic underdevelopment of the Islamic world as the principal fuel for fundamentalism. As one economist noted:

There exists no workable Islamic economic system. Government-championed 'economic Islamization' efforts in Sudan, Pakistan, and Iran have all ended in failure. Leading Islamist writers rationalize these disappointments by arguing that no properly Islamic economy can exist so long as the world is rife with corruption. Some add that none has existed in history, except during the initial few decades of the first Islamic state founded fourteen centuries ago in Western Arabia. After that 'Golden Age', corruption took over, breeding unfairness, injustice, and inefficiency.[18]

Many scholars have pointed to the restraints that autocratic governments in the Muslim world impose on political expression as a major contributor, if not the main one, to the rise of Islamic extremism. They argue that in these societies, many activists turn towards religion as the only arena that remains relatively open, as all other channels for serious opposition are blocked by the repressive state. With no real political parties, a gagged press and few possibilities to air alternative views, the mosque becomes the primary, and often only, forum for expression of dissent. This was indeed the case in Iran under the Shah in the 1970s, where his crackdown on dissent left the mosque as the only substitute for a civil society, opening the way for Khomeini's meteoric rise to power. There have been similar examples in Arab countries. An American correspondent quoted an Arab human rights activist in Cairo as saying: 'Politics is prohibited in this society in general, but the government can't close the mosque. If you can't gather people to discuss issues in the appropriate place, such as the headquarters of the opposition party, the only place you can gather people is the mosque.'[19] And then, of course, there is a plethora of international factors, such as the impact of the 1991 Persian Gulf War or the bloody conflict in the Balkans, particularly the atrocities committed against the Muslims and Belgrade's policy of ethnic cleansing. These and many other events across the Islamic world have, according to many observers, fuelled a widespread perception among Muslims that the West is irreconcilably hostile towards Islam and Muslims. This in turn has helped the recruitment drive of fundamentalists and fanatics and has provided Iran's clerical rulers with much-needed propaganda.

While most of the factors cited by scholars to explain the rise of Islamic fundamentalism in recent times are indeed relevant and, to varying degrees, can account for this phenomenon, they fail both to unveil the real cause and nature of the ascent of fundamentalism and to pinpoint the critical turning point in its development over the past few decades. Islamic fundamentalism has spread with alarming speed in Muslim societies across the world, but as scholars such as Ankie Hoogvelt point out, the defining moment in this trend was clearly the creation of the modern world's first theocratic Islamic Republic in Iran in 1979 in the wake of the overthrow of the Shah's pro-Western monarchy.[20] Middle East expert Daniel Pipes observed in an article entitled 'Death to America': 'America's war on terrorism did not begin in September 2001. It began in November 1979. That was shortly after Ayatollah Khomeini had seized power in Iran, riding the slogan "Death to America" – and sure enough, the attacks on Americans soon began. In November 1979, a militant Islamic mob took over the U.S. embassy in Tehran, the Iranian capital, and held 52 Americans hostage for the next 444 days.' In all, 800 persons lost their lives in the course of attacks by militant Islam on Americans before September 2001 – more than have been killed by any other enemy since the Vietnam War.[21] Pipes contended that America's weak response to the first acts of terrorism by the clerical regime only emboldened the fundamentalists and extremists in Iran and other Islamic countries and the 11 September attacks were a consequence of the failure to deal with this threat at a much earlier stage of its development. Bruce Hoffman, a terrorism expert in the USA, notes that a review of the historical development of modern-day terrorism shows that 'the latest manifestation of this trend began in 1979, when the revolution that transformed Iran into an Islamic republic led it to use and support terrorism as a means of propagating its ideals beyond its own border'.[22]

A twin phenomenon

It would be misleading if in trying to understand what prompted the 11 September attacks, we confined ourselves to the study of personalities, attitudes and even the specific beliefs of those who perpetrated the attacks. In the contemporary world, terrorism is the other side of the coin of Islamic fundamentalism, the heart of which beats in Tehran. Terrorism is a tactic, a function, and a method powered by an ideological and political driving force. In the 1960s and 1970s, terrorism was based largely on nationalist and secular views. In the 1980s and 1990s, however, Islamic fundamentalism became the most important driving force behind terrorism. After coming to power in Iran in 1979, Khomeini coined the motto of 'export of Islamic revolution' to the rest of the world, transforming the idea of creating a global Islamic rule from a pipe dream of nostalgic Islamic extremists to an achievable goal for many fundamentalists, who had been until then rather isolated in the Islamic world at large.

Some researchers see the influence of mullahs' terrorism as extending even beyond the Islamic world. In a think-tank paper titled *A Brief History of Terrorism*, researcher Mark Burgess noted:

> Before long, the trend had spread beyond Iran to places as far afield as Japan and the United States, and beyond Islam to every major world religion as well as many minor cults. From the Sarin attack on the Tokyo subway by the Aum Shinrikyo in 1995 to the Oklahoma bombing the same year, religion was again added to the complex mix of motivations that led to acts of terrorism. The al Qaeda attacks of September 11, 2001, brought home to the world, and most particularly the United States, just how dangerous this latest mutation of terrorism is.[23]

Historically, Tehran's role in fomenting Islamic fundamentalism in the past two decades could be compared with Moscow's role in giving viability to communist movements across the world for seventy years, from the 1917 October Revolution until the demise of Soviet power. So long as the Bolsheviks were in power in Russia, even those Marxist parties that had ideological differences with the Kremlin mattered only because the Soviet Union was there. The demise of the Soviet bloc was a mortal blow even to communists avowedly opposed to Moscow. A conservative estimate shows that during the 1980s and 1990s, at least 90 per cent of all major terrorist attacks in the world were linked to the Iranian regime.[24] The mullahs have, of course, paid a price for their notorious role in exporting terrorism. Tehran has been dubbed 'the most active state sponsor of terrorism'[25] and condemned by many governments, parties and personalities the world over, but Iran's rulers felt the price was worth the effort, given the enormous windfall that such rogue behaviour brought to their regime.

The perils of appeasement

The policy of appeasement and rapprochement pursued by Western governments in the past two decades towards Tehran has had two clear consequences. It has emboldened the Iranian regime's most extremist and hard-line factions, leading to stepped-up repression at home and the export of terrorism and fundamentalism abroad. The 'engagement' of the mullahs' regime by Western governments – whether in the form of overt negotiations or secret deals – has also always been to the detriment of the Iranian resistance and particularly the PMOI. These two consequences have led to one outcome: a strengthening of fundamentalism in Iran and across the Islamic world.

The irony is that Western governments' soft approach to Iran's ruling mullahs is providing a badly needed shot in the arm for the religious regime at a time when it is in steep decline. As the myth of Khatami's moderation fades away, earlier illusions about reform of the religious dictatorship have evaporated. United Nations sources and international human rights organizations report a marked deterioration of the human rights situation in Iran. The *Economist* reported on 8 February 2003: 'Few people now believe that Mr Khatami can deliver on his seductive promise to reconcile Islamic values with democratic ones. But the EU's defence, when charged by Americans with helping to legitimise a dishonourable regime, is that its engagement with Iran helps the reformists to fulfil their pledges. As Mr Khatami shrinks in stature, that defence sounds hollow.'

Public executions, torture, arbitrary arrests, medieval punishments, violent suppression of women, ethnic and religious discrimination and inquisition continue unabated. In 2002 alone, 474 executions were announced, while most death sentences were carried out in secret. The United Nations Human Rights Commission's Working Group on Arbitrary Detention reported, after visiting Iran in 2003, that Iran's judicial system lacks many important principles laid down in international conventions, including the presence of counsel during trials. The report said, 'In ward 209 of Evin prison, referred to as "a prison within a prison", dialogue with prisoners was quickly brought to a halt by two unidentified individuals who appeared to be from the intelligence services. Without identifying themselves, these two individuals demanded that the delegation leave that area ... What this showed was that they had something to hide.'[26] After the report was published, French jurist Louis Joinnet, who headed the UN delegation to Iran, told reporters: 'In Ward 209, we visited several members of the People's Mojahedin Organization of Iran. It is likely that there were many more members of this organization in Ward 209 that we could simply not visit. It is our view that the treatment of prisoners in this ward is not only inhumane, but also clearly in breach of their human rights.'[27]

Mullahs' sponsorship of terrorism, too, shows no sign of let-up. US officials reported 'strong evidence' of links between the perpetrators of the deadly bombing in Riyadh on 12 May 2003 and terrorists based in Iran.[28] In the occupied territories and Israel, the Iranian regime sponsored at least fifteen terror attacks in the year preceding August 2003. Fifty civilians were killed and 105 wounded in these attacks.

Appeasement also allowed the clerical regime to engage freely in the procurement of nuclear weapons. Before the National Council of Resistance of Iran blew the cover of two secret nuclear sites in Natanz and Arak in central Iran and revealed significant advances in Tehran's nuclear efforts in August 2002, Western governments made no serious attempt to confront this matter; indeed some European countries continued their technical co-operation with Tehran, thereby assisting the mullahs to advance their ominous nuclear ambitions. This numbness to the danger of the 'godfather of international terrorism' arming itself with nuclear weapons was not rooted in ignorance or neglect, but was a direct result of the policy of engagement *vis-à-vis* the Iranian regime. The consequence, as a confidential report by the French government published in the *Los Angeles Times* on 4 August 2003 warned, was that 'Iran is surprisingly close to having enriched uranium or plutonium for a bomb'. In the report, 'The French warned other governments to exercise the most serious vigilance on their exports to Iran and Iranian front companies.'

Appeasement apologists, who represent business interests that promote trade with the mullahs, insist on improving ties with Tehran despite the policies and conduct of the Iranian regime, but it is no coincidence that, almost in the same breath, they lash out at the Iranian Resistance. More often than not, such virulent attacks on the Resistance serve as justification for 'engaging' the high priests of Islamic fundamentalism in Iran.

A case in point

The Clinton administration's policy towards the clerical regime and the PMOI serves as a vivid example of such an ill-fated approach. The urge to appease Tehran went so far that the US government decided to sit on specific information on the role of Tehran in the Khobar Towers bombing in Saudi Arabia in June 1996, which killed nineteen US servicemen. Washington chose not to pursue the matter, lest it 'undermine' the 'moderates' in Tehran and ruin the chances of a thaw in US–Iranian ties. The *New Yorker* magazine wrote in June 2001 that FBI Director Louis Freeh had prepared a list of those responsible for the deadly attack. He submitted it, containing the names of several Iranian officials, to the government for prosecution, but the Clinton administration chose to shelve Freeh's report. In May 2003, free from the constraints of officialdom, Freeh told his story in an article carried by the *Wall Street Journal*.[29] Writing in the immediate aftermath of the 12 May bombing in Riyadh, Saudi Arabia, he noted:

> Impervious to the new order against terrorism are the terrorists who maintain their regime in Tehran. While the horrific bombing scenes were still smoldering and littered with their victims in Riyadh, Iranian President Mohammad Khatami received a rousing welcome in Beirut, where he vowed to support 'resistance' against Israel and called the U.S. occupation of Iraq a 'great mistake' and a 'dangerous game.' Meanwhile, Mr. Khatami's atomic-energy chief denied that Iran had a nuclear weapons program but told the U.N. that his country was not willing to submit to tougher inspections.
>
> Make no mistake; Iran's terrorist leaders are well versed in 'martyrdom operations' against Americans. Hezbollah, the exclusive terrorist agent of the Islamic Republic of Iran, has killed more Americans than any other group besides al-Qaeda ...
>
> On June 25, 1996, Iran again attacked America at Dhahran, Saudi Arabia, exploding a huge truck bomb that devastated Khobar Towers and murdered 19 U.S. airmen as they rested in their dormitory ... More than 400 of our Air Force men and women were wounded in this well-planned attack ...
>
> Over the course of our investigation the evidence became clear that while the attack was staged by Saudi Hezbollah members, the entire operation was planned, funded and coordinated by Iran's security services, the IRGC [Islamic Revolutionary Guards Corps] and MOIS [Ministry of Intelligence and Security], acting on orders from the highest levels of the regime in Tehran.
>
> Unfortunately, the White House was unable or unwilling to help the FBI gain access to these critical witnesses. The only direction from the Clinton administration regarding Iran was to order the FBI to stop

photographing and fingerprinting official Iranian delegations entering the U.S. because it was adversely impacting our 'relationship' with Tehran. We had argued that the MOIS was using these groups to infiltrate its agents into the U.S.

Freeh stated that when the FBI was finally able to interview six of the Hezbollah members who actually carried out the attack, 'All of them directly implicated the IRGC, MOIS and senior Iranian government officials in the planning and execution of this attack. Armed with this evidence, the FBI recommended a criminal indictment that would identify Iran as the sponsor of the Khobar bombing. Finding a problem for every solution, the Clinton administration refused to support a prosecution.'

The Clinton administration's appeasement of the mullahs' regime did not stop there. To further please the mullahs, it took a singularly harsh and unwarranted action against the PMOI. In a snub to members of the United States Congress, the State Department designated the PMOI as a 'foreign terrorist organization' on 7 October 1997. The next day, a senior Clinton administration official told the *Los Angeles Times*, 'The inclusion of the People's Moujahedeen [*sic*] was intended as a goodwill gesture to Tehran and its newly elected moderate President Mohammed Khatami.' At the time of the redesignation of the PMOI in the 1999 list, US Assistant Secretary of State for Near Eastern Affairs Martin Indyk said in a speech to the Asia Society on 14 October 1999 that the designation was at the behest of the Iranian regime. *Newsweek* magazine later quoted Indyk as saying, '[There] was White House interest in opening up a dialogue with the Iranian government. At the time, President Khatami had recently been elected and was seen as a moderate. Top Administration officials saw cracking down on the [PMOI], which the Iranians had made clear they saw as a menace, as one way to do so.'[30]

The policy of appeasement that began with a 'goodwill gesture' – the terror tag on the PMOI – to mollify the Iranian regime quickly led to covering up the role of Tehran in one of the deadliest attacks on America before the 11 September tragedy. Those in hot pursuit of lucrative oil and business deals with Tehran stopped at nothing in their efforts to beautify the image of the theocratic regime in Iran and, at the same time, to demonize the Iranian Resistance.

In recent years, the European Union has been following a similar policy towards Iran, giving priority to trade over all other issues, including the Iranian regime's abysmal human rights record and sponsorship of terrorism. In an interview with the Tehran-based daily, *Entekhab*,

Spain's ambassador to Iran acknowledged that the EU had blacklisted the PMOI at the request of the Iranian regime. He said: 'There were three issues that Iran wanted to address with the EU. When Spain was the President, the two sides were able to resolve these differences. One of the major issues was including the People's Mojahedin Organization in the list of terrorist groups by the EU.'[31]

These examples, and many others, demonstrate a persistent trend in the Iranian regime's priorities in dealing with foreign governments: it is always demanding action against the PMOI. Since the late 1970s, the ruling ayatollahs sensed through first-hand experience that Western governments lacked the political will to stand firm in the face of the threat posed by fundamentalism and terrorism and would invariably prefer a 'soft approach' to confrontation. Former World Bank senior vice-president and Clinton adviser Joseph Stiglitz candidly criticized US trade and economic policies in the 1990s in his 2003 book, *The Roaring Nineties: Seeds of Destruction*:

> The policies we pushed and the way we pushed them generated enormous resentment. The already visible results include growing anti-Americanism in Asia and Latin America. Even if our economy had not faltered, our global strategy was not likely to succeed. It was based on putting aside principles – principles of social justice, equity, fairness, that we stressed at home – to get the best bargain we could for American special interests.

When it came to Iran, the 'best bargain' meant appeasement of the ruling theocracy. The mullahs were not blind to these calculations. They soon discovered that the export of terrorism and fundamentalism was one of the most effective tools in their arsenal for gaining concessions from other governments. In March 2000, Secretary of State Madeleine Albright announced the lifting of US sanctions on certain Iranian exports and stressed the Clinton administration's willingness to develop ties with Tehran. A few months later, State Department officials were quoted as saying that there had been 'a noticeable increase' in the Iranian regime's terrorist activities in the region. Clearly, the ayatollahs in Tehran felt that the more they caused problems for Western governments, the more concessions they would be able to extract.

The mullahs also discovered that beyond the rhetoric aimed at the voting public in their own countries, governments in the West competed with each other in finding ways of appeasing Tehran's rulers so as to encourage further trade and keep terrorists off their own territories. This allowed the clerical regime to use Western hostages in Lebanon throughout the 1980s as bargaining chips in its dealings with Western governments, demanding and receiving major concessions in heinous *souq* deals that were euphemistically called 'negotiations'. Even as recently as 2003, Iranian rulers have been playing the same game with Western governments, making tantalizing offers of 'exchanging' Al-Qaeda operatives in Iran for members of the PMOI in Iraq.[32]

Islamic fundamentalism is a grave threat to peace and tranquillity across the world. While there is debate as to its roots and characteristics, there is a quasi-consensus among experts and observers that this is a global menace that not only threatens the stability of the Middle East, but also has wide adherence throughout Africa and Asia and gives rise to terrorism worldwide. The fervour of Islamic fundamentalism is far greater than it was for communism in its heyday. This fundamentalist movement, whose heart beats in Tehran, is both expansionist, with a vision to revive the Islamic caliphate, and militaristic. With Tehran moving rapidly to acquire the technological capability to make nuclear bombs, Khomeini-style fundamentalism is set to become the most important threat to global peace and security in the coming years.

Notes

1. Daniel Defoe, *The True-Born Englishman* (1701), pt 2.

2. Mohammad Mohaddessin, *Islamic Fundamentalism: The New Global Threat*, Washington, DC: Seven Locks Press, 1993.

3. Ibid., p. 53.

4. President George W. Bush, address to a joint session of Congress and the American people, 20 September 2001.

5. Zachery Karabell in John T. Rourke, *Taking Sides*, Connecticut: McGraw-Hill/Dushkin, 2001, p. 277.

6. Ibid., p. 282.

7. Leon P. Hadar, 'What Green Peril?', *Foreign Affairs*, Spring 1993.

8. Alexander Kronemer, 'Understanding Muhammad', *Christian Science Monitor*, 9 December 2002.

9. Samuel Huntington, *The Clash of Civilisations and the Remaking of World Order*, London: Touchstone Books, 1996.

10. William Pfaff, 'Stop Calling Islam the Enemy', *International Herald Tribune*, 5 December 2002.

11. Ankie Hoogvelt, 'Globalisation and the Postcolonial World: The New Political Economy of Development', ch. 9, *Islamic Revolt*, London: Macmillan.

12. Hilal Khashan, 'The New World Order and the Tempo of Militant Islam', *British Journal of Middle Eastern Studies*, vol. 24, no. 1, May 1997.

13. Elaine Sciolino, 'Radicalism: Is the Devil in the Demographics?', *New York Times*, 9 December 2001.

14. Ibid.

15. Ibid.

16. Cedric Gouverneur, 'The Enemy Within', *Le Monde Diplomatique*, March 2002.

17. Robert Nolan, 'Sowing the Seeds of Fundamentalism', *U.S. Foreign Policy Association*, 23 October 2001.

18. Timu Kuran, *The Religious Undercurrents of Muslim Economic Grievances*, Social Science Research Council, 10 December 2001.

19. Karl Vick, 'Arab States' Restraint: The Root of Extremism?', *International Herald Tribune*, 29 October 2001.

20. Hoogvelt, 'Globalisation ... '.

21. Daniel Pipes, 'Death to America', *New York Post*, 8 September 2002.

22. Bruce Hoffman, *Inside Terrorism*, New York: Columbia University Press, 1988, p. 87.

23. Mark Burgess, *A Brief History of Terrorism*, Centre for Defence Information, 2 July 2003.

24. Mohaddessin, *Islamic Fundamentalism*, p. xxiv.

25. *Patterns of Global Terrorism*, US State Department, April 2003.

26. Report of the United Nations Human Rights Commission's Working Group on Arbitrary Detention on its visit to the Islamic Republic of Iran, E/CN.4/2004/3/ADD.2, 20 June 2003.

27. BBC Persian Section, interview with Louis Joinnet, 20 June 2003.

28. CBS news, 16 May 2003.

29. Louis Freeh, 'Remember Khobar Towers', *Wall Street Journal*, 20 May 2003.

30. *Newsweek*, 26 September 2003.

31. *Entekhab*, 28 October 2002.

32. See, for example, Barbara Slavin, 'Iran Might Swap Terrorists for Help from U.S.', *USA Today*, 3 August 2003.

2 | Mullahs and the bomb

We should fully equip ourselves both in the offensive and defensive use of chemical, biological, and nuclear weapons. From now on, you should make use of the opportunity and perform this task. *Ali-Akbar Hashemi Rafsanjani*[1]

Hashemi Rafsanjani was the acting Commander in Chief of the Armed Forces when he made the above remarks to the Revolutionary Guards in October 1988. Rafsanjani was effectively Khomeini's right-hand man while the founder of the Islamic Republic ruled Iran and he has been one of the two most powerful figures in the clerical regime ever since. A flamboyant powerbroker, Rafsanjani is also the principal architect of Tehran's weapons of mass destruction programme. It was Rafsanjani who revived Iran's nuclear power programme, which had been cancelled after the overthrow of the Shah's regime. Under his aegis, the Iranian regime entered secret talks in the first half of 1980s with several countries, including China, Pakistan, Russia, North Korea, Argentina, India and South Africa, to enlist their assistance in its nuclear project.[2] In October 1988, Rafsanjani addressed a conference of expatriate Iranian nuclear scientists in Tehran and urged them to return to the country, underlining the 'critical importance' of developing the nuclear industry.[3] It was Rafsanjani who secured China's co-operation to build a nuclear research centre four kilometres outside Isfahan and equip it, by the mid-1980s, with a 'training reactor' and, two years later, with a rudimentary calutron for experimental uranium isotope separation.[4] And again it was Rafsanjani who, in June 1989 and as the newly elected president, went to Moscow to seal Soviet participation in Tehran's nuclear project, a strategic step that gave an unprecedented boost to the mullahs' dreams of acquiring nuclear weapons.[5] His deputy at the time, Ataollah Mohajerani, said in 1991, 'Since the enemy has atomic capabilities, Islamic countries must be armed with the same capacity.'

As the storm over Iran's nuclear ambitions gathered pace in 2003, Rafsanjani was back in action, playing a key role in co-ordinating the clerical regime's response to the growing international chorus calling for Iran's immediate and unconditional accession to the Additional Protocol to the Nuclear Non-proliferation Treaty. In a speech in July 2003, Rafsanjani made thinly veiled terrorist threats against the West: 'We must prepare ourselves to confront the enemy's new aggression. We shall respond to this aggression by striking at their heartland.'[6] In another speech in September 2003, marking the anniversary of the Iran–Iraq war, Rafsanjani said, 'Those who threaten Iran ought to know that the situation is very different from the past. Our country is now more ready to defend itself than it was before ... Today we manufacture many weapons inside the country and have built missiles which have worried our enemies.'[7]

By the middle of 2003, little doubt remained that the Iranian regime was moving to the final stages of nuclear weapon development. A confidential report prepared by the French government in May 2003 concluded that Tehran was 'surprisingly close to having enriched uranium or plutonium for a bomb'. The French warned other governments to exercise 'the most serious vigilance on their exports to Iran and Iranian front companies', according to a copy of the report given to the *Los Angeles Times* by a foreign intelligence service.[8] The same newspaper also reported that 'in recent months, Iran has approached European companies to buy devices that can manipulate large volumes of radioactive material, technology to forge uranium metal and plutonium and switches that could trigger a nuclear weapon'. The paper added: 'European intelligence sources said Tehran's shopping list was a strong indication that Iran has moved to the late stages of weapons development.'[9]

Mullahs' Manhattan Project

The nuclear weapons programme began in earnest in the mid-1980s, but since the summer of 2002, the clerical leaders have been pressing the military officers and nuclear experts running the programme to speed full steam ahead to complete the project, now in a highly advanced stage, as quickly as possible. The added urgency had a reason behind it. The startling revelation of secret nuclear sites in Iran by the National Council of Resistance (NCRI) in August 2002 shocked the clerical hierarchy in Iran. All of a sudden, the centrepiece of a closely guarded secret project – the key uranium enrichment and heavy water plants – was exposed to the world, bringing Tehran's nuclear programme under unprecedented international scrutiny. Information on the precise location of the two elaborately camouflaged sites and their exact functions came from the People's Mojahedin network inside Iran, which obtained the top-secret documents from its sources within the mullahs' regime. The revelations came at a time when the Iranian regime felt most vulnerable: its long record of sponsorship of terrorism and export of Islamic fundamentalism had also come under the spotlight in the wake of the 11 September attacks. Almost a year after the attacks in the United States and the war in Afghanistan, and with a US military attack on Iraq looking increasingly likely, the clerical regime's leadership was deeply worried about its own future in the midst of this growing turmoil.

The stakes were high and urgent action was needed. The Supreme National Security Council, the Iranian regime's highest decision-making body in security and defence areas, held a series of extraordinary sessions in September 2002 to review a new military doctrine devised by the Islamic Revolutionary Guards Corps on the orders of Supreme Leader Ali Khamenei. The SNSC is chaired by the president of the Islamic Republic and is charged, in accordance with Article 176 of the constitution, with the following tasks:

1. to determine the national defence/security policies within the framework of general policies laid down by the Leader;
2. to co-ordinate political, intelligence, social, cultural and economic activities in relation to general defence/security policies;
3. to exploit material and non-material resources of the country for facing internal and external threats.[10]

All decisions by the SNSC must be endorsed by the Supreme Leader before being implemented. Its members include the heads of the executive, legislative and judiciary branches of power, the top commanders of the Revolutionary Guards and the Army, the ministers of foreign affairs, interior, and intelligence and security (MOIS), as well as two representatives directly appointed by Khamenei.[11]

At the end of its sessions, the SNSC approved the 'doctrine of asymmetric warfare' proposed by the Revolutionary Guards command. The clerical regime's military strategists argued that since the Iranian armed forces did not stand a chance in any conventional confrontation with the USA and its allies, particularly in the age of highly advanced military technology and ultra-modern weapons, they must resort to other tactics, including terrorist attacks on US interests and other Western targets, and the use of weapons of mass destruction and their means of delivery, ballistic missiles. These unconventional means were what was meant by 'asymmetric warfare'.

After the adoption of this military strategy, Brigadier General Mohammad-Ali Jaafari, commander of the Revolutionary Guards' ground forces, announced: 'As the likely enemy is far more advanced technologically than we are, we have been using what is called "asymmetric warfare" methods. We have gone through the necessary exercises and our forces are now well prepared for this.'[12] Of far greater strategic significance was the clerical leadership's decision that the nuclear weapons programme must be completed at all costs. The combined experience of North Korea and Iraq – even prior to the war that toppled the Iraqi regime – convinced the Iranian rulers that nuclear weapons were the best guarantor of survival for their regime, now finding itself on the defensive both on the domestic scene and in the regional and international arena. A project that had been launched in the 1980s with the strategic aim of facilitating Tehran's demarche to dominate the Islamic world and strengthening the mullahs' regional leverage through the intimidation of Iran's neighbours had by now become an irreplaceable tool of political survival.

No one is more acutely aware than Iran's rulers of the power that nuclear weapons would bestow on their enfeebled, faltering regime, helping the mullahs to terrorize the restive population into submission and advance their long-standing regional political aspirations. Tehran has never given up the goal of becoming the leader of the Islamic world and aspires to be the dominant power in the Persian Gulf. Iran is a state driven by an expansionist ideology, in a way that Saddam Hussein's regime never was. Weapons of mass destruction, and above all the nuclear bomb, are a necessity, not a luxury, for such a regime. They are the most effective deterrents, and at the same time serve as the best means of intimidating Iran's less powerful and more vulnerable neighbours. This point is never lost on the rulers in Tehran. When, on 18 April 2001, the clerical regime fired seventy-seven surface-to-surface missiles at seven camps of the Iranian Resistance in Iraq, Khamenei's adviser Brigadier General Ali Larijani told Tehran's Friday prayers congregation that this was a warning to the region's 'small countries not to step on the lion's tail'.[13]

The turning point

With so much international attention and world-wide concern focused on Iran's nuclear weapons programme, it is hard to imagine that prior to August 2002 all was quiet on the Iranian front. That changed when the National Council of Resistance of Iran revealed the precise location and functions of two top-secret and well-camouflaged nuclear sites in central Iran: a hexafluoride gas uranium enrichment centrifuge facility at Natanz and a heavy water facility near Arak. The NCRI's revelations prompted the International Atomic Energy Agency to request a visit to the two sites by its inspectors. Despite months of foot-dragging by Tehran to 'sanitize' the sites, a senior United Nations official said IAEA director general Mohamed ElBaradei and his inspectors found the Natanz site and the Iranian nuclear programme 'to be surprising in their sophistication' when they visited Iran in February 2003.[14]

Caught red-handed by the Resistance's revelations, the Iranian regime embarked on a 'damage-control' exercise. President Mohammad Khatami made a lengthy speech on 9 February, acknowledging the existence of more sites in Iran's nuclear project, including a uranium extraction plant in Saghand, 200 km from the southern city of Yazd:

> If we need nuclear plants, which we have already started, we need a complete fuel cycle, from uranium discovery and extraction to production of uranium oxide and its use in nuclear reactors and the management of the spent fuel. This is a very sensitive and important cycle and this government, following in the footsteps of its predecessor which had already taken steps along this path, has decided to see this through.
>
> Providing fuel for this process is very important and we must be self-sufficient. These are steps that we have taken ... Nobody has the right to protest against us. If there is anybody to protest it is us, who have been denied the use of international facilities through rumour-mongering and noise-making and biased methods.[15]

The Natanz uranium enrichment facility has, according to the IAEA, about a hundred completed centrifuges, and the equipment to build at least 5,000 more. When this plan is realized, the IAEA estimates, the clerical regime will have the capability of making at least two uranium-based bombs per year. Both the uranium mining and the centrifuge capabilities will give Tehran an entirely native ability to produce both nuclear fuel and bombs.

In February 2003, the NCRI exposed two newly discovered nuclear facilities near Tehran. They were two small laboratories that operate as satellite plants to the larger nuclear facility in Natanz.[16] Following these revelations, the New York Times quoted 'a senior United Nations official' as saying: 'This [opposition] organization has been extremely on the mark in the past ... They are a group that seems to be privy to very solid and insider information.'[17]

The Iranian regime insisted that its intention for the sites is to make fuel for a civilian nuclear power programme, but US and European officials and independent analysts rejected the claims. White House spokesman Ari Fleischer said, 'Iran now openly says that it is pursuing the complete nuclear fuel cycle. We completely reject Iran's claim that it is doing so for peaceful purposes.'[18] 'Iran admitted the existence of these facilities only after it had no choice, only because they have been made public by an Iranian opposition group,' Fleischer added. His comments were echoed by State Department spokesman Richard Boucher, who told journalists, 'Iran admitted to constructing a uranium enrichment plant and heavy water plant only after it had no choice because this had been [made] public, as you know, starting with an Iranian opposition group.'[19]

Buying time

Ever since it was caught red-handed, the clerical regime has shifted gear from a state of complete denial to a stalling strategy designed to buy time for the completion of its weapons project. By using every device in its diplomatic armoury to 'divide and thwart' the international community over the mullahs' nuclear ambitions, the Islamic Republic's stratagem closely resembles a diplomatic 'rope-a-dope', as Tehran hunkers down in the face of growing international pressure, trying to draw the world community to long deliberations, while pressing ahead with its nuclear development. It refuses to take a clear stance, speaking with many voices, but none authoritatively or decisively making Tehran's response to the world clear.

The clerical rulers have been playing, so far, a cat-and-mouse game at which they excel. They took a seemingly hard-line position on the issue of accession to the NPT's additional protocol, but already, they were busy building more secret and smaller sites to frustrate even a more stringent inspection regime by the IAEA. This would allow the Iranian regime to gain maximum concessions from Western countries before signing the additional protocol.

Gary Samore, a former US official who negotiated with the Iranian government and is now with the International Institute for Strategic Studies (IISS) in London, told the BBC: 'Iran can sign the extra protocol and retain its weapons option. All it has to do is to allow the inspections and continue its programme. The IAEA has no powers to stop it. It can then give 90 days' notice to leave the NTP.'[20] The mullahs' double-talk approach was evident during the visit to Tehran in July 2003 by Dr ElBaradei. President Khatami told the IAEA chief: 'While Iran is undoubtedly willing to co-operate with the IAEA, it is adamant to clear all misunderstandings and to defend its national interest and pride and will not buckle under undue pressures and baseless claims.'[21] Khatami's remarks made it clear that the clerical leadership in Tehran may be divided over the tone and form of approach to the question of nuclear weapons, but not over the content and substance. ElBaradei told reporters after the meeting: 'We have not discussed a time frame for signing the protocol, but we agreed that a team of experts would come to Iran to discuss with Iran the areas that Iran needs clarification on.'[22]

The IAEA chief's tone was decidedly more subdued than when he told reporters in Germany on the way to Iran that the clerical regime was willing to sign the additional protocol.

A deadline

By the end of summer 2003, the world was simply too alarmed by the rapid progress of Tehran's nuclear project to be lulled into inaction. In June, the IAEA's governing board chided the clerical regime for its failure to live up to its international commitments in the nuclear field. The IAEA noted that Tehran secretly imported 1.8 tons of nuclear material from China in 1991 and processed some of it to manufacture uranium metal, which would be of no use in Iran's commercial programme but would be integral to weapons production.[23]

The leaders of the Group of Eight industrial nations, meeting for an annual summit in the French resort of Evian in June, came up with a strongly worded statement on Iran's nuclear gambit and called for a 'comprehensive IAEA examination' of Tehran's nuclear programme. The European Union summit in Thessalonika in Greece also demanded that Tehran sign the additional protocol without preconditions and further delay. Similarly, the EU–US joint statement on 25 June expressed 'serious concern at Iran's nuclear programme, in particular as regards the pursuit of a full nuclear fuel cycle'.

In July, Tehran's claim that it was seeking only to develop a civilian nuclear power industry was dealt a serious blow when IAEA inspectors detected traces of highly enriched, weapons-grade uranium at a nuclear facility in Natanz. In a change of stories that has now become a hallmark of Tehran's cheat-and-conceal efforts, the Iranian regime claimed that the enriched uranium came from contaminated nuclear devices it had purchased on the international black market. In its September meeting in Vienna, the IAEA governing board decided to put an end to the Iranian regime's delaying tactics and set a 31 October deadline for Tehran to prove to the world that it was not secretly building nuclear weapons. The IAEA said in a resolution that passed without dissent, 'It is essential and urgent ... that Iran remedy all failures identified by the agency and cooperate fully.'[24] The agency called on Iran to provide a 'full declaration' of its nuclear programme, to open all nuclear sites for inspection, and to agree to environmental testing in advance of an IAEA meeting scheduled for 20 November 2003. The resolution urged the Iranian authorities immediately to end the uranium enrichment programme as a sign of good faith. A similar request by the IAEA in June was ignored by Tehran.

The clerical regime's representatives to the IAEA walked out in protest after the agency's thirty-five-nation governing board unanimously approved the deadline. The head of Iran's delegation warned that Tehran may cease its 'co-operation' with UN nuclear inspectors, following in the footsteps of North Korea in renouncing international treaty obligations that prohibit nuclear weapons research. 'We will have no choice but to have a deep review of our existing level and extent of engagement with the agency,' Ali Akbar Salehi said in a brief statement before walking out.[25] The Iranian regime had to choose between granting UN inspectors greater access to its nuclear facilities and documents, or being brought before the UN Security Council for possible sanctions.

Barely two weeks after the IAEA issued its ultimatum to Tehran, UN nuclear inspectors found further traces of weapons-grade uranium in Iran, reinforcing the international community's suspicions that the mullahs are trying to build a nuclear bomb.[26] Environmental samples taken at the Kalaye Electric plant outside Tehran in August showed traces of highly enriched weapons-grade uranium. The Iranian regime had concealed the Kalaye Electric site as a watch factory, before it was unveiled by the NCRI as a top-secret nuclear site. The discovery at the Kalaye Electric plant followed months of a cat-and-mouse game, with the inspectors initially being barred from taking samples at the plant. The inspectors were allowed to visit the site in August and finally took swab samples of dust. They found that the plant had been substantially rebuilt in order to hamper the inspectors' work and to 'sanitize' the facility. After months of stalling, the Iranian authorities also admitted that the site was central to their uranium enrichment projects and had been used as a testing centre between 1997 and 2002.

Even before the new discovery was announced, IAEA chief ElBaradei warned that Tehran faced a stark choice: 'either implement its obligations under the [nuclear Non-proliferation Treaty] ... or try to walk out of its international obligations'. ElBaradei said that an IAEA board meeting in November would probably refer the crisis to the UN Security Council in New York if he was unable to affirm that Iran's nuclear programme was purely for electricity generation. Western diplomats in Vienna, the IAEA headquarters, told journalists that some of the findings by inspectors in Iran were alarming. One diplomat told the *Guardian*, 'They are getting results that are raising tremendously high eyebrows at the agency ... In the coming weeks this will raise even bigger questions.'[27]

Failure of 'engagement'

The world had known for a long time about the Iranian regime's nuclear ambitions and its secret atomic weapons programme. The

Iranian Resistance first released inside information about the secret project in 1991. Since then, it has exposed a substantial amount of important information on the mullahs' drive to acquire nuclear weapons. In October 1992, for example, the NCRI announced that Tehran had clinched a deal to buy four nuclear warheads from newly independent Kazakhstan.[28] The clerical regime was also negotiating to purchase large quantities of low enriched uranium (LEU) and beryllium from Kazakhstan's Ulba Metallurgical Plant. The revelation was strenuously denied by the Iranian regime, the Kazakh government and several other parties, but Kazakh authorities cancelled the deal. Four years later, the Kazakh ambassador to the United States confirmed the truth of the NCRI's revelations and said that his government had stopped the transfer of the warheads to Iran. Ambassador Nurgaliyev, who was chief of Kazakhstan's national security and arms control at the time, told the Washington press that 'Iran attempted to buy unidentified materials from a major Soviet nuclear facility in his country'.[29] The ambassador said that in 1992, 'Iranian representatives made contact with the Ust-Kamenogorsk facility and sought certain "things"'.[30]

FBIS reported in 1993:

Two Iranian diplomats discussed via telephone the acquisition of four nuclear warheads by Iran from one of the Central Asian republics of the former Soviet Union. The two diplomats are identified as an Iranian Foreign Ministry official Abdolrahmani, who is in charge of relations with the Central Asian republics of the former Soviet Union, and Iranian Deputy Sirus Nasiri Tabatabai-Kia, who is second in command in the Iranian delegation to United Nations institutions and international organizations in Geneva. In the tapped phone conversation between Abdolrahmani and Tabatabai-Kia, which is obtained from a European intelligence service, Abdolrahmani confirms that one of the Muslim republics of the former Soviet Union sold four warheads to Iran. Tabatabai-Kia notes that the purchases 'completed their mission in the best possible way'. Abdolrahmani says that the warheads had not arrived because of a problem with transportation, and that he does not know how much the warheads cost because 'some other guy arranged the issue of the payment'. In the course of the conversation, the names of Iranian President Rafsanjani's brother-in-law Hajj Mohsen Rafiqdust, and the Iranian defence minister Akbar Torkan are mentioned in connection with the sale.[31]

In September 1992, the NCRI office in Washington, DC, held a news conference to announce that the government in Tehran had increased the nuclear project's budget from $200 million in 1991 to $800 million in 1992. The NCRI's information was based on intelligence gathered by members of the People's Mojahedin inside Iran.

Information was also released on Tehran's systematic efforts to buy centrifuges, heavy water, and other parts needed to start a nuclear weapons programme from several countries in Europe, Russia, China and Argentina. The clerical regime also tried to obtain other components for uranium enrichment, including uranium hexafluoride; this pattern of acquisition and Tehran's drive to self-sufficiency for nuclear production clearly signalled military intent. The theocratic regime organized a network of front organizations throughout Europe to buy nuclear and missile technology.

The policy clearly has the blessing of both factions in the clerical regime. President Khatami declared on 1 August 1998 that 'Iran will not ask for anyone's permission to develop its defence capabilities.' For his part, Supreme Leader Ali Khamenei told a gathering of Iranian ambassadors in August 2003: 'The position of the United States and certain Western countries, which require Iran to give up nuclear technology, is unjust and oppressive, and the Islamic Republic of Iran will never accept these requests ... Any weakness and surrender on our part would be the greatest strategic error.'[32]

Few people doubt that a radical fundamentalist regime such as the Islamic Republic of Iran would pose a far greater danger to regional and global peace and security if it acquired nuclear weapons. The big question is why, despite the stream of information that had been divulged about the mullahs' nuclear project, the international community failed to react appropriately to the rising threat. The Iranian nuclear file is a clear manifestation of the failure of engagement and rapprochement when the interlocutor is a religious tyranny that has no respect for the fundamental rules of international relations. By 2003 it had become clear even to the most ardent supporters of dialogue with, and engagement of, Iran's ruling ayatollahs that these policies had for over a decade only aided Tehran in its quest to develop a secret nuclear project. Iranian operatives and front companies were allowed to roam Western markets to procure sensitive information and materials for Tehran's nuclear project.

Ironically, even at this stage, some governments in the West contend that by granting mullahs greater concessions, they could be dissuaded from pursuing their nuclear ambitions. What advocates of appeasement fail to see or acknowledge is the fact that the concessions would greatly embolden the clerical leaders and signal to them the lack of political will on the part of the international community.

Hide and cheat

The mullahs' regime, feeling the threat that would be posed to its nuclear facilities if they were uncovered, and drawing lessons from the raid on Iraq's Tammuz nuclear facilities in 1981, has adopted a two-fold method to foil such surgical military strikes by showcasing the nuclear site in Bushehr and turning it into the focal point of outside attention, thus providing cover for the development of other nuclear sites in the country. At the same time, the regime built up other nuclear laboratories and uranium enrichment sites in different parts of Iran by various agencies, so that even if one or two sites were destroyed in an attack, the project would survive and be continued at other sites.

This policy has meant that there are three types of nuclear sites or centres operating in Iran:

1. open sites such as Bushehr, which the regime intentionally places under the monitoring of the International Atomic Energy Authority as a ruse;
2. secret sites, such as the uranium enrichment plant in Natanz and the heavy water production plant in Arak and the uranium mining project in Saghand near Yazd (these sites were critical for the regime's efforts to reach its ultimate goal and it tried very hard to keep them secret);
3. smaller, more dispersed sites used for uranium enrichment. These sites not only act as complementary to principal sites such as Natanz, but they also ensure that in the case of air attacks or more intrusive intervention by the IAEA which might suspend activities in places like Natanz, these sites would still allow the mullahs to continue enriched uranium production.

The clerical regime engages in deception and concealment to keep its nuclear facilities away from the eyes of international inspectors. The Iranian authorities use a large array of front companies to cover up their procurement activities abroad and sensitive sites inside the country. The Iranian Atomic Energy Organization began setting up front companies in the mid-1990s. A sub-directorate called Companies Oversight Office was established in the IAEO for this purpose. Its front companies include:

- Kalaye Electric Company
- Hasteh Farayed Company
- Kavoshyar Company
- Energy Novin Company
- Novin Puneh Company

- Mesbah Energy Company
- Tavan Gostar Company
- Noor-Afza-Gostar Company
- Sakht Iran company
- Mesbah Energy Company
- Hasteh Sarayand Company
- Kan Iran Company
- ICS

All domestic and foreign procurements for the Centre for Atomic Research (CAR) of the IAEO are conducted by Kavoshyar Company.

Concealment is a widely used tactic to keep sensitive information and materials away from UN inspectors. For example, in late May 2003, Morteza Ostad Ali Makhmalbaff, the head of intelligence security of the Defence Industry Organization, and Brigadier General Mohammad Beig Mohammadlou, deputy co-ordinator of the Defence Industry Organization (involved in the enrichment of uranium), hid a number of containers related to the pilot facility of the DIO at a warehouse measuring 80 metres (260 feet) by 25 metres (80 feet). These containers are sealed and there have been strenuous efforts made to ensure that no one should know of the existence of these containers. This warehouse is surrounded by an auto junk yard and is located at the Martyr Kazemi complex of the Defence Industry Organization, next to Kolahdouz complex.

Peripheral sites

The mullahs' regime began the construction of two nuclear sites west of Tehran in the year 2000. One site is located at Lashkar-Abad village and another 5 km away at Ramandeh village. Both have been under the direct supervision of the director of Iran's Atomic Energy Organization and operate under the cover of Noor-Afza-Gostar Company, one of the front companies of the IAEO. The Lashkar-Abad site is situated between Karaj and Hashtgerd, 40 km west of the Iranian capital. The walled compound is known among the local people as 'the Presidential Orchard'. It has a surface area of 80 hectares. The site has been developed by a construction firm called Jahad-e Tosseye Silou. This was the same company that built part of the principal nuclear facilities in Natanz. Its employees and experts are ex-officers of the Revolutionary Guards. All the workers, even manual labourers, were brought in from Tehran and no indigenous construction worker was hired, a practice highly unusual in Iran. In a hall 50 by 30 metres, several centrifuge machines have been installed for testing. The hall is similar to the laboratory in Natanz, but is smaller and has fewer machines.

The site at Ramandeh village is a walled compound protected by armed guards. Inside the walled area, there are several orchards, concealing the building where the site is located. The sites are laboratories which in normal circumstances work as sub-stations for the main site in Natanz in the nuclear enrichment process. Their other function is to be used as substitutes for Natanz in case of military strikes or any interruption in its operations.

A giant machine

The Iranian regime's secret nuclear weapons project is a giant apparatus that has three main components: a uranium extraction facility in Saghand, uranium enrichment facilities being conducted in a large number of sites across the country, but centred on the one in Natanz, and a heavy water production plant in Arak.

Tehran's plan for a complete uranium enrichment cycle is made up of these components:

- mining uranium in Saghand (200 km from Yazd), from a depth of 350 metres;
- preparing yellow cake in Ardekan near Yazd, at a site known as Ardekan Nuclear Fuel Unit;
- the Uranium Conversion Facility (UCF) in Isfahan will then use the yellow cake prepared in Ardekan to produce a number of products, including uranium hexafluoride (UF_6), metallic uranium, and uranium oxide (UO_2). These are later used for uranium enrichment.

Natanz uranium enrichment facility

Natanz was the crown jewel in the mullahs' secret nuclear programme. The uranium enrichment facility in Natanz is' to use the yellow cake and the products of the Isfahan UCF unit to enrich uranium through the use of gas centrifuge equipment. Nuclear fuel pellets will eventually be produced in Natanz. These pellets could then be used to form fuel rods. Natanz's role is crucial, because it is where the Atomic Energy Organization of Iran (IAEO) is developing a series of centrifuges, which could be used to produce enriched uranium. The revelation of the facility's location and its function by the Iranian Resistance prompted UN inspectors to visit the site. The *New York Times* (22 February 2003) reported that 'after the work on the plant was publicly disclosed by an Iranian opposition group, the National Council of Resistance of Iran, Dr. ElBaradei, asked that it be included in his visit to Iran'. The *Washington Post* wrote two and a half weeks later (10 March) that when in the months following the Iranian Resistance's revelations details of the Natanz complex began to emerge, US officials described the progress of the regime's nuclear programme as 'startling' and 'eye-opening'.

The Natanz project is directly supervised by the clerical regime's Supreme National Security Council. The site was built for uranium enrichment as part of a self-sufficient nuclear fuel production capability. To prevent its discovery, the project was disguised as a station for combating desertification. The site is located on the old Kashan–Natanz highway, near Deh-Zireh village, some 40 km south east of Kashan. The site, with a surface area of nearly 250,000 acres (100,000 hectares), is protected by barbed wire. The area under construction is nearly 25 acres (10 hectares) with two large halls, each nearly 6 acres (2.5 hectares) in an area near several administrative and technical buildings capable of holding 1,000 personnel. Part of the site is underground and heavily reinforced to withstand air attacks. Each of the halls is about 25 feet (8 metres) deep underground, protected by concrete 8 feet (2.5 metres) thick, and surrounded by another protective shield to make it resistant to explosions. Inside the halls, strong foundations have been laid to instal the proper equipment. The construction of the buildings of this project began in 1998, undertaken by two construction companies, Jahad-e Towse'eh and Towse'eh- Sakhteman, and is near completion. Installation of technical facilities began subsequently. The site will be completed by the end of 2003. Next to the main buildings, they have built a smaller building for testing the equipment. It is located in the site in between five warehouses, which are used simply for storage. This small site is evident in satellite photographs, but has been camouflaged as a warehouse. The person is charge of the Natanz project is an engineer by the name of 'Nobari'. Before him, another engineer known as 'Aghajani' and prior to him another engineer called 'Madani' had been in charge of the project. The project has cost 950 billion rials so far. Its budget has been allocated by the Supreme National Security Council and is not overseen by the Budget and Planning Organization.

To create a better cover, the Atomic Energy Organization set up a front company, Kalaye-Electric, through which it has been procuring all the requirements of the project. Kalaye-Electric executives, including CEO Davood Aqajani, made several trips to China and India in 2001. The company's communications and contacts with the Atomic Energy Organization are made directly through the office of IAEO chief Gholamreza Aghazadeh.

Arak's heavy water site

The Atomic Energy Organization began the construction of this heavy water facility in Arak's Khondaub region in 1996. The project is considered top-secret within the IAEO and is supervised by Dr Mohammad Qannadi, Aghazadeh's deputy for nuclear fuel production. The site is located at Qatran Workshop, close to the banks of Qara-Chai river, on the Arak–Khondaub highway. The site requires a lot of water and has been built on a river bank. The heavy water facility has several cooling towers about 3 metres in diameter and 48 metres in height.

To keep tight tabs on the project, the Atomic Energy Organization has been using a front company, the Mesbah Energy Company, affiliated with the IAEO. The company's CEO, Daryoush Sheibani, runs the project. The project's operational manager is Behnam Asgarpour, based at Khondaub. Given the clandestine nature of the Arak site, its budget does not fall under the supervision of the State Organization for Planning and Budget. Its staff are not registered in the IAEO personnel and management departments' data. Secret projects such as Arak are directly overseen by Gholamreza Aghazadeh and the IAEO's Security and Intelligence Office.

After the NCRI exposed the Arak site in August 2002, the Iranian regime stopped a project to expand the site further. Officials finally concluded, however, that the project was in such an advanced stage that they could not dismantle the machinery or change its location. It was decided to continue the project and justify it by saying that it addressed the country's industrial needs.

Missile development

Nuclear arms or other types of weapons of mass destruction (WMD) would give the clerical regime far greater intimidating or deterrent power if it also possessed the means to deliver them. Tehran has been developing medium- and long-range missiles in tandem with the work on WMD programmes. In February 2003, Navy Commander Abbas Mohtaj announced: 'We are now capable of building missiles with a range of 1,500 km.' He added: 'Our enemy has weak points known to us, so if there is a war, we can inflict serious damage on the enemy.'[33]

In a comprehensive report in October 2002, the NCRI's Defence and Strategic Studies Committee revealed that the Iranian regime had completed tests on the Shahab-4 missile, with a range of 2,000 km, both with aluminium and a cast-iron body. The Iranian military is currently trying to improve Shahab-4's guidance components. The Shahab-4 would be capable of hitting targets as far away as Germany and western China.

The missile is a modified version of the Sandaĺ (SS-4) missile, carrying a 1.5 ton warhead. The Shahab-4 is 22 metres long and weighs around 42 tons.

The tests were carried out at a missile firing range facility located 80 km south of Semnan in eastern Iran, in May and August 2002, by the Revolutionary Guards' Fifth Raad Missile Brigade. Revolutionary Guards Air Force Commander Ahmad Kazemi, the IRGC's Missile Force Commander Hassan Tehrani Moqaddam and several other senior military commanders were present. When in May 2002 Iran's Defence Minister Ali Shamkhani was asked about the test, he referred to a Shahab-3 test, to keep the Shahab-4 test secret. This missile is assembled at Hemmat industrial complex on the Damavand–Tehran highway. The plant belongs to the Revolutionary Guards.

After the completion of the Shahab-4, Tehran has now begun work on the Shahab-5 missile, with a range of 4,000 km, and the Shahab-6, an intercontinental ballistic missile (ICBM). The latter has been codenamed Kowsar. The Shahab-3 missile is the same as the Nodong I of North Korea, with an increased range of 1,300 km. It was concluded that the missile should be equipped with chemical and biological warheads in order to make it effective in any confrontation. On 26 September 1998, when Shahab-3s were displayed for the first time in a parade, Khomeini's quotations had been prominently written on their bodies: 'The U.S. cannot do a damn thing' and 'Israel must be wiped off the face of the earth'.

Iran's neighbours and others in the region could not have found much comfort in the statement by Revolutionary Guards Commandant General Rahim Safavi, who said, 'Iran's ballistic missile capabilities have increased and the country has become a major missile power in the region.'

Notes

1. Ali-Akbar Hashemi Rafsanjani, acting Commander in Chief of the Armed Forces, addressing Islamic Revolutionary Guards Corps on 6 October 1988, quoted in 'The China-Iran Nuclear Cloud', *Middle East Defence News*, 22 July 1991.

2. Reza Amrollahi, head of Iran's Atomic Energy Organization in the early 1980s, a Rafsanjani protégé.

3. *Middle East Defence News*, August 1992, p. 42.

4. Mark Hibbs and Neel Patri, 'U.S. to Ask New Delhi to Back Off on Research Reactor Offer to Iran', *Nucleonics Week*, vol. 32, no. 47, 21 November 1991, pp. 2–3.

5. Mark Hibbs, 'Iran Negotiating with USSR for Supply of "Several" PWRs', *Nucleonics Week*, vol. 41, no. 43, 25 October 1990, pp. 1–2.

6. Rafsanjani, IRNA, 16 June 2003.

7. Rafsanjani speech marking 'the Week of Sacred Defence', *Jomhouri Islami* daily, 20 September 2003.

8. Douglas Frantz, 'Iran Closes in on Ability to Build a Nuclear Bomb', *Los Angeles Times*, 4 August 2003.

9. Ibid.

10. Constitution of the Islamic Republic of Iran, Article 176; see <www. salamiran.org>.

11. Ibid.

12. Interview with Brigadier General Mohammad-Ali Jaafari, IRNA, 9 October 2002.

13. Ali Larijani, speech at Tehran's Friday prayers, IRNA, 20 April 2001.

14. Bellona news service, 28 May 2003.

15. 'Iran Mining Uranium', *Arms Control Today*, March 2003.

16. Text of NCRI press conference in Washington, DC, 20 February 2003, on NCRI foreign affairs committee website, <www.iranncrfac.org>.

17. *New York Times*, 20 February 2003.

18. Associated Press, 'U.S. Rejects Iranian Claim that Nuke Facilities are for Energy', 11 March 2003.

19. Ibid.

20. Paul Reynolds, 'Iran: Nuclear Squeeze is On', BBC World Service, 16 June 2003.

21. IRNA, 9 July 2003.

22. Ibid.

23. Statement on Iran, IAEA board of governors, 16–20 June 2003, cited on IAEA website, <www.iaea.or.at>.

24. Joby Warrick, 'UN Sets Nuclear Deadline for Iran', *Washington Post*, 13 September 2003.

25. Ibid.

26. Ian Traynor, 'New Iran Uranium Find Reinforces Bomb Fears', *Guardian*, 26 September 2003.

27. Ibid.

28. Nick Ludington, 'Iran Buying Nuclear Warheads from Kazakhstan Says Opposition Group', Associated Press, 21 October 1992.

29. 'How Iran Nearly Got Nuke Gear', *Washington Times*, 2 November 1996.

30. Ibid.

31. FBIS, 'Tapped Line Said to Reveal Deal on Warheads', 15 January 1993, pp. 61–2.

32. Ali Khamenei addressing a gathering of Iranian ambassadors, IRNA, 19 August 2003.

33. Revolutionary Guards Rear Admiral Abbas Mohtaj, interview with *Kayhan* newspaper, 2 February 2003.

PART II
Clash of Islams

3 | Anti-fundamentalist Muslims

> Tyranny, like hell, is not easily conquered; yet we have this consolation with us, that the harder the conflict, the more glorious the triumph. What we obtain too cheap, we esteem too lightly.
>
> *Thomas Paine*[1]

The conflict that has dominated Iranian politics for a quarter of a century can be seen, from one perspective, as the clash of two Islams. On one side of the conflict, Shiite clerics have been ruling Iran since 1979, offering Muslims around a world a fundamentalist model of government. Throughout this time, the main opposition to clerical rule in Iran has come from the People's Mojahedin Organization of Iran (PMOI), a movement that also purports to be Muslim, but advocates a secular, democratic and pluralist form of government that is at odds with the present theocracy.

The People's Mojahedin Organization of Iran is the oldest and largest anti-fundamentalist Muslim group in the Middle East. From its intellectual roots in the 1960s, the PMOI has grown into a mass movement with an avowedly anti-fundamentalist interpretation of Islam. Since its foundation in 1965, the PMOI gradually succeeded in offering a new, comprehensive and credible interpretation of Islam and its outlook on freedom, human rights, social justice, gender equality, ethnic and religious minorities' rights and other problems facing modern societies. This interpretation, diametrically opposed to the fundamentalists' religion, is compatible with progress, social development and human civilization. The most important distinction between the PMOI's interpretation of Islam and that of Khomeini-inspired fundamentalists is that the PMOI's version relies on freedom, democratic rights of all citizens and secularism.

In contrast to fundamentalists, who view the *vali-e faqih* (Supreme Leader) as 'God's representative on Earth', and consider his legitimacy entirely 'divine', the Mojahedin insist that nothing is legitimate unless confirmed by the ballot-box and that elections and public suffrage are the sole indicators of political legitimacy. The PMOI make it quite clear that Islam defends freedom and popular sovereignty. In a meeting attended by 200,000 people in Tehran in June 1980, PMOI Secretary General Massoud Rajavi said:

Freedom is a divine blessing. No one has given it as charity. We gain freedom with the force of our blood and would not abandon it to our last breath. Anyone trying to restrict human freedom has neither understood Islam nor mankind and the [anti-monarchist] revolution. Freedom is indispensable to the survival of mankind as human beings. Otherwise, human beings would be no different from animals and could not be held responsible for anything.[2]

Reactionary clerics, led by Khomeini, were alarmed by the PMOI's appeal, particularly among the young. Repeated calls by religious personalities and the public at large on the clerics to support the PMOI in its confrontation with the Shah's regime compelled them either to express that support openly or, in the case of Khomeini, do so implicitly by referring to the Mojahedin as 'young Muslims fighting the Shah's dictatorship'.[3] When he first took the helm, Khomeini sought to exploit the Mojahedin's prestige and influence among young people to solidify his power. From Paris, his son Ahmad contacted Massoud Rajavi, who had just been released from prison, to tell him: 'You have a lot of support in Iran. If you form a party, millions would join you.' Shortly after Khomeini's return to Iran, Ahmad Khomeini met Rajavi and told him: 'If you support the Imam and oppose his opponents, all gates would be open before you and you would receive every thing you want.' Rajavi rejected the offer, saying that the PMOI sought a democratic government and that if Khomeini were to choose that path, the Mojahedin would not hesitate to support him.

Khomeini's demand was clear: either the Mojahedin would submit totally to his power, or face a ban on their activities. Rajavi's response left Khomeini in no doubt: there would be no room for the PMOI in the Islamic Republic. After the 200,000-strong rally in Tehran's Amjadieh stadium on 12 June 1980, where Massoud Rajavi attacked the creeping dictatorship, Khomeini lashed out two weeks later. On 25 June he said on state radio that the PMOI was 'the main enemy', adding, 'Our enemy is neither in the United States, nor the Soviet Union, nor Kurdistan, but sitting right here in Tehran under our nose.' He went on:

The Monafeqin [meaning hypocrites, mullahs' pejorative term for the Mojahedin] are worst than infidels. They say they are Muslims, but they act against Islam. The Quran has condemned them more than it has condemned others. We have a chapter of the Quran that is called Monafeqin, but there is no chapter called infidels. Islam has always been plagued by such groups ... These people wanted to deceive me. I was in Najaf and they came to deceive me. For more than twenty days, these people who claim to be Muslims came in Najaf. I gave them time to say what they wanted. They thought they could fool me. Regrettably, some honourable and learned clergymen had written to me, saying that these people were 'brave young men'. Today, we clergymen are being called reactionaries. Now, our clerics are being called reactionaries and those people are being called the intellectuals.[4]

Mehdi Karrubi, a close confidant of Khomeini who is now the Iranian regime's Majlis Speaker, recounted the events of that period:

If the Imam [Khomeini] were to be influenced, he would have been influenced when he was in the holy city of Najaf, in exile. Friends, confidants and supporters inside and outside could have influenced him and compelled him to write a letter on behalf of the so-called Mojahedin Organization. All revolutionary groups and Muslims, first and foremost among them the most distinguished cleric Ayatollah Montazeri, tried to compel the Imam to say one word or write a single line about this organization, but he single-handedly refused to do so and did as he thought was right.[5]

Clearly, the face-off between the PMOI and Khomeini was not over power sharing, but a deep, irreconcilable ideological and political divide that separated them. In early 1980, the Interior Minister Hashemi Rafsanjani, who later became President, met with Massoud Rajavi, who had requested to see him to complain about the widespread vote-rigging in the first post-revolutionary parliamentary election. Rafsanjani admonished Rajavi: 'If you were willing to accept Imam [Khomeini's] supreme authority, all the gates to the government would have been open to you and we would not have had to appoint expatriates as ministers and senior officials.'

In an affidavit to the US Court of Appeals in the District of Columbia, the prominent orientalist, Dr Khalid Duran, wrote: 'The Mojahedin's differences with Khomeini date back to the 1970s, and stem from their opposition to what is known today as Islamic fundamentalism. The antipathy was mutual; Khomeini was the only opposition religious figure who refused to endorse the Mojahedin.'

A lexicographic note

The roots of the term Mojahedin go back to the history of Iran's nationalist and constitutionalist movement at the turn of the twentieth century. For the first time in Iran's contemporary history, revolutionaries in the 1906 Constitutional Movement, the first major social revolution in the East, called themselves the 'Mojahedin'. Sattar Khan[6] and Baqer Khan[7] were the leaders of the Mojahedin in the north-western province of Azerbaijan. When the Qajar Shah ordered the army to shell the newly established parliament in a bid to defeat the Constitutional Movement, the Mojahedin resisted the attack and forced the Shah to flee. The revolutionaries in that movement were mostly Muslim. Politically, they believed in democracy and the separation of mosque and state.

Massoud Rajavi, the PMOI's Secretary General from the onset of the mullahs' rule until 1989, said the following about the Mojahedin's historical background:

> The Iranian people's experience in the past century shows clearly that the road to freedom and people's sovereignty in our contemporary history began with the standard-bearers and the Mojahedin at the time of the Constitutional Movement. It passed through the Mojahedin around Mirza Khuchek Khan[8] and then to the oil nationalization movement under Dr Mossadeq's[9] leadership. It suffered a setback during the 19 August 1953 coup and the martyrdom of Dr Hossein Fatemi,[10] but the founders of the People's Mojahedin took it to new heights ... Hanifnejad's[11] breakthrough gave rise to a movement that served as guarantor of our nation's historic struggle to achieve freedom and popular and national sovereignty in the face of the reactionaries. The message of this pioneering mindset is to understand Islam's liberating message, which heralds freedom and social justice.[12]

Mojahedin versus Islamic fundamentalists

Sazeman-e Mojahedin-e Khalq-e Iran, or the People's Mojahedin Organization of Iran, was founded in 1965 by Mohammad Hanifnejad and two other young, university-educated intellectuals, Sa'id Mohsen and Ali Asghar Badi'zadegan. Until 1971, however, the PMOI was involved in formulating a new interpretation of Islam that rejected traditional and reactionary understanding of the religion. In six years, the Mojahedin succeeded, for the first time in the modern-day Islamic world, in presenting a new, systematic and comprehensive vision of Islam that was entirely independent of what was espoused and advocated by the fundamentalist mullahs who considered the interpretation of Islam their exclusive domain.

The Shah's secret police, SAVAK, arrested all PMOI leaders and most of its members in 1971. In April and May 1972, the three founders and all the Central Committee members were executed. Massoud Rajavi's death sentence was commuted to life imprisonment after a campaign by his Geneva-based brother Dr Kazem Rajavi (assassinated in April 1990 in

Geneva by mullahs' agents) and the personal intervention of the French President Georges Pompidou and François Mitterrand (Kazem Rajavi, *La Révolution iranienne et les Moudjahidin*, Paris: Anthropos, 1986).

During his seven-year incarceration, Rajavi faced a struggle on three fronts: the Shah's dictatorship, fundamentalist mullahs and opportunist communists who had, through a creeping coup, taken control of the already weakened PMOI network outside prisons and declared a 'leap' from Islam to Marxism. They usurped the PMOI's name and all its assets. Mojahedin members who resisted their pressures and threats to declare their 'conversion' from Islam to Marxism were expelled; several of them were brutally murdered. The coup by the communists against the PMOI quickly became a pretext for the mullahs to lash out at the Mojahedin. Prior to the coup and the virtual disintegration of the PMOI, these clerics, most of whom were destined to become key figures in the Islamic Republic, had accepted the predominance of the Mojahedin in the opposition to the Shah's regime. In a trip abroad at the time, Hashemi Rafsanjani told PMOI representatives that 'without the blessing of the Mojahedin, Khomeini cannot even move a finger'. Within a few years, however, the strongest opposition organization inside Iran, the Mojahedin, fell into complete disarray in the wake of SAVAK's devastating blows and the communist takeover of its network. Conversely, a Khomeini-led Islamic fundamentalist current gained strength. These developments took on greater significance in November 1976, when Jimmy Carter was elected as the thirty-ninth President of the United States on a platform that included a pledge to end support for dictators who ruled in the name of US allies.

Pressurized by the Carter administration, the Shah slowed down executions and torture in Iran. For the first time after twenty-five years of iron-fist rule, people in their millions dared to pour out on to the streets and shake the regime to its foundations. On 16 January 1979, the Shah fled Iran, never to return. All democratic opposition leaders had by then either been executed or imprisoned, and could exert little influence on the trend of events. Khomeini and his network of mullahs across the country, who had by and large been spared the wrath of SAVAK, were the only force that remained intact and could take advantage of the political vacuum. In France, Khomeini received maximum exposure to the world media and assistance from the French government. With the aid of his clerical followers, he hijacked a revolution that began with calls for democracy and freedom and diverted it towards his fundamentalist goals. Through an exceptional combination of historical events, Shiite clerics assumed power in Iran.

Years later, Rajavi said:

When the spell of SAVAK's repression was broken and popular protests coalesced into a momentous upheaval, Khomeini was sitting under an apple tree in Paris, smiling. He equivocated about the future instead of presenting a specific programme or pledge. He only engaged in generalities. He completely lied about people's sovereignty. With respect to the role of clerics in government, he said, 'Clergymen, like other sectors of society, would have representatives.' As to his own role, he said, 'Once the revolution succeeds and the Shah falls, I will return to Qom to continue my religious studies.' But as soon as he assumed power, he began to monopolize power and concentrated everything in the hands of the clerics around him. He rejected the election of a constituent assembly and instead formed a clergy-dominated Assembly of Experts. He also imposed the *velayat-e faqih* constitution on the Iranian people. Step by step, the fundamentalist ogre began to wipe out the achievement of the revolution and solidify an autocratic theocracy in the name of Islam.

Thus, after Khomeini assumed power, the historical face-off between the Mojahedin and the ruling fundamentalists began to take shape, albeit in a qualitatively much wider and comprehensive scope. For Khomeini had regrettably targeted our homeland, our people, our ideals and our beliefs ...

This was an inevitable and necessary, but patently unequal, confrontation. Khomeini, as a well-known Marjaa Taqlid [senior Shiite religious leader], combined temporal and ecclesiastical power in a way Iran had not experienced in its thousands of years of history. He had usurped political power and the legitimacy of a popular revolution in one stroke and rode on the wave of illusion of a people who saw his face in the moon.

Despite all the pressures and assaults by Khomeini and his clique, one year after the fall of the Shah, the Mojahedin emerged as a major political and social movement across Iran with branches and offices in more than 250 cities. The PMOI's daily newspaper, *Mojahed*, had a circulation of 600,000 copies, the largest-ever for an Iranian daily.[13]

The Mojahedin had recognized the rising threat of Islamic fundamentalism before Khomeini assumed power. In the mid-1970s, while in prison, Rajavi voiced concern in his teachings and books at the coming to power of an Islamic fundamentalist current. In dozens of articles and treatises, he and his colleagues systematically formulated the marked differences between a democratic and a fundamentalist Islam in the realms of history, philosophy, economy, society and politics. Rajavi described Islamic fundamentalism as 'the main threat within the opposition movement' and warned particularly of Khomeini's reactionary and totalitarian views. He wrote, 'We believe this backward religious current is the antithesis of, and the principal threat to, all groups who struggle in the name of Islam.'[14]

The Mojahedin never acquiesced in describing the anti-monarchist revolution as an 'Islamic revolution'. It considered such a name an attempt to exclude the secular currents which fought against the Shah's regime. This prompted Khomeini and his entourage to attack the PMOI for 'being opposed to Islam'.

Rajavi was released from prison in January 1979, after the Shah fled Iran. He reconstructed the PMOI's organizational structure and moved quickly to present the organization's political platform to the public. In his first speech on 24 January 1979, at Tehran University, Rajavi said,

I have not come here to approve of the spontaneous trend of events. We have not come here to confirm the status quo. We must think about what is needed to happen. It must be said clearly that everyone has the right to struggle. The sanctity and the right to resist must be safeguarded. The right to struggle is the natural and divine right of any human being. We must, therefore, respect each other and avoid disunity.

An anti-fundamentalist platform

On 23 February 1979, eleven days after the mullahs took power, Rajavi announced the Mojahedin's political programme under the new government at a rally in Tehran University. He voiced alarm about threats to political freedoms. The next day, Tehran dailies (e.g. *Kayhan*, 24 February 1979) wrote that the PMOI had presented itself as the opposition to the new regime. Rajavi's speech in Tehran University was in fact the Mojahedin's anti-fundamentalist manifesto. The prestige and credibility that years of struggle against the Shah bestowed on the PMOI made it a prime candidate to challenge the mullahs' power in the country. The PMOI's emphasis on political freedoms as the most important issue of the day put it on a collision course with Khomeini and his supporters, including the KGB-controlled Tudeh Party. 'The History of Iran', published by the United States Library of Congress, described the Tudeh Party's collaboration with the ruling fundamentalists against the Mojahedin thus: 'The Tudeh had secured itself a measure of freedom during the first three years of the Revolution by declaring loyalty to Khomeini and supporting the clerics against liberal and left-wing opposition groups.'[15]

The clerical regime's leaders and their Tudeh allies sharply attacked the PMOI, claiming that by insisting that fundamental freedoms should be put on top of the agenda, the organization had put itself in the service of the United States and was acting against the 'Islamic Revolution'. In an open letter to senior clerical officials written 18 May, Tudeh Party Secretary General Nourreddin Kianouri wrote: 'The Tudeh Party of Iran has acted and acts with all the forces at its disposal against groups and grouplets who are either deliberately collaborating with the counter-revolutionaries or have done so unwittingly due to a misguided vision of the nature of the Islamic Revolution.' Tudeh Party leaders sank deeper into collaboration with the mullahs, to the point where they began to spy on the Mojahedin for the regime. Many members of the Mojahedin were arrested and executed as a result of information provided by the Tudeh Party. When Massoud Rajavi went to Paris in 1981, the Tudeh Party wrote, on 30 July, to senior French government officials, 'We endorse the Iranian regime's demands and emphatically call for the extradition of Rajavi.'

From the onset, the mullahs began a systematic campaign aimed at the step-by-step elimination of all opposition forces. Only a few weeks after the Shah's overthrow gangs of club-wielders, known as Hezbollah and organized by the ruling Islamic Republican Party, began to attack the offices, rallies and supporters of the Mojahedin. The PMOI called for broad participation in a democratic government. This objective formed the basis for its political strategy and was reconfirmed in its minimum expectations programme in early 1979. Brutal attacks against the Mojahedin only increased their popularity. The PMOI became identified for its steadfastness against religious tyranny and the regime's efforts to impose its fundamentalist Islam on the country. Despite the harshest crackdown on the Mojahedin, the organization, its members and sympathizers remained resolute in their decision to engage in a peaceful struggle to establish democracy and freedom in Iran.

Fundamentalist constitution

In January 1980, the PMOI took part in the first presidential election after the Shah's overthrow. Its candidate, Massoud Rajavi, was supported by a large sector of Iranian society, including several other parties, ethnic and religious minorities (such as the Kurds, Sunnis, Christians and Jews), students, young people, secular groups and women. Khomeini considered Rajavi a serious threat, particularly if he were allowed to run in the presidential election. A week before elections were held, he issued a fatwa, vetoing Rajavi's candidacy. He said those who did not vote for the constitution in December 1979 could not stand as candidates in the presidential election. Clearly this fatwa applied only to Rajavi. He and his organization refused to take part in the referendum on the *velayat-e faqih* constitution. The PMOI's refusal to endorse Khomeini's constitution, while he still wielded vast popular support, was a bold but necessary act, for the new constitution was a fundamentalist declaration that enshrined the principle of *velayat-e faqih*.

The French daily *Le Monde's* correspondent Eric Rouleau reported from Tehran on 29 March:

> Had Imam Khomeini not vetoed his candidacy in the presidential election last January, Mr Rajavi would have obtained several million votes. He was, moreover, assured of the support of the religious and ethnic minorities – whose rights to equality and autonomy he defended – and a good part of the female vote, who seek emancipation, and the young, who totally reject the 'reactionary clergy' ...
>
> The Mojahedin have not ceased denouncing, documenting and issuing calls about 'the rigging, fraud and violence' surrounding the first round of elections. Two thousand five hundred of their supporters were wounded, 50 of them gravely, by armed bands of 'Hezbollah' in the course of the election campaign ... Observers appointed by the Mojahedin who protested the election fraud were expelled from the premises, beaten, and sometimes arrested ...

Shaul Bakhash, Professor of History at George Mason University in Virginia and an expert on the Middle East, wrote about the events of that era in his book, *The Reign of the Ayatollahs*:

> In February 1980, 60,000 copies of Mojahed were seized and burned. In Mashad, Shiraz, Qa'emshahr, Sari, and dozens of small towns, club wielders attacked and looted Mojahedin headquarters, student societies, and meetings. Since the Mojahedin meetings were often large, these attacks turned into huge melees. Some 700 were injured in the attack on the Mojahedin headquarters at Qa'emshahr in April, 400 in Mashad. Ten members of the organization lost their lives in clashes between February and June 1980.
>
> Preachers were often the instigators of these attacks. In Qom, anti-Mojahedin marches took place after sermons by Mohammad Taqi Falsafi and Mohammad-Javad Bahonar. In Behshahr, the Mojahedin were attacked after a sermon by Fakhr ad-Din Hejazi. Hojjat ol-Eslam Khaz'ali moved from town to town to preach against the Mojahedin. 'If they do not repent,' he told a crowd in Shahrud, 'take them and throw them in

the Caspian Sea.' He accused the Mojahedin of being communists, taking part in the Kurdish uprising, killing Revolutionary Guardsmen, and misleading young girls. 'Even if they hide in a mouse hole,' he told a Mashad congregation, 'we will drag them out and kill them ... We are thirsty for their blood. We must close off their jugular.' ...

[Khomeini] was suspicious of the Mojahedin's growing strength and disapproved of their attempts, as laymen, to appropriate to themselves the authority to interpret Islamic doctrine. In June 1980, Khomeini publicly denounced the Mojahedin as polytheists and hypocrites and contemptuously referred to Rajavi as 'this lad who calls himself the leader'. The Mojahedin responded by quietly closing all their branch offices and retreating further underground.[16]

Attacks against Mojahedin offices and meetings continued in the first half of 1980. On 12 June, in a famous speech before a crowd of 200,000 at Tehran's Amjadieh Stadium, Rajavi urged the Iranian people to 'defend freedoms, freedom of speech, associations and gatherings'. The Revolutionary Guards tried to disrupt the meeting with tear gas and live ammunition. Their assault left one dead and hundreds wounded. In an article on 14 June about that meeting, Rouleau wrote:

The objective of the popular gathering on Thursday afternoon, called by the People's Mojahedin, was to protest against attacks on their supporters and activists in the past few days ...

Tens of thousands of the party's sympathizers had lined up at the entrance gates an hour before the gathering [at Amjadieh Stadium] when groups of Hezbollah began loudly protesting against the Mojahedin ,... chanting, 'There is only one party, the Party of God, and only one Leader, Imam Khomeini.'

The Hezbollah claims no precise political organization. They are notorious among the public as the shock troops ... and serve as the tool of the extreme right faction of the Islamic Republican Party, directed by Beheshti ...

Things being as they stand, the choice, according to observers, is between reconciliation and civil war.

In an unclassified report on the PMOI in December 1984, the US State Department referred to the events of 1979–81:

The Mujahedin have never accepted the Khomeini regime as an adequate Islamic government. When Khomeini took power, the Mujahedin called for continued revolution, but said they would work for change within the legal framework of the new regime. The Mujahedin publications emphasized their unique role as an urban guerrilla force that promised to enter candidates for the highest offices under the new political system. The Mujahedin also entered avidly into the national debate on the structure of the new Islamic regime. The Mujahedin unsuccessfully sought a freely elected constituent assembly to draft a constitution.

The Mujahedin similarly made an attempt at political participation when Mujahedin leader Masud Rajavi ran for the presidency in January 1980. Rajavi was forced to withdraw when Ayatollah Khomeini ruled that only candidates who had supported the constitution in the December referendum – which the Mojahedin had boycotted – were eligible. Rajavi's withdrawal statement emphasized the group's efforts to conform to election regulations and reiterated the Mojahedin's intention to advance its political aims within the new legal system.

In March and May 1980, Rajavi and several other Mujahedin ran in Tehran for the Islamic Assembly (Majlis). Moussa Khiabani, Rajavi's deputy, ran in Tabriz, and others ran in the north, where the group was strong. The Mujahedin attempted to demonstrate their broadened appeal by running on their ticket several moderate political figures ...

Between the two election rounds, the Mujahedin announced that its members would disarm to prove that they were not initiating the clashes with the fundamentalists that had become endemic during the campaign. The fundamentalists responded by once again banning Mujahedin representatives from the university campuses. The group's allegations, that vote tallies had been altered to deny Rajavi and Khiabani victories, were ignored.

Rajavi then began to hint that the Mujahedin were considering active opposition to the Khomeini regime. In the early summer of 1980 the Mujahedin staged several rallies in Tehran, drawing up to 150,000 people to hear Rajavi promise to carry on the opposition to fundamentalist domination. On June 25 Khomeini responded by a major statement against the Mujahedin, claiming their activities would derail the revolution and bring back 'U.S. dominance'.

'Worse than infidels'

After Khomeini's 25 June speech in which he said the Mojahedin were 'worse than infidels', he set the stage for outright suppression of the PMOI. His decree gave a green light not only to the Revolutionary Guards and club-wielders, but also to the judiciary and the religious judges across Iran. Responding to a letter of complaint by Mojahedin supporters in August 1980, when the organization still engaged in public activities, Mullah Allameh, head of the revolutionary court in Bam, in southern Iran, wrote: 'According to the decree of Imam Khomeini, the Mojahedin of Iran are infidels and worse than blasphemers ... They have no right to life.'[17]

This type of 'punishment en masse' for the followers of a party or a political organization with mass following across the nation can only be described as genocidal. A decade later, Mohammad Yazdi, the head of the regime's judiciary, referred to Khomeini's order to massacre the Mojahedin and their supporters, issued months before it became public, as follows: 'The Imam's hand-written judicial order condemned the [Mojahedin] – the totality of the organization and its infrastructure, and not individuals – so that there would be no hesitation in terming the activities by these individuals as waging war on God and corruption on Earth [and carrying out their execution orders]'.[18]

In summer 1988, Khomeini issued a fatwa physically to annihilate the Mojahedin. Some 30,000 political prisoners were massacred in the course of several months. The full text of the fatwa was made public years later by his deposed successor Ayatollah Hossein-Ali Montazeri. This fatwa did not attract as much attention as the one issued a few months later against British author Salman Rushdie. It is, none the less, an important historical document, for it shows, above all else, that Islamic fundamentalism in power has ultimately no recourse other than physically to eliminate its opponents. This is one of the many characteristics that transform Islamic fundamentalism to fascism under the cloak of religion, and renders it comparable with the Nazis' 'final solution' and their use of concentration camps. The text of Khomeini's fatwa was as follows:

> As the treacherous Monafeqin [Mojahedin] do not believe in Islam and what they say is out of deception and hypocrisy, and as their leaders have confessed that they have become renegades, and as they are waging war on God ... and as they are tied to the World Arrogance [the United States], it is decreed that those who are in prison throughout the country and who remain steadfast in their support for the Monafeqin, are waging war on God and are condemned to execution. It is naïve to show mercy to those who wage war on God. The decisive ways in which Islam treats the enemies of God is among the unquestionable tenets of the Islamic regime ... Those who are making decisions must not hesitate nor should they show any doubt or be concerned with details. They must try to be most ferocious against infidels ... To have doubts about the judicial matters of revolutionary Islam is to ignore the pure blood of martyrs.[19]

Following the fatwa, the Chief Justice Abdolkarim Moussavi Ardebili asked Khomeini, through his son, Ahmad, whether the decree also applied to those who had already been tried and who had received limited jail terms. Khomeini's response was chilling: 'If the person at any stage or at any time maintains his [or her] support for the Monafeqin, the sentence is execution. Annihilate the enemies of Islam immediately. Use whichever criterion that speeds up the implementation of the [execution] verdict.'

In an article on 4 February 2001, entitled 'Khomeini Fatwa "Led to Killing of 30,000 in Iran"', the *Sunday Telegraph* wrote:

Children as young as 13 were hanged from cranes, six at a time, in a barbaric two-month purge of Iran's prisons on the direct orders of Ayatollah Khomeini, according to a new book by his former deputy. More than 30,000 political prisoners were executed in the 1988 massacre. Gruesome details are contained in the memoirs of Grand Ayatollah Hossein-Ali Montazeri, one of the founders of the Islamic regime. The most damning of the letters and documents published in the book is Khomeini's fatwa decree calling for all Mojahedin (as opponents of the Iranian regime are known) to be killed ...

Mr. Kamal Afkhami Ardakani, a former official at Evin Prison, said in testimonies to human rights rapporteurs of the United Nations: 'They would line up prisoners in a 14-by-5-metre hall in the central office building and then ask simply one question, "What is your political affiliation?" Those who said the Mojahedin would be hanged from cranes in position in the car park behind the building.'

He went on to describe how, every half an hour from 7.30am to 5pm, 33 people were lifted on three forklift trucks to six cranes, each of which had five or six ropes. He said: 'The process went on and on without interruption.' In two weeks, 8,000 people were hanged. Similar carnage took place across the country.

Many of those in the ruling council at the time of the 1988 massacre are still in power, including President Mohammed Khatami, who was the Director of Ideological and Cultural Affairs.

The clerical regime's campaign of physical annihilation of dissidents has led, in the past two decades, to the execution of more than 120,000 members and supporters of the PMOI. The names and particulars of some 20,000 of them have been published.

Absolute repression

From the start of 1981, it became quite clear that attacks against the PMOI would rise and grow more serious. On 24 April 1981, the PMOI organized a protest demonstration against the killing of its members and sympathizers. Some 150,000 Tehran residents took part in the rally. On 7 May 1981, the Mojahedin organized another demonstration in which 150,000 families of PMOI supporters and members tortured or imprisoned in jails across Iran took part. PMOI women supporters in particular participated in this demonstration. These peaceful protests sought to encourage the clerics to stop violence and respect the minimum democratic rights of the Iranian people. Regrettably, these peaceful efforts failed.

Finally, the turning point for the Mojahedin and the Iranian people in their struggle for democracy and freedom came on 20 June 1981. The PMOI organized a half-a-million-strong demonstration in Tehran to protest against repression. The Revolutionary Guards, on Khomeini's direct orders, violently crushed the protest; hundreds were killed or wounded. Khomeini had decided once and for all to eliminate the Mojahedin, because he saw its rising popularity as a serious threat to clerical rule. The next day, the regime executed hundreds of those arrested. Some, including twelve young girls, were executed without their identities being established. On 24 June, the daily *Ettela'at* published the pictures of the under-age girls executed en masse. Noting that their identities had not been established at the time of their execution, it asked their parents to go to the officials to receive the bodies of their loved ones.

The US historian Ervand Abrahamian, who worked closely with State Department officials involved in Irangate, referred to the June 1981 events in his book, *The Iranian Mojahedin*:

On 20 June, vast crowds appeared in many cities, especially in Tehran, Tabriz, Rasht, Amol, Qiyamshahr, Gorgan, Babolsar, Zanjan, Karaj, Arak, Isfahan, Birjand, Ahwaz and Kerman. The Tehran demonstration drew as many as 500,000 determined participants. Warnings against demonstrations were constantly broadcast over the radio-television network. Government supporters advised the public to stay at home: for example, Nabavi's Organization of the Mojaheds of the Islamic Revolution beseeched the youth of Iran not to waste their lives for the sake of 'liberalism and capitalism'. Prominent clerics declared that demonstrators, irrespective of their age, would be treated as 'enemies of God' and as such would be executed on the spot. Hezbollahis were armed and trucked in to block off the major streets. Pasdars were ordered to shoot. Fifty were killed, 200 injured, and 1,000 arrested in the vicinity of Tehran University alone. This surpassed most of the street clashes of the Islamic Revolution. The warden of Evin Prison announced with much fanfare that firing squads had executed twenty-three demonstrators, including a number of teenage girls. The reign of terror had begun.[20]

Until then, the PMOI had taken part only in peaceful demonstrations against the clerical regime, putting forth its platform for democracy and freedom in Iran in a non-violent manner. Nevertheless, from February 1979 until June 1981, the regime murdered seventy-one PMOI members. Until 20 June 1981, more than 2,500 Mojahedin sympathizers had been arrested and imprisoned. The violent repression unleashed after 21 June 1981 was clearly a turning point in Iranian political history. Peaceful struggle against the clerical regime was no longer possible. In the face of such an onslaught, the democratic opposition, including the Mojahedin, had no choice but to resort to all-out resistance.

The US Library of Congress, in 'History of Iran', wrote: 'The executions were facilitated by a September 1981, Supreme Judicial Council circular to the revolutionary courts permitting death sentences for "active members" of guerrilla groups. Fifty executions a day became routine; there were days when more than 100 persons were executed.'

The 'reign of terror' that began in 1981 has gone through different phases, but has continued for more than two decades. The clerical regime has executed more than 120,000 of its opponents and tortured and imprisoned hundreds of thousands more. It has applied more than 170 forms of physical and psychological tortures in its prisons. It has been hunting down its opponents across the world. The repression has not just targeted political groups and dissidents, it has permeated the entire society, as everyone, particularly women, young people and students, find themselves the favourite targets of this unparalleled inquisition. Revolutionary Guards and security forces enter homes at will and detain people on such bogus charges as taking part in mixed parties. They harass women and young people in the streets. Any violation of *hejab* (compulsory dress rules for women) can result in the arrest of the offender. Extensive purges have taken place in government offices and ministries to ensure that anyone remotely connected with dissidents will not be hired.

Through this reign of terror, the clerics succeeded in maintaining their grip on power. The price was losing any popular legitimacy. For years, the mullahs tried to convince the outside world that the vast majority of Iranians still supported the regime despite its brutal suppression. Today, even ardent apologists of the ruling theocracy have stopped making such claims. Ali Ansari, a fervent proponent of the clerical regime in Britain, commented after the anti-government demonstrations in Iran in June and July 2003: 'The situation is incredibly fragile ... What has been striking in the last year, is the rapidity of the collapse of social popularity of the regime. People are no longer saying "Tinker with the edges, and it will be OK." People say: "Let's get rid of them."[21]

A quarter of a century of repression has exacted a heavy price from the Iranian nation; no Iranian family has been spared the crimes of the mullahs. At the same time, however, this situation has brought about the ideological demise of Islamic fundamentalism in Iran, making its downfall somewhere down the line inevitable.

Notes

1. Thomas Paine, 'The Crisis', no. 1, *The Writings of Thomas Paine*, ed. Moncure D. Conway (1894), vol. 1, p. 170.

2. PMOI daily, *Mojahed*, 15 June 1980, Tehran.

3. Ayatollah Montazeri wrote in a secret letter to Khomeini, who was in Najaf at the time: 'As you are aware, a large number of Muslim and pious young men are in prison and some face execution. They are practising Muslims who have a broad and profound knowledge of Islam and all the clerics here have taken note of that. It would be appropriate for Your Eminence to write something in their support to save their lives.' From the 'Memoirs of Grand Ayatollah Hossein-Ali Montazeri', published by the underground press in Tehran, 2001.

4. Published in *Saheefeh Nour* (Book of Light), a collection of Khomeini's lectures, compiled by the Ministry of Islamic Guidance and Culture, vol. 12, pp. 192–202, 25 June 1980.

5. *Jomhouri Islami*, Tehran, 18 August 1999.

6. Haji Hassan Qarajeh-Daghi, popularly known as Sattar Khan, was a leader of the Constitutional Movement of 1906 against the Qajar dynasty. He was from the north-western city of Tabriz. Sattar Khan defeated the siege of the Czarist and pro-monarchy forces in Azerbaijan province and later on attacked Tehran and toppled the government of the Qajar monarch, Mohammad Ali Shah. After the victory of the Constitutional Movement, leaders of the Old Guard usurped the leadership and conspired to disarm Sattar Khan and his fighters, known as the Mojahedin. In the ensuing battles, Sattar Khan was wounded. He passed away several years later, in 1913 (Mohammad Mo'in, *A Persian Dictionary*, Tehran: Amir Kabir Publications, 4th edn, vol. 5, p. 733).

7. Baqer Khan was another leading figure in the Constitutional Movement. He, along with Sattar Khan, was instrumental in the defeat of the pro-monarchy forces in Tabriz.

8. Mirza Younis bin Mirza Bozorg, known as the Mirza Khuchek Khan Jangali, was originally a clergyman. He founded an association of the clergy, vowing to stop foreign domination over Iran. He played an important role in the victory of the Constitutional Movement and later on liberated the entire province of Gilan and declared a republic. After the coup in 1920 that brought Reza Shah to power, government forces attacked his bases in the jungles of Gilan. He eventually died in 1921 after getting caught in a snowstorm. A government soldier cut his throat and took his head to Reza Shah (Mo'in, *A Persian Dictionary*, vol. 6, p. 1619).

9. Prime Minister Dr Mohammad Mossadeq, who nationalized Iran's oil industry, was ousted in the US-British coup of 19 August 1953.

10. Prime Minister Mohammad Mossadeq's Foreign Minister. After the August 1953 coup that toppled Dr Mossadeq's government, Dr Fatemi was arrested, tortured and ultimately executed by the SAVAK.

11. Mohammad Hanifnejad, the founder of the People's Mojahedin Organization of Iran. An agricultural engineer, Hanifnejad was born in 1938 in Tabriz, capital of the north-western province of East Azerbaijan. As a Muslim intellectual, he had been politically active against the Shah's dictatorship and was imprisoned in 1963. After his release, he founded the Mojahedin in 1965. Until 1971, he concentrated on expanding the organizational network across Iran and formulating the movement's ideology, tactics and strategy. In September 1971, the Shah's dreaded secret police, SAVAK, arrested the organization's leaders, including Hanifnejad. After months of brutal torture, all but one of the members of the Leadership Committee, Massoud Rajavi, were executed. Hanifnejad was executed on 25 May 1972.

12. Massoud Rajavi's speech at the ceremony commemorating the anniversary of the founding of the People's Mojahedin Organization of Iran, *Mojahed* weekly, special issue, 23 September 1998.

13. Massoud Rajavi's speech on the thirty-fifth founding anniversary of the People's Mojahedin, *Mojahed* weekly, issue no. 456, 7 September 1999.

14. A twelve-point statement, Ettelaye Taeen-e Mavaze-e Sazeman-e Mojahedin-e Khalq-e Iran (Statement on the Position of the People's Mojahedin Organization of Iran), was drawn up in autumn 1975 to define the Mojahedin's stance vis-à-vis the Marxist coup that led to the organization's temporary disintegration in the mid-1970s, paving the way for Khomeini's rise to power.

15. 'History of Iran', Library of Congress, <www.countrystudies.us/iran>.

16. Shaul Bakhash, *The Reign of the Ayatollahs*, New York: Basic Books, 1984, p. 123.

17. *Mojahedin* daily, 30 December 1980.

18. *Ettela'at* daily, Tehran, 30 May 1990.

19. Khomeini's fatwa, cited in *Crime Against Humanity*, publication of the Foreign Affairs Committee of the National Council of Resistance of Iran, 2001, pp. 2, 3.

20. Ervand Abrahamian, *The Iranian Mojahedin*, New Haven, CT: Yale University Press, 1989, pp. 218–19.

21. *Christian Science Monitor*, 16 June 2003.

4 | Two Islams in conflict

Let there be no compulsion in religion. *The Quran*[1]

Since 1979 and the rise of Shiite clerics to power, two 'Islams' have been at war in Iran. The confrontation between Khomeini's fundamentalist vision of Islam and the Mojahedin's modernist vision began long before the 1979 revolution, but the mullahs' rise to power brought it to a head. Once fundamentalist Islam grabbed the reins of power, the campaign for the establishment of democracy and secularism in Iran became inseparable from the fight against the ideology and outlook of medieval clerics who claim that their views represent the 'only' and the 'pure' Islam.

It is of critical importance to note that the Mojahedin have criticized and discredited the fundamentalist ideology of Khomeini and his disciples on the basis of their interpretation of the Quran and the traditions and teachings of Prophet Muhammad and the Shiite Imams and leaders. The experience in Iran shows clearly that Islamic fundamentalism was able to weather all kinds of attacks and criticisms from non-Muslims or those not respectful of Islam. In Iran itself, there has been no shortage of such attacks on the mullahs and their fundamentalist outlook over the past century. But none ever came close to the effectiveness and influence of the PMOI's systematic critique and rejection of fundamentalist Islam, because the PMOI did not, as many others did and still do, equate fundamentalism with Islam itself, but set out to prove that Islam is not only fully 'compatible' with democracy, human rights and the values of modern-day civilization, but that it is an inherently tolerant and democratic religion. In this chapter, we throw a glance at the PMOI's understanding of Islam.

The most striking distinction between PMOI's Islam and Khomeini's is the former's stance on the issue of free will and individual volition and choice, which in the social realm manifests itself in democracy and a government by the people, of the people and for the people. Khomeinism is adamantly opposed to this. The PMOI has unambiguously explained in its teachings and positions that spreading the word of God and Islam would be meaningless without freedom and respect for individual will and the right to choose. The Quran says that the most important attribute that distinguishes human beings from animals is their free will and the concept of individual responsibility, a major theme in

Islam, is based on the freedom of the individual to choose. It is on this basis that human beings are held accountable for their actions.[2]

Unadulterated Islam

Contrary to those who claim that Islam is intrinsically incompatible with democracy, unadulterated Islamic teachings, particularly the Quran and the traditions of Prophet Muhammad and such leaders as Ali ibn Ali Taleb, the first Shiite Imam, both of whom ruled the nascent Islamic state, underscore the necessity to hand over power to the people. These teachings highlight the need for progress, social and economic justice, and respect for human rights principles. References to such values are abundant in Islamic teachings, dating back fourteen centuries.

Like all other religions and ideologies, Islam has had its share of distortions and misinterpretations, which began in the early decades of Islam, as men perverted and changed the message of religion to justify self-interest. The Kharajites who distorted the meaning of the Quranic phrase, 'no rule, but that of God', to advocate anarchy and became the archetypal fundamentalists, and the aristocratic clique who turned the early Islamic state into a type of monarchy, are examples of those who diverted Islamic teachings from the original path laid down by the Quran and practised by Prophet Muhammad.

Contrary to the impression created by the likes of the mullahs ruling Iran, Islam is an ideology with a comprehensive view on existence, society and history, rather than a mere collection of edicts and rules of conduct on social, political and economic matters, which naturally evolve over time. It defines each of these concepts within the philosophy of *towhid*, or monism. Out of 6,200 verses in the Quran, more than 5,500, or 90 per cent, deal with these basic questions of philosophy – existence, history and human beings – and the interpretations, examples and allegories related to them.

One fundamental and central theme, derived from Islam's monistic approach to existence, is equality among human beings. It is explicitly emphasized in the Quran that all human beings are equal, regardless of gender, race or nationality. According to this principle, the only criterion for differentiating among people is the extent of their cognizance, emancipation and sense of responsibility, which in Quranic terminology is called *taqwa*. Taqwa is commonly translated as 'fear of God', but the concept, if studied throughout the Quran, implies far more: 'O mankind, We have created you male and female, and appointed you races and tribes, that you may know one another. Surely, the noblest among you in the sight of God is the one with the greatest *taqwa*.'[3] These constitute the primary teachings of the Quran.[4] The purposefulness of the universe, namely, its evolution from the realm of contradiction to the realm of unity and oneness (towhid); the inexorably one-way direction of history (in contrast to spontaneity), which explains the role of prophets in human history; and human beings' sense of responsibility are three principles that form the essence of Islamic ideology.

Dynamic interpretation

The Quran itself divides its verses into two categories: *mohkamat* and *motashebihat*. The word mohkamat (plural of mohkama) is derived from the root 'uhkima' which means 'to decide between two things'. It is a verbal noun in the plural, meaning judgements or decisions. Motashebihat (plural of motashabiha) is derived from the root 'ishtabaha' meaning 'to be doubtful'. It is a verbal noun in the plural, meaning the uncertain or doubtful things.

In so far as edicts and rules of conduct on social and economic issues are concerned, neither the Quran nor Islam claims they are unalterable and must be implemented at all times. The Quran emphasizes that social and economic edicts must be formulated in each particular era to prevent decadent and counter-evolutionary forces from halting the advancement of human society. The key, therefore, is to grasp the spirit and genuine outlook of the Quran. In Sura 3, Al-e Imran ('The Family of Imran') verse 7, the Quran says: 'He has sent down to you the Book: In it are verses fundamental (Mohkamat); they are the foundation of the Book: others are allegorical (Motashebihat). But those in whose hearts is perversity follow the part thereof that is allegorical, seeking discord.'[5] The fundamentalists and reactionaries interpret all the edicts, precepts and temporal rules as unchangeable dogma. This interpretation contradicts the Quran's own definitions and categorization. Mohkamat are the fundamental principles of Islam, definite and unchangeable. They contain the philosophical essence of Islam's worldview on humankind. Motashebihat are relative, dynamic and flexible. They relate to the methods and rules of conduct in everyday life. As such, they are never rigid and they can and must be adapted to human progress, technological advancement and the social norms of the times, while preserving the same monistic essence and spirit of Islam. Otherwise, they would become a useless and rigid set of canonical laws. Thus, the rigid and reactionary interpretation of Islam, exemplified in our times by Khomeinism, is un-Islamic and contrary to the spirit of Islam.

Imam Ali's views on the Quran and the religious precepts further underline the dynamism of the Quran. He says:

The Quran has spelled out what is lawful and unlawful; what is obligatory and recommended; what is renewing and outdated; what is general and specific; what is fundamental and allegorical. The Quran has proclaimed some things as obligatory, but they have been annulled by the Prophet's tradition. There are also certain matters that have been considered as obligatory in the Prophet's tradition, but the Quran allows their annulment. There are also matters that were obligatory in their own time, but were later abolished.[6]

The Mojahedin believe that genuine Islam is so dynamic it never impedes social progress; it does not oppose science, technology and civilization; it cherishes and promotes them.

The basic principles of Shiite theology accentuate this point. The concept of *ijtihad* (contemporary interpretation of motashabih verses by qualified scholars) makes it imperative for Islamic scholars to develop methods and rules appropriate to the times. This mandate, contrary to the prevalent view propagated by the mullahs, is not the exclusive domain of the clergy. Far from it, it is the guiding principle for all Muslims, encouraging public participation in running the affairs of society.

During Prophet Muhammad's twenty-three-year mission, we come across Quranic verses that were declared *mansoukh* (outdated). Some verses on social and economic matters in the early years of the Prophet's rule changed, consistent with changes in society and advancements in culture and social relationships. In the latter years of Prophet Muhammad's life, new verses that were more advanced in dealing with such issues were revealed to him.

This explains why only 600 verses in the Quran, less than 10 per cent, deal with edicts. This shows that the purpose of the Quran was not to legislate for society and mankind instead of human beings themselves. It came to remove obstacles to social evolution. As it says, it came to remove the chains and shackles from human beings, already subjugated by oppressive rules and regimes,[7] so that they could formulate their way of life consistent with their specific historical juncture, within an evolutionary and progressive framework and in complete freedom and consciousness.

A social revolution

In the seventh century AD, Islam brought about a major social change at a time when Europe was in the Dark Ages. Even in the advanced civilizations of the time, such as the Persian and the Byzantine empires, the situation was appalling. In Iran (Persia), the rule of the Sassanid dynasty

(224–640 AD), despite its outward splendour and majestic pomp, was brutal, corrupt and oppressive with a rigid caste system. Ordinary people had no right to education; only members of the court, the aristocracy and the church could learn to read and write. 'In both Persia and Byzantium, it was an age of intolerance,' H. G. Wells noted in his *Short History of the World*. 'Both empires were religious empires in a new way, in a way that greatly hampered the free activities of the human mind.'

Life on the harsh, barren deserts of desolate Arabia was far more backward. Against this backdrop, Islam brought about a social revolution that changed life drastically in societies that came under its rule. An examination of the Quran's 600 verses on social and economic issues and of the tradition of the Prophet and Imam Ali shows clearly the manner in which the philosophical and ideological framework of Islam paved the way for progress in tapping society's economic and social potential. To understand this, let us look at a number of these edicts.

Take the rule on inheritance, for example: fourteen centuries ago, a woman's share was set at half a man's.[8] If the historical circumstances are ignored and this edict is interpreted as permanent, then its significance at the time cannot be appreciated. Furthermore, the unrealistic conclusion would be that Islam opposes the equality of women and men. In fact, Islam accorded women a share in inheritance at a time when they inherited nothing, and were themselves inherited. They were part of their husband's property, to be owned by his heirs or other men of their tribe. Moreover, in none of the contemporaneous civilizations were women economically independent from their husbands or fathers. Therefore, the very idea of according women the right to inheritance, in and of itself, was a revolution.[9] The same holds true for many other precepts on social or legal issues, such as testimony, the payment of fines, etc. Consider the precept on testimony, whereby the testimony of two women is equal to that of one man. In this case, too, a dogmatic interpretation would presume that this decree is immutable and eternal. Again, that would mean inequality attributed to Islam, whereas fourteen centuries ago, when women had no rights in primitive societies and female infants were buried alive, such decrees were important, bold initiatives towards establishing women's rights and independent political identity.

At a time when slavery was the dominant world order, edicts in the Quran and rulings by the Prophet were attempts to limit slavery to the maximum extent and set the stage for its eradication.

In the case of moral offences, the Quran called for the lashing of adulterers. This was at a time when men were completely unrestrained in promiscuous relationships, while women were easily murdered by their clans, husbands, fathers or brothers if suspected of the slightest promiscuity. Contrary to what the mullahs later attributed to Islam, the Quran has never called for stoning adulterers. Indeed, the Prophet made it a mortal sin to slander a woman, and set the most stringent standard of proof: to prove the accusation, one had to produce four witnesses, making such accusations practically impossible to prove.

As regards homicide, when the Quran calls for retribution in kind, it does so to prevent the revenge killings of whole tribes prevalent at the time. It said homicide was among the most serious crimes and called for the punishment, under very restrictive conditions, of only the murderer. This is in dire contrast to the criminal sentences issued in Iran today on the pretext of retribution. The mullahs have violated numerous verses of the Quran, which call for mercy and compassion, and tried to justify their atrocities in a few edicts that sought to promote tolerance consistent with the cultural and social development of fourteen centuries ago.

The Prophet's governance and treatment of people at that time similarly represents a significant departure from the prevailing norms. Vast empires, such as Iran, were unable to withstand the newly converted Arab Muslims who did not match them in weapons and military hardware, but had brought with them the message of fraternity and equality. On the treatment of opponents, the Quran is unequivocal. 'God only forbids you, with regard to those who fight you for (your) faith, and drive you out of your homes, and support (others) in driving you out, from turning to them (for friendship and protection). It is such as turn to them (in these circumstances), that do wrong.'[10] The meaning of this verse, which was revealed to the Prophet when he was ruling over much of Arabia, is that so long as opponents have not taken up arms against the legitimate and legal government and acted peacefully, they shall enjoy security and be accorded their rights. In the middle of the seventh century, Imam Ali agreed to be the caliph (political and religious leader) of the Islamic world, only when he was convinced that an absolute majority wanted him to assume that post. He emphasized that if the people had not made such a demand, he would not have accepted that position.[11] Once in power, Ali told everyone, including his close associates, how they should interact with him:

> Do not speak to me as if you are speaking to despots. Do not come to me with a false face. Do not hide any issue from me, as one would from a furious crowd or oppressive rulers. Do not engage in stage-managing with me. Do not believe that I cannot believe the truth. How can one implement the truth when one does not have the capacity to listen to it?[12]

Imam Ali's instructions and recommendations to, and criticisms of, his commanders and subordinates when they neglected people's problems point up a social change that was possible only in the context of new values that Islam had brought. An example of this is the covenant that Ali asked Malek Ashtar, whom he appointed as the governor of Egypt, to sign. Many aspects of this covenant, a de facto manifesto for governing an Islamic society drafted in the mid-seventh century, resemble the content of the Universal Declaration of Human Rights.

In the covenant, Ali emphasized restraint:

Control your personal whims. Refrain from what is not allowed for you, as this is the equivalent of justice and fairness (for he who rules) ... Make your heart home to kindness and love for the people. If they do you bad, forgive them and pray for them and ask for their counsel in case of war. God forbid you from treating them as a wild beast, for all the subjects under your rule belong to one of two groups, either they are your brothers in religion or they are your peers in creation ... Those who tell you more about the bitter truth and say less in your praise, when they think your speeches and deeds are not aimed at acquiring God's satisfaction, they should be the selected and the most highly placed with you, even though their bitter tone and their lack of praise might appear injurious to you.[13]

Although many companions of Imam Ali urged him to act decisively against the Kharajites in the seventh century, or at least restrict their freedom and political activities, Ali replied, 'So long as they do not harm us, we will not take any action against them. If they debate us, we will do likewise. We will continue to pay them their share of public funds. We will allow them to go to the mosque to pray. Only if they resort to violence and killing will we reluctantly fight them.'

Such a major social, political and economic revolution became possible on the Arabian Peninsula fourteen centuries ago only in the framework of the philosophy and worldview of Islam. These views are totally alien to the policies and practices of the mullahs who rule Iran in the name of Islam.

Islam and democracy

Consistent with the teaching of Prophet Muhammad and Imam Ali, the Mojahedin believe that the 'freedom of an individual or that of a group must face no restriction up to the point of taking up arms against the legitimate and legal system of the country'.[14] This has been specified in the programme of the National Council of Resistance of

Iran: 'The attainment of popular sovereignty through the provisional government will be the most valuable achievement of the just Resistance of the Iranian people. In the view of true Muslims, God's will, as far as societies are concerned, is historically realized through democratic governance.'[15] Khomeini's worst crime was that he 'usurped the Iranian people's most fundamental right, the right to popular sovereignty'.[16] If the Iranian people had had the possibility to exercise that right, use the ballot-box and take part in a free election, there would have been no need for armed resistance; peaceful political struggle would have continued. Precisely because those rights were denied to the Iranian people, resistance to attain them became necessary, legitimate and just. Whenever there might be a chance for a referendum and the holding of a 'free election, public suffrage would be the only criterion for legitimacy'.[17] The NCRI's programme, to which the PMOI has been a signatory, emphasized this issue.

In 1981, Massoud Rajavi stressed the Mojahedin's viewpoints on the programme of the NCRI and said, 'Contrary to Khomeini, the Islam that we believe in is far too rich to need to acquire political legitimacy through coercion and force. We profoundly believe that Islam would only blossom in the absence of any discrimination, privilege and political and social compulsion.'[18] He emphasized that 'the Provisional Government rejects all gender, ethnic and ideological privileges'.[19] 'In our country, one must make fundamental freedoms the guarantee and criterion of genuine social progress. Otherwise, the stage would be set for the emergence of dictatorships that cannot remain independent. Freedom is not a luxury but an indispensable imperative.'[20]

For the Mojahedin, freedom and gender, ethnic and religious equality, human rights and peace are not merely political commitments, but ideological principles. The lives and the struggles of all great prophets, such as Moses, Jesus and Muhammad, are examples of unrelenting commitment to these principles. Contrary to what the mullahs ruling Iran preach, these great pioneers of humanity never advocated cruelty, war, aggression, suppression and ruthlessness. All but one chapter[21] of the Quran begin with the phrase, 'In the name of God, the Merciful, the Compassionate'. This God is the exact opposite of the God Khomeini and his clique preach to the people.

In summer 1982, Massoud Rajavi said:

With the victory of our Resistance, we will overcome one of the major obstacles to the success of contemporary revolutions. This same obstacle has been the most important factor in their deviation and failure. It is the concept of invading (under any pretext) the sacred limits of freedom. Our worldview is monistic, and the eminence of our species lies precisely in mankind's freedom of choice; hence, the revival of freedom is in essence the revival of mankind and man's vanquished revolutions ... We are not anyone's liberator. For a nation to appreciate the value of its freedom, it must free itself. Everyone, both as an individual and as a member of society, can free himself only if he tears apart the chains of coercion and compulsion on his own.[22]

These principles have guided the PMOI in the social, political and economic arenas. In this ideology, God alone is perfect, devoid of deficiency and shortcomings. Man influences and is influenced by circumstances. The Quran gives glad tidings to those 'who listen to all that is said and follow the fairest of it'.[23] Prophet Muhammad ruled over large parts of the Arabian Peninsula for ten years (622–32 AD). Yet he never took any important decision without consulting the Muslim umma (society), oftentimes submitting, against his better judgement, to the views of his disciples.

Committed to the principle that the sole criterion for political legitimacy is the ballot-box, and that resistance is legitimate only against repression and dictatorship, the PMOI proposed a maximum tenure of six months for the Provisional Government to take power after the mullahs, during which time sovereignty will be transferred to the people. The proposal was accepted by other members of the National Council of Resistance of Iran and became part of the NCRI platform. The experience of other movements which refused, under various pretexts, to respect the people's vote after the overthrow of dictatorship, shows that free elections and commitment to the vote are the only means of safeguarding democratic movements from deviating from their original paths. The Mojahedin profoundly believe that to avoid the deviations that beset contemporary revolutions throughout the world, they must remain wholeheartedly committed to the will of the people and democracy.

It is the PMOI's view that all the legitimacy bestowed on its cause by its long decades of struggle under repression and the suffering, imprisonment, torture and execution of its members and supporters under the Shah and the mullahs does not give it the right to govern or participate in government, unless it receives the backing of the electorate. It is the electorate, expressing itself in a free and fair election that gives a party, a group, a coalition or an individual the mandate to govern. Any party that attempts to make up for the lack of popular mandate by relying on its past sacrifices, organizational prowess or arms, will soon discover that a vibrant, creative, lively and democratic organization would soon become a hollow, rotten bureaucracy. That is the reason why the PMOI has emphasized: 'If the people don't vote for us (after we have overthrown the mullahs' regime), we shall remain in the opposition and hold firmly to our principles.'[24]

Establishing democracy in a country ruled for several decades by despotic regimes and chafing under two dictatorships for eighty years is no easy task. The difficulties have been compounded by the mullahs' attempts to disrupt and destroy all secular civil institutions and social relationships through brutal suppression and religious tyranny. All vestiges of democratic institutions and civil society in Iran have withered away under the clerical dictatorship's omnipresent repression. A difficult and long road looms ahead in trying to heal the open wounds and to universalize democracy in a society whose rulers sought to imprison even human emotions within their narrow, intolerant bounds. Khomeini's betrayal of Iranians' hope for freedom underlines the need to revive the people's trust; they need assurances that past experiences will not be repeated.

Religious totalitarianism

Khomeinism rests upon the totalitarian precept of *velayat-e faqih*, which is the guiding principle of the regime's constitution. This concentration of political and religious powers in the hands of the clerics denies popular sovereignty. The *velayat-e faqih* system invests the law, power and legitimacy in one man, the so-called Supreme Leader. The clerical regime is totalitarian, because it does not recognize freedom and the right of political activity for anyone other than those who fit within its narrow definition of 'loyal to the Islamic state'. This loyalty, the leading mullahs have stated openly, must be demonstrated both by 'heartfelt belief in, and practical demonstration of, the principle of *velayat-e faqih*'.

The religious regime suppresses not only political freedoms, but freedom in all aspects of social, individual and family life. Inquisition in the form of a most pervasive invasion of people's privacy to search for any sign of 'heresy' or 'anti-Islamic behaviour' is routine; there is no freedom of thought. In contrast, the PMOI sees democracy as indispensable to Islam, which tolerates its opponents and treats them fairly. Islam blossoms only in a spirit of freedom and truthfulness, and therefore cannot trample upon the legitimate rights of the people. Political power in itself does not constitute the goal in this version of

Islam, which is committed to an ethical approach to power and politics. In accordance with this spirit, all members and organizations of the National Council of Resistance of Iran, including the Mojahedin, regardless of their strength, political status and so forth, have an equal vote. In the decision-making process, therefore, the PMOI, though a nationwide political party with a considerable following, has only one vote, as does every other organization and personality in the council. The NCRI embodies a historic democratic experience for Iran.

In accordance with the council's programme, after the overthrow of the clerical regime, a provisional government will be in power for a maximum of six months, its main task being to hold free elections for a National Legislative and Constituent Assembly. Once the assembly is formed, the provisional government will submit its resignation to it. The people's elected representatives will then determine the country's mode of government and the new republic's constitution.[25]

The NCRI's programme and the provisional government emphasize 'recognizing the people's right to make decisions and determine their own destiny'. The programme underscores complete freedom of belief and expression and a ban on censorship and inquisition; complete freedom of the press, parties, assemblies, political associations, and various unions, societies and councils; and the right to dissent at all civil and military levels and positions.

The emphasis on the need for a popular mandate to govern and the rejection of the fundamentalists' claim of 'divine legitimacy' is not unique in Islamic history. There are important precedents set by Muslim clerics and laymen who argued passionately against the notion that elections have no place in an 'Islamic' rule. Years before Khomeini came to power, respected clergymen like Ayatollah Mirza Hussein Na'ini and Ayatollah Seyyed Mahmoud Taleqani warned against the danger of religious tyranny. Ayatollah Na'ini stressed this point in his writings at the time of the Iranian Constitutional Revolution at the turn of the twentieth century:

> Among the forces safeguarding despotism are the religious tyrants. They adopt certain words and components of religion to appear appealing to the naïve. They deceive the ordinary people, unfamiliar with the principles and basics of the religion and the essence of the Prophet's mission. They make these people obey their rule. They claim to safeguard the religion and to be looking after the interests of the religion, but in fact, they spread the shadow of Satan over the public and keep them under this ominous shadow of ignorance and wretchedness.
>
> Because they manipulate the pure emotions of the people and take

cover behind the strong fortifications of religion, they are much more dangerous and harder to repel. Although religious tyranny differs from political tyranny in appearance, in essence they act similarly and lead in the same direction. Both utilize the financial and spiritual resources of the people to preserve power. As stipulated in the Quran, obedience to them constitutes dualism.[26]

Women's emancipation

Iranian women are the biggest victims of the religious dictatorship ruling Iran, which considers them as second-class citizens. The clerical regime relies on gender discrimination and distinction to negate women's human identity. Its constitution, to which all factions adhere, denies women the right to leadership,[27] presidency and judgeship.[28]

The theocratic regime has turned family life into a setting where women are tortured and humiliated. Discrimination against women has been written into the law, but the plight of women goes far beyond discrimination. Under this regime, they are subjected to a painful process of character destruction. Husbands can divorce their wives any time they so choose. After divorce, the father takes custody of the child. The father and paternal grandfather have the right to guardianship. They even have the right to wed their baby girl to anyone they wish. Once the daughter becomes an adult, she has no right to protest.

The regime has executed tens of thousands of women for political reasons and tortured many more. Religious judges issue fatwas that allow the torturers to rape their victims. When Zahra Kazemi, a fifty-four-year-old Canadian-Iranian photojournalist, was arrested for taking a few pictures outside a prison in Tehran in July 2003, she was viciously raped, tortured and murdered. The world watched in disgust as the pleas of her Canadian son and the Ottawa government fell on deaf ears and the Iranian authorities had her buried in Shiraz to cover up forensic evidence of their crime.[29] If this is what they can do to a Canadian citizen in broad daylight, it is not hard to imagine what happens to dissident women in torture centres.

The Iranian Resistance's President-elect Maryam Rajavi says:

Just as racial supremacy formed the leitmotif and the cornerstone of Hitler's Nazism, gender apartheid and discrimination make up the foundation of the thinking and culture of Khomeini-style theocracy and fundamentalism. This is, if one day, they give up their ideology of eternal male domination over women, they would no longer be what they were before. Gender-based outlook plays the central role and is the highest priority in all their values and concepts, from piety and punishment to vice and virtue.[30]

For the Iranian Resistance, the realization of the democratic rights of different sectors of society and the establishment of democracy is tested by the realization of the rights of women. All NCRI members, including the PMOI, have ratified a plan on the rights and freedoms of women,[31] which not only recognizes gender equality in highest government, judicial and political positions, but also in inheritance, testimony and custody. It includes:

- the right of women to elect and be elected;
- the right to employment and freedom of choice in profession and careers and the rights to hold any public or government position, office or profession, including judgeship in all tribunals;
- the right to free political and social activity and travel without the permission of another person;
- absolute freedom of choice regarding spouse and marriage, and equal right to divorce;
- the right freely to choose one's dress and manner of clothing; and
- the right to use, without discrimination, all educational, athletic, and artistic resources, and the right to participate in all athletic competitions and artistic activities.

The role of women in the Iranian Resistance is unparalleled in contemporary resistance movements. Women comprise half the members of the NCRI. The PMOI's leadership council is made up exclusively of qualified women. Women also play a major role in the NLA's General Command and its chain of command. They have also taken charge of many of the Resistance's organizational, political, international, public relations and executive affairs and heralded a new world of emancipation and responsibility for Iranian women. Maryam Rajavi explained this presence: 'We are fighting against a regime whose most distinct hallmark is its misogynous character, and we are its antithesis. If we want to uproot it and draw up a new design, we should have a new message and a new conduct in the area of women's emancipation. We must have new ideas, and most importantly, translate them into action.'[32] Rajavi formulated what she considered to be the key points in the process of women's emancipation and empowerment in Iran:

- If relationships based on gender oppression are to be uprooted, then women must, before all else, pave the way by engaging in political and social activism.

- Along the same lines, it is necessary to have a revolution in thinking and get rid of every value based on gender discrimination and male dominance. Since every revolution requires a leading goal and indicator, women must take on responsibilities of political and social leadership. Affirmative action for a period will compensate for the historical deprivation of women. To this end, it is imperative to have quotas promoting ever greater roles by women in responsible positions in society. The spirit and intention of such privileges, in any case, are to liberate and enhance the ability of men and women to take on responsibility and to do away with exploitation and gender discrimination.
- Liberation of men depends on the liberation of women and the emancipation of women should result in the emancipation of men. Solutions that simply switch their places and reinforce the male/female conflict will not result in the liberation of women. Because of the inherent unity and humanity of women and men, realistic and feasible solutions are those that promote humane interaction and true equality between women and men.
- Women's rights are human rights. We cannot overemphasize this, even though it is exactly what the backward misogynists detest most strongly. These rights encompass all the individual and social freedoms cited in the Universal Declaration of Human Rights, according to which women are masters of their own bodies and feelings.
- The twenty-first century is the century for freedom of women and abolition of discrimination. This is the century of prosperity and democracy. Yet the reactionaries who belong to the Dark Ages are trying to turn the tide of history backwards with their misogyny. What they do not realize is that they would be uprooted from all over the world, including in Iran, by free and liberated women and will vanish from the face of history.[33]

Pluralism versus totalitarianism

Totalitarianism and the tendency to monopolize every aspect of Iranian society as its own exclusive domain are a hallmark of the Islamic fundamentalist regime in Iran. The ruling body at first included secular groups and personalities in addition to the mullahs, but Khomeini first eliminated the liberal faction in the regime back in 1980 and 1981. The ruling clerics then began the process of destroying or expelling from power other factions and groups; a process that seemed to fulfil the maxim that 'a revolution devours its own children'.

The mullahs have approached economic, cultural and social issues with the same totalitarian outlook, banning every activity that does not conform strictly to their own narrow vision of how things should be run. But contrary to the mullahs' approach, the PMOI has proved its allegiance to pluralism over the past two decades. The very flourishing and continuing viability of the NCRI, the longest-lasting political coalition in Iran's history, is a definitive affirmation of PMOI's belief in pluralism. Massoud Rajavi announced the formation of the National Council of Resistance of Iran in Tehran in July 1981. He asked all democratic forces opposed to the ruling theocracy to join it. Members of the NCRI include five political organizations and parties and more than 500 political, cultural and social dignitaries. The NCRI also includes specialists, lawyers, artists, intellectuals, sports champions and scientists. The renowned author Manouchehr Hezarkhani; Moslem Eskandar Filabi, one of Iran's most popular sporting champions in recent memory; Marzieh, the legendary diva of Iranian music; Mohammad Shams, a distinguished composer and conductor, and Parviz Khazai, Iran's former ambassador to Norway, are among NCRI members.

Until the holding of free and fair elections within six months of the mullahs' overthrow, the NCRI will be in power as a coalition government, representing a wide spectrum of Iranian political and social forces, including secularists, liberals and nationalists, as well as representatives of ethnic and religious minorities, such as the Kurds, Baluchis, Turkmens, Arabs, Jews, Christians and Zoroastrians. Twenty-two years after its inception, the NCRI has evolved into a viable alternative to the fundamentalist regime in Iran.

Notes

1. Quran, Sura 2, Verse 256.
2. Quran, Sura 33, Verse 72.
3. Quran, Sura 49, Verse 13.
4. Quran, Sura 3, Verse 7.
5. Ibid.
6. Nahj-ol Balagha (The Road to Eloquence), Section 38 of Sermon 1.
7. Quran, Sura 7, Verse 157.
8. Quran, Sura 5, Verse 176.
9. Quran, Sura 2, Verse 282.
10. Quran, Sura 9, Al-Mumtahina, Verse 8.
11. Nahj-ol Balagha (The Road to Eloquence), Section 17 of Sermon 2.
12. Nahj-ol Balagha (The Road to Eloquence), Section 12 of Sermon 207.
13. Nahj-ol Balagha (The Road to Eloquence), Imam Ali's Covenant to Malek bin Hareth Ashtar.
14. Programme of the National Council of Resistance and the Provisional

Government of the Democratic Islamic Republic of Iran, Chapter 3, Section 2, 'On Freedom', 27 September 1981.

15. Programme of the National Council of Resistance and the Provisional Government of the Democratic Islamic Republic of Iran, Chapter 2, 'Basic Viewpoints of the Provisional Government', 27 September 1981.

16. Programme of the National Council of Resistance and the Provisional Government of the Democratic Islamic Republic of Iran, Chapter 1, 'Provisional Situation, Principal Tasks of the Transitional Period', 27 September 1981.

17. Programme of the National Council of Resistance and the Provisional Government of the Democratic Islamic Republic of Iran, Chapter 4, Section 4, 27 September 1981.

18. Ibid.

19. Ibid.

20. Programme of the National Council of Resistance and the Provisional Government of the Democratic Islamic Republic of Iran, Chapter 3, Section 2, 27 September 1981.

21. Quran, Sura 9, A Tauba.

22. Massoud Rajavi, Appraisal of the First Year of the Resistance, summer of 1982.

23. Quran, Sura 39, Verse 18.

24. Massoud Rajavi, interview, weekly publication of the Union of Muslim Students' Associations Abroad, 9 January 1983.

25. Programme of the National Council of Resistance and the Provisional Government of the Democratic Islamic Republic of Iran, Chapter 1, 'Provisional Situation, Principal Tasks of the Transitional Period', 27 September 1981.

26. Ayatollah Mirza Hussein Na'ini, *Tanbihol Umma va Tanzihol Millah* (Raising the People's Awareness and Purifying the Ideology).

27. Constitution of the Islamic Republic, Article 115.

28. Mohammad Yazdi, Ressalat, 15 December 1986.

29. Zahra Kazemi was arrested on 23 June 2003 when photographing families of prisoners in front of the notorious Evin prison. The journalist was beaten during her arrest and finally died because of the beating on 11 July 2003 in Baghiatollah military hospital. After first efforts by the authorities to hide the real cause of the death of the journalist, Khatami's deputy Ali Abtahi announced on 16 July that Zahra Kazemi had died because of a 'brain haemorrhage'. Her body was buried with great respect on 23 July in her birthplace, Shiraz. Mrs Ezzat Kazemi, Zahra's mother, said in an interview on 30 July that she had undergone immense pressure by the authorities to consent to her daughter's being buried in Iran. Excerpts from a report by the Reporters sans frontières.

30. Maryam Rajavi, interview, 8 March 2001, published in *Price of Freedom*, a publication of the Women's Committee of the National Council of Resistance of Iran, Paris: 2001, p. 28.

31. NCRI's plan on Freedoms and Women's Rights, 17 April 1987.

32. Ibid.

33. Ibid.

5 | Terrorism: victims or villains?

If the clerical regime yields to a free election under the auspices of
the United Nations, the Mojahedin will immediately lay down their
arms to take part in it and will accept the outcome without any
hesitation. *PMOI Secretary General Mojgan Parsai*[1]

For years the Tehran regime has been pressing governments around the
world to limit, hamper or even shut down the activities of the People's
Mojahedin Organization of Iran (PMOI) and the National Council of
Resistance of Iran (NCRI). To achieve this goal, the clerics have accused
the PMOI of terrorism. In a speech at Tilburg University in the Netherlands in November 2002, United Nations Secretary General Kofi Annan
warned against the use of the terror tag by various governments to
demonize their opposition. He said:

> Internationally, we are beginning to see the increasing use of what I call
> the 'T-word' – terrorism – to demonize political opponents, to throttle
> freedom of speech and the press, and to de-legitimize legitimate politi-
> cal grievances.
>
> We are seeing too many cases where states living in tension with
> their neighbours make opportunistic use of the fight against terrorism
> to threaten or justify new military action on long-running disputes.[2]

It is a tragedy of our times, as far as international law and moral
rectitude in politics are concerned, that certain governments have kow-
towed to the mullahs' demands and subscribed to the use of the 'terrorist' label against the PMOI. A tragedy because these governments know
very well that the organization has never targeted civilians; has never
carried out a military operation outside Iran; and has declared its full
commitment to international humanitarian law, including the Geneva
Conventions. These are key issues that we shall explore in greater detail
in this chapter, but these facts, if nothing else, are enough, as prominent
international jurists and fair-minded political pundits have testified, to
make it untenable to describe the PMOI as a terrorist organization.

In considering the nature of the PMOI's military activities, it is also
necessary to consider the context in which they have taken place, namely
the regime making it impossible to engage in any form of peaceful,
political opposition and continuously and relentlessly persecuting the

PMOI and indeed all the regime's opponents, to the point of public mass executions and brutal tortures. So why have some governments chosen to ignore international law and political ethics to brand the PMOI as terrorist? The move is invariably motivated by political and economic considerations and has nothing to do with terrorism or law. Indeed, senior US officials are on record as saying that the purpose of including the PMOI in the list of terrorist organizations has been to send 'a goodwill gesture' to Tehran.

That the mullahs' regime, the chief patron of international terrorism in the world today, should accuse its principal opposition movement of terrorism is no surprise. Through this move, the theocratic rulers seek to justify their chilling record of human rights violations in Iran and, at the same time, divert attention from Tehran's prominent role in international terrorism. What is surprising, though, is the willingness of some Western governments to accept those allegations and acquiesce in Tehran's outrageous demands that they blacklist the PMOI. Indeed, many prominent politicians, parliamentarians, jurists and scholars in the West have expressed surprise and dismay that the terrorist label has been pinned on the PMOI at the behest of a regime that is itself the protagonist and sponsor of international terrorism. They rightly pose the question: 'Who is the real terrorist, the mullahs, or their principal victims, the Mojahedin?'

The distinguished British jurist and former chair of Amnesty International and vice-chair of the Anti-Slavery Society, Lord Archer of Sandwell QC, posed this question to the House of Lords:

> So where are the terrorists? Are they among the Mujaheddin or among the leadership of the regime? Not surprisingly, most of the Iranian community [in this country] have supported the resistance, not all of whom are members of the Mujaheddin. But some of them do applaud the Mujaheddin; some even help it financially. They are in good company. Members of the Mujaheddin have been welcomed as guests at the Labour Party conference where there is always sympathy for victims of persecution.[3]

In the same parliamentary debate, Lord Avebury, vice-chairman of the British Parliamentary Human Rights Group and a veteran campaigner for human rights around the world, noted the blatant contradiction in Western governments' approach to the question of terrorism and defended the legitimacy of the PMOI:

> The West has not always taken such a rigid stance against armed oppositions in other countries combating repressive regimes. At one time

the United States backed UNITA in Angola. Of course the outstanding example which we live to regret is the mujaheddin in Afghanistan. President Bush senior tried to persuade the Shi'a of Iraq to rise against Saddam in 1991 after operation Desert Storm. So there are plenty of examples in the recent past where states and our own governments have supported armed oppositions which are fighting repressive regimes.[4]

Lord Avebury went on:

> The People's Mojahedin of Iran cannot pursue its goal of a secular democratic state by peaceful means when the supremacy of the religious leader is the fundamental principle of the Islamic revolution and anybody rash enough to question that idea is a criminal. As the noble Lord, Lord Alton, mentioned, the president himself said that that person is guilty of treason and 30,000 of the members of that organisation were slaughtered in cold blood in 1988 on the orders of Ayatollah Khomeini.

The crux of the issue in the case of the PMOI is neither terrorism nor international law, but the basic right of the Iranian people to end the rule of fundamentalist despots in Iran. Those governments with a stake in keeping the mullahs' regime in power also deny the Iranian people's right to resist dictatorship and establish democracy in their country.

Yardstick of legitimacy

The students of Iran's contemporary history know that it was the mullahs' regime that banned all peaceful political activities by the democratic opposition through a reign of terror unprecedented in Iranian history (see Chapter 3, 'Anti-fundamentalist Muslims', for a more detailed treatment of events that led to the absolute suppression of opposition parties in 1981).

The mullahs had every incentive to prevent their opponents from carrying out political activities, because they saw how in twenty-eight months – from the overthrow of the Shah's regime in February 1979 to the massacre of peaceful demonstrators and beginning of mass executions in June 1981 – Khomeini's popularity slumped as the democratic opposition, led by the PMOI, saw their following and influence in society grow day by day. In those first twenty-eight months of their rule, the mullahs quickly learned the first 'law' of Islamic fundamentalism in power: lacking any real solutions to the complex problems of a modern society, fundamentalists cannot survive in power without resorting to violent repression and export of domestic crises beyond the borders of their country.

Khomeini and his mullahs had every interest in banning all activities by their opponents and forcing them underground, calculating that after a few months of daily executions and pervasive repression, the opposition would die down and its rapidly growing challenge to the mullahs' tyranny would be stifled. In the twenty-eight months prior to June 1981, the PMOI and its allies in the democratic opposition were doing everything to prevent the mullahs from achieving their goal of denying all opposition parties the possibility of conducting political activities. Even after the mass executions began in 1981, and the ferocious repression left no room for open activities, the PMOI consistently called on the ruling mullahs to allow free elections under United Nations supervision, but the clerics have consistently refused all such offers, not least because they already know the result would be an overwhelming rejection of their rule. In an interview with the French journal *L'Unité* on 1 January 1984, Massoud Rajavi said:

> The Islam that we profess does not condone bloodshed. We have never sought, nor do we welcome confrontation and violence. To explain, allow me to send a message to Khomeini through you ... My message is this: if Khomeini is prepared to hold truly free elections, I will return to my homeland immediately. The Mojahedin will lay down their arms to participate in such elections. We do not fear election results, whatever they may be.
>
> Before the start of armed struggle, we tried to utilize all legal means of political activity, but suppression compelled us to take up arms. If Khomeini had allowed half or even a quarter of the freedoms presently enjoyed in France, we would certainly have achieved a democratic victory.

The PMOI's firm commitment to accept the results of a free and fair election in Iran is significant, because it proves that it was the mullahs who imposed armed resistance on the democratic opposition and that, even today, it is the regime that can instantly resolve the conflict by agreeing to hold a free election under UN supervision. This, after all, is the basic right of the Iranian people, persistently denied by the ruling theocracy: the right to elect a government of their choice that is accountable to them. The demand for a UN-supervised election in Iran has been repeated throughout these years, not just by the PMOI, but by the resistance movement on a broader scale. When Maryam Rajavi, the Iranian Resistance's President-elect for the transitional period, returned to her residence at Auvers-sur-Oise on 3 July 2003, she told some 2,000 Iranians who had come from across the world to welcome her: 'We said from day one and repeat now that as soon as the mullahs accept a free election in Iran on the basis of popular sovereignty and not mullahs' sovereignty, and under United Nations' monitoring, we will immediately accept it and resistance would no longer be an issue.' In a message to 20,000 Iranians attending a rally in Brussels on 13 May 2002 to protest against the listing of the PMOI as a terrorist organization by the EU, Mrs Rajavi said the ruling mullahs could

> take their chance against the National Council of Resistance of Iran by holding a free presidential election, or elections to choose a national constituent assembly with proper guarantees and under the auspices of the United Nations. So I would repeat that the Iranian resistance has the capability and capacity of proving its legitimacy or for the final show-down with the enemy, to commit itself to any peaceful test including a referendum or free elections with proper international guarantees to prove the illegitimacy of the anti-human regime in its totality to everyone.

Inviolable rules

PMOI operations inside Iran have been carried out by autonomous operational cells that operate independently in selecting their tactics, targets and timings of operations. The last of these operations was in summer 2001 and since then, no more operations have been carried out at the request of the Mojahedin Command inside Iran. What distinguishes the record of the PMOI and renders the 'terrorism' label inapplicable and unjustified in its case is the fact that it has laid down and consistently and meticulously abided by three inviolable rules governing its operations throughout the past two decades:

1. Zero-tolerance approach to civilian casualties: the PMOI has never targeted civilians and has taken stringent precautions to ensure that no civilian would be harmed in its operations. The targets of Resistance operations have always been military and armed, from the main agencies of suppression in the direct command structure responsible for executions, torture and suppression of the Iranian people. The PMOI has refrained from any operation that could even inadvertently inflict any damage on civilians. It has refrained categorically from any operation that could have endangered the welfare of civilians.
2. No military operation outside Iran: the PMOI has not committed or engaged in any military activity outside Iran. Military operations described above were carried out exclusively within Iranian territory. Despite the fact that the Iranian regime's terror squads have carried

out at least 200 terrorist attacks on the PMOI and other components of the Resistance outside Iran, from Pakistan and Iraq to Italy, Switzerland, Germany, Turkey, Britain, France and other parts of the world, the PMOI has never retaliated.

3. Full compliance with international humanitarian law: the PMOI has declared in writing to the International Committee of the Red Cross (ICRC) and other relevant international authorities that it is committed to international humanitarian law (IHL), including the provisions of the Geneva Conventions of 12 August 1949, and additional Protocols 1 and 2. In its choice of targets, its treatment and release of prisoners of war, and its respect for the immunity of civilians, the PMOI has always respected the international humanitarian law and this has been acknowledged by the relevant international authorities and experts.

The PMOI cells inside Iran have shown great restraint in their modus operandi and choice of targets. They have never chosen targets such as bridges, factories and power plants which, despite being categorized as 'legitimate military targets' by most interpretations of international law, may result in 'collateral damage'. On many occasions, PMOI cells have decided not to carry out operations because of the proximity of the proposed target to population centres or in order to prevent accidental casualties.

Lord Alton, in the British House of Lords debate on 27 March 2001, quoted Mr Massoud Rajavi's public announcement, in which he said: 'I pledge on behalf of the Iranian Resistance that if anyone from our side oversteps the red line concerning absolute prohibition of attacks on civilians and innocent individuals, either deliberately or unintentionally, he or she would be ready to stand trial in any international court and accept any ruling by the court, including the payment of compensation.' All those killed or wounded in clashes between PMOI military units and the regime's security forces across the country have been considered legitimate military targets by the PMOI under its strictest definition of a military target. The PMOI has never attacked barracks that house lower-ranking members of the Iranian regime's armed forces. Many of these people are in fact sympathizers of the PMOI. The PMOI has targeted only those officials and commanders with the highest responsibility in oppression, who are in fact guilty of crimes against humanity. Indeed, PMOI's target selection and criteria for identifying legitimate military targets are far more stringent than those employed by any other military outfit in the world. The United States military and NATO, among others, accept civilian casualties in military operations as 'collateral damage'. For example, paragraph 8.1.2.1. of the US Navy's 'Commander's Handbook on the Law of Naval Operations' unambiguously states, 'It is not unlawful to cause incidental injury to civilians, or collateral damage to civilian objects, during an attack upon a legitimate military objective.'

Sadeq Seyyedi, a commander of PMOI operational units inside Iran until autumn 2000, submitted a sworn affidavit to the US Court of Appeals in the District of Columbia. He emphasized that in the directive given by the PMOI command inside Iran to subordinate operational units it was made clear that 'whenever the commander of an operational unit deems that for whatever reason the planned operation might, contrary to the proposed plan, put civilians in harm's way, he or she must immediately call off the operation and [once again] review the plans fully, until he or she is satisfied that no civilian would be harmed'.

Another important principle to which the PMOI has firmly adhered is that throughout the past two decades, its activities outside Iran have always been in accordance with the laws of the host country. This has been acknowledged publicly by security and intelligence agencies in several countries, including Germany, the Netherlands, Norway and Australia. This principle applies not only to the PMOI, but to the broader Resistance movement. In her speech before 2,000 Iranians in Auvers-sur-Oise on 3 July 2003, Mrs Maryam Rajavi reiterated this point:

> We have always been on the side of peace, democracy, stability and security. We have never engaged and will not engage in unlawful actions in Europe, in the United States and in any other country. The supporters and sympathizers of the Iranian Resistance and Iranian refugees have only engaged in legal and peaceful activities outside Iran. It would be the same in the future, too.

Legitimate resistance, not terrorism

The right of the Iranian nation to resist and to seek the overthrow of the religious dictatorship that has deprived them of their most basic rights is a prima facie case of a nation's legitimate rebellion against tyranny and is therefore universally acknowledged. The only ones denying this right have a vested interest in maintaining the status quo in Iran. This inalienable right is stipulated in the 1990 preamble to the Universal Declaration of Human Rights, which stipulates, 'If man is not to be compelled to have recourse, as a last resort, to rebellion against tyranny and oppression, human rights should be protected by the rule of law.' This right has also been recognized by the Catholic Church, which in general opposes the use of violence. In a press conference in 1986, Cardinal Joseph Ratzinger, President of the Pontifical Biblical Commission, introduced a document called 'Christian Liberty and Liberation', wherein it was stated, 'Armed struggle is the last resort to end blatant and prolonged oppression which has seriously violated the fundamental rights of individuals and has dangerously damaged the general interests of a country.'⁵

The US Declaration of Independence, too, recognizes a people's right, and indeed duty, to topple a tyrannical regime: 'But when a long train of abuses and usurpations, pursuing invariably the same Object evinces a design to reduce them under absolute Despotism, it is their right, it is their duty, to throw off such Government, and to provide new Guards for their future security.' In his inaugural address on 4 March 1861, Abraham Lincoln said, 'This country, with its institutions, belongs to the people who inhabit it. Whenever they shall grow weary of the existing Government, they can exercise their constitutional right of amending it or their revolutionary right to dismember or overthrow it.' Thomas Jefferson, one of the founding fathers of the United States of America, said in 1776: 'The oppressed should rebel, and they will continue to rebel and raise disturbance until their civil rights are fully restored to them and all partial distinctions, exclusions and incapacitation are removed.'⁶

Clearly, if the French people were entitled to resist Hitler's Nazism and Americans could wage the War of Independence, the right to resist and to overthrow the clerical regime, one of the most vicious dictatorships of recent times, is the undeniable right of the Iranian people. Even those in contemporary times have reiterated that, faced with no possibility of peaceful political activity, people have the right to use all means available. The late US President John F. Kennedy said, 'Those who make peaceful revolution impossible will make violent revolution inevitable.'

Views of experts and official agencies

There is a wide body of expert opinion vehemently opposed to the basic premise of the use of the terrorism label against the Iranian Resistance. The research services of the US Congress and the Australian parliament have both concluded, in separate studies, that the PMOI has not targeted civilians. After extensive research, the US Congressional Research Service wrote in a 1999 report that 'the group (People's Mojahedin) does not appear to purposely target civilians'.⁷ In a research paper on the PMOI in June 2003, the Australian parliament's research service noted that 'the mass indiscriminate killing associated with some terrorist groups does not appear to have ever been the MeK's objective or favoured tactic'.[8]

When, in June 2003, the Australian Federal Police raided the homes of ten Iranian families who had been living in that country as political refugees, newspapers reported that the Australian security service was dismayed by the police action. The *Sydney Morning Herald* reported on 14 July: 'Significantly, the nation's top domestic security watchdog, the Australian Security Intelligence Organisation (ASIO), was invited to join the raids [on PMOI supporters] but declined. "ASIO saw nothing to be gained from getting involved," said one source. "It told the AFP [Australian Federal Police] it had previously investigated the MeK and did not see it as a threat to Australian security."'

British Home Secretary Jack Straw, in a report to Parliament on 28 February 2001, acknowledged that 'the MeK has not attacked UK or Western interests'.

Yves Bonnet, the former director of France's counter-espionage agency, DST, who was also a member of parliament and the prefect of a department, said in a speech to Iranian demonstrators in Brussels on 13 May 2002:

I have been battling against terrorism for years; terrorism that was nothing but violent destruction and eradication. In other words, terrorism meant involvement in a violent act, to the point of death and terror with the objective of making other countries unstable ... A terrorist movement and organization could be defined with two criteria: first, they want to terrorize and for that reason they target ordinary citizens. The second criterion of a terrorist movement is that it wants to destabilize regimes. Neither of these two criteria permits one to describe the People's Mojahedin as a terrorist movement.

The only targets of the PMOI have been the military and security infrastructure of the ruling regime in Iran. No one has been able to show, no one has even been able to imagine that the People's Mojahedin would resort to violent acts outside Iran or would perpetrate operations against civilians. They simply have not done so. Even within the territory of a country as large as Iran, I could say that the People's Mojahedin has been engaged in terrorizing the ruling terrorists.

In an interview with the daily *Le Parisien* on 18 June 2003, a day after the French police raid on the office of the National Council of Resistance of Iran in France, Bonnet said:

I know the Iranian resistance very well. I even visited their camps in Iraq when I was a member of the French Parliament. Describing them as terrorists has been rejected by dozens of U.S. senators and French parliamentarians ... A terrorist organization is an organization that carries out violent acts against civilians within a country or against people outside that country. A movement that acts solely against the government apparatus within a country could not be described as terrorist, otherwise one has to eliminate the word resistance from lexicons.

We must also bear in mind the nature of the Iranian regime, which is one of the most repressive and fanatical regimes of its kind. All legislative, executive and judicial powers are under the control of the supreme leader.

In an official testimony before the US Court of Appeals for the District of Columbia, ex-congressman Dr Mervyn M. Dymally mentioned that he had visited PMOI camps in Iraq in 1989 as a subcommittee chair of the US House of Representatives' Foreign Affairs Committee and was very familiar with the Iranian Resistance and the situation in Iran due to his extensive contacts with the large Iranian community in his home state of California and other parts of the USA. Dymally told the court:

> The PMOI does not represent a threat to United States nationals or US national security. There is absolutely no evidence for that. PMOI is very much respected in the Congress. In 1992, after the Persian Gulf crisis, 219 Members of the House of Representatives endorsed a statement which emphasized that support for this movement would contribute to the achievement of peace and stability in the region. Their activities have been against our own sworn enemy. To the contrary, they prove most helpful to protecting us from terrorism and weapons of mass destruction. It is clear that the Mojahedin do not belong to any list of foreign terrorist organization. (written affidavit to the US Federal Appeals Court, District of Columbia, 15 October 2001)

He added:

> In our battle against terrorism, we must disarm our enemies from taking advantage of both the religion of Islam as well as the people's religious sentiments. To this end, the PMOI is an anti-fundamentalist movement that advocates a moderate, tolerant, pluralistic and democratic Islam. The movement, because of its support among the people in the region, is potentially an effective asset for us. Therefore, considering that we have a long war ahead of us to uproot terrorism, we need to treat the PMOI as a partner and not an enemy.

Professor Raymond Tanter, who served on the US National Security Council during the Reagan administration and is an eminent scholar on Iran and Iraq, told the Washington Post on 6 July 2003: '[The PMOI's] status should be re-examined. I have seen no evidence that justifies them being on the list, in the sense of the deliberate targeting of civilians for political gain.' Patrick Clawson, deputy director of the Washington Institute for Near East Policy, and Daniel Pipes, a board member of the US Institute of Peace and director of the Middle East Forum, wrote in a joint article on 22 May 2003, that the People's Mojahedin is not a terrorist organization. 'For the last 15 years, [PMOI] has been organized as an army, and its only violent actions have been directed against the Iranian regime.'

Michel Juneau-Katsuyo, a former member of the Canadian Security Intelligence Service, noted in a press article that having 'observed' the PMOI in Canada for a long time, he came to the conclusion that the movement 'has deep roots in Canada' and 'did not fit the profile that's been put on it'. 'This particular group was targeting specifically Iranian government officials and military targets,' Juneau-Katsuyo noted. 'They were not specifically going after civilian targets and were actually quite careful in not going after such a thing.' Juneau-Katsuyo said the real Iranian threat to Canadian security was more likely to come from the Iranian embassy, which has operated as a base for spying on Canada's large Iranian community.

An American scholar, Professor Thomas M. Ricks, director of international studies and professor of history at the Centre for Arab and Islamic Studies of Villanova University, has been monitoring the activities of the People's Mojahedin in Iran and in the USA for thirty years. Professor Ricks lived in Iran for several years during the Shah's reign and has written several books on the Middle East. In a court affidavit on the PMOI, he said:

> While the PMOI is adamant in its defence of armed resistance and is the only viable alternative for bringing serious change within Iran today, it has vowed, since the days of the Shah, not to put civilians in harm's way. I myself witnessed Mojahedin peacefully passing out literature and posting 'wall letters' in Tehran despite being beaten, pushed to the ground and kicked by the Islamic Guardians or Pasdaran. They also stated that in a democratic environment, they would lay down their arms and accept the results of a truly free and fair election under the auspices of the United Nations with the presence of international election observers, which lends credibility to Mojahedin's commitment to the principles

of political activism and democracy. PMOI, therefore, is not a terrorist organization ... They appear to me to act peacefully and legally in the US. Some of their detailed information on issues sensitive to the national security of the US, including state-sponsored terrorism and stockpiling of weapons of mass destruction by Tehran, have been well published and well received. The PMOI offered reliable reports from within the clerical hierarchy and it remains a creditable source of news on Iran.

Bruce McColm, chairman of the board and president of the Institute for Democratic Strategies (IDS), and former Executive Director of Freedom House, gave this opinion on the PMOI after noting that he has known the People's Mojahedin for almost two decades and has also heard the views of their detractors:

> The PMOI is not a terrorist organization. It does not target civilians and it does not engage in or sponsor international acts of terrorism. It has stated publicly throughout the years that its military actions are limited solely against the repressive agencies of the Iranian government such as the Pasdaran (the Revolutionary Guards), the Intelligence Ministry as well as other agencies with a direct role in the political killings that have plagued that country. A review of their various military actions over the past decades would bear this out.
>
> The PMOI has been at the forefront of the fight against the ominous phenomenon of Islamic fundamentalism ... The PMOI's leaders and their allies in the NCRI coalition, over the years, have constantly warned us about the threat of terrorism by fundamentalist groups ...The advice of the PMOI on this subject has been sought by our public policy institutes, various congressional offices, agencies of the United States Government and nongovernmental organizations. During this time, they have provided most valuable information about some of the terrorist acts carried out by such fundamentalist groups. They were the first to provide details about the perpetrators of the Khobar Tower bombing in 1996 in Saudi Arabia as well as the bombing of the Jewish Community Centre in Argentina in 1994, to name a few.[9]

Dr Khalid Duran, a USA-based expert on the Middle East and Islam who has taught in universities in the USA, Europe and Asia and has written five books on Islam, wrote in an affidavit to the Court of Appeals in the District of Colombia:

> The PMOI is not a terrorist organization, and does not represent a threat to the United States nationals or U.S. national security. Indeed, the PMOI has contributed extensively to the fight against terrorism and the effort to

curb the proliferation of weapons of mass destruction by exposing sensitive information on the Iranian regime's terrorist networks in the Middle East, Europe and elsewhere ... If by terrorism one means indiscriminate violence which resulted in the deaths of, or injury to, innocent civilians, none of the incidents referred to the People's Mojahedin qualifies ... By definition, terrorism is a resort to violence that puts civilians in harm's way in order to achieve a certain political objective. I have looked very carefully at the PMOI's military activities. To the best of my knowledge, all the targets struck by the PMOI's military units have been military in nature or involved in government-sponsored repression of dissent.[10]

Another Middle East expert, Professor Marius Deeb of the School of Advance International Studies at Johns Hopkins University, also rejected the use of the terrorism label against the PMOI:

I think it would be very unwise not to cultivate a sort of relationship with the Mojahedin-e Khalq vis-à-vis Iran. By giving in to Iran, you get nothing in return. This is the experience with Iran. The idea that we will go and have a dialogue with Iran and reach an agreement is all nonsense. Unfortunately one of the negative side-effects of the war in Iraq has been the spread of Iran's influence. So we need more than ever to cultivate relationships with all groups that oppose the Iranian regime, especially the Mojahedin-e-Khalq.[11]

Professor Deeb informed members of Congress of his views on this subject in an address to a meeting on Capitol Hill on 18 June 2003, titled, 'Does Washington Need a New Policy Towards Tehran?' Professor Deeb told the law-makers and congressional staff:

One can't understand how we conduct our diplomacy, we bomb the Mojahedin-Khalq which is fighting the terrorist supporters and then we have talks with the terrorist supporters in Geneva, to the Iranians ... There is no logical frame to this policy. Of course in this way the Iranian regime will not listen to you.

We are just beginning the war on terrorism. What happened with Islamic revolution in Iran, it started that process. Bin Laden is just one of the greatest creations but it is not the end of it. I wanted to emphasize that we had to deal with the issue of terrorism and we have to find allies everywhere, all the allies we need, and the Mojahedin-Khalq organization is definitely an ally in our struggle against terrorism and their terror masters.

Addressing the same meeting in Congress, James Aikins, a fellow of the Council on Foreign Relations and a former US ambassador to Saudi Arabia, said:

The Mojahedin remain the only organized group still trying to bring about real change in Iran. Unlike the mullahs, they favour a just peace between the Arabs and the Israelis. Unlike the mullahs, who bear direct responsibility for the hundreds of Americans killed in Lebanon 20 years ago and the dozens killed more recently in Riyadh, the Mojahedin have taken no action against America or American interests in the Middle East, in Europe or in America. They have suffered tremendously at the hands of the mullahs – having lost some 30,000 members. And because they have fought against the mullahs, they are characterized by the Iranian government as 'terrorists'.

It would seem reasonable to assume that the United States Government would tacitly support the Mojahedin or at least would take no action to inhibit them. Yet, strangely, the opposite is taking place. They have been placed on the list of 'terrorist' organizations ...

Our efforts to place the Mojahedin on our list of 'terrorist organizations', to try to force it to close its offices and to stop its political activities in the United States, and to curry favour with the mullahs are both immoral and politically stupid. The State Department itself has made it explicitly clear that 'making a friendly gesture to Iran' is the sole reason for our placing the Mojahedin on the list of organizations supporting terrorism. It has never shown that the Mojahedin has ever engaged in anti-American activity; its meetings are carefully monitored by the FBI and never has any evidence been found of any plot against any American citizen or property. If the State Department has such evidence it should be revealed to American judges. The mullahs may call the Mojahedin attack on the building in Tehran where political prisoners are held, tortured and murdered 'an act of terrorism', but no one else in the world would.

Dr Neil Livingstone, a top terrorism expert, told the congressional gathering that the PMOI should never have been included in the list of terrorist organizations:

While it once launched attacks against Iranian government installations, the MEK has spent most of the last decade placing political pressure on the regime in Tehran, striving for the freedom they cherish ... The Central Intelligence Agency lists the Mujahedin e Khalq as a political pressure organization 'almost completely repressed by the government', and in its profile of Iran's political makeup, the CIA does not associate the MEK with terrorism.[12]

The United States must now change its policy and support organizations seeking more liberty and more freedom for the Iranian people. America should also express its support for a free Iran by removing the MEK from the State Department's list of terrorist organizations, making it a partner in the liberation of Iran, not an adversary.

International support

The broad, long-term political support the PMOI has enjoyed in the parliaments of different European countries, the United States Congress and elsewhere in the world is due not only to the fact that it has suffered so greatly at the hands of the brutal clerical regime, but also because the PMOI does not, in their informed estimation, even remotely resemble a group of terrorists. It is in this light that in the past twenty years, the PMOI has enjoyed vast support among many political dignitaries, parliamentarians and government officials across the world, despite the Iranian regime's repeated pleas that the PMOI's activities outside Iran be banned and the organization be branded terrorist. Such support goes back to the early years when the PMOI took up arms against the Tehran regime. Resistance leaders and PMOI delegations were invited to many party congresses, met government and party leaders, members of parliaments and attended the United Nations and European Parliament sessions. This support continues to the present.

Three weeks after the US State Department first included the PMOI in its terror list, an international parliamentary seminar in London announced a policy initiative on Iran endorsed by 2,000 members of parliament from sixteen countries who declared their support for the Resistance. They included a majority of the US House of Representatives (224 members) and parliamentary majorities in Britain (331 members of the House of Commons and 119 peers), Italy (326 MPs), Switzerland (116 MPs), Norway (84 MPs), Luxembourg (43 MPs), San Marino (32 MPs) and 250 members of the European Parliament, 115 Italian senators, and dozens of parliamentarians from Sweden, Denmark, the Netherlands, Australia, Germany, France, Belgium, Jordan, Egypt and Palestine.

Support for the PMOI and the Iranian Resistance among members of Congress is overwhelming. In November 2002, 150 members of the US Congress made a bipartisan declaration: 'As a majority of our colleagues in the House (of Representatives) have repeatedly underscored, the Mojahedin is a "legitimate resistance movement"; as a prominent anti-fundamentalist organization adhering to tolerant Islam, it is a major player in confronting this ominous phenomenon and terrorism emanating from it.'

After the State Department first designated the PMOI a foreign terrorist organization, a majority of the House of Representatives said the designation violated the spirit of the anti-terrorism law. In a bipartisan statement issued on 16 September 1998, they stated:

> It was not Congress's intent that a legitimate opposition to the Iranian regime be included within that particular list of terrorist groups. This has essentially had the effect of opening up the main opposition group in Iran to further attack by the Iranian regime's state-sponsored terrorism machine ... This designation is indeed a wrong-headed approach, and appears to directly contradict the spirit of the anti-terrorism law, and we believe the decision should be reviewed immediately.

Similarly, when the State Department redesignated the PMOI in October 1999, US law-makers again criticized the move and called for a change. On 14 October 1999, almost a third of the US Senate urged the State Department to 'look afresh towards the possibilities that exist within Iran's democratic opposition, including the people's Mojahedin'. In their joint letter to the Secretary of State, the senators expressed their support for the statement by the House majority recognizing the PMOI as 'a legitimate resistance movement even though they remain on your agency's list of terrorist organizations'. In June 1995, some 202 members of Congress wrote to President Clinton to voice their support for the Iranian Resistance. In September 1989, 186 members of Congress expressed their support for the movement in a joint letter to Secretary of State James Baker. And in July 1990, 162 members of Congress endorsed the movement's peaceful and democratic aims in a letter addressed to Mr Rajavi. In October 2000, 228 members of the US House of Representatives issued a joint statement on Iranian policy, reiterating the position by a House majority and the Senate a year earlier that the PMOI was 'a legitimate resistance movement'. Eight members of the House from both sides of the aisle took part in the press conference, attended also by the NCRI's US representative, to announce the statement.

Showing another kind of support, dozens of US law-makers, including some of those who drafted the Anti-Terrorism and Effective Death Penalty Act, have taken part in many gatherings and events organized by the PMOI and different Iranian-American communities and associations across the United States, both before and after the designation. That would not have occurred if they had any doubts about the legitimacy of the PMOI.

The impact of such widespread support for the PMOI was clearly not confined to politics. In considering a motion on the legality of using

PMOI's designation to prosecute individuals, a Federal judge in California ruled on 21 June 2002 that such prosecution was void, because the designation of the People's Mojahedin as a terrorist organization violated the US Constitution. Judge Robert M. Katasuki of the US District Court for the Central District of California found that the designation was 'unconstitutional on its face'. 'Accordingly, such designation is a nullity and cannot be relied upon in a prosecution,' he stated, adding that 'the argument for national security should not serve as an excuse for obliterating the Constitution'. Judge Katasuki added:

> Members of Congress have opined that the MEK (PMOI) is a legitimate resistance movement fighting the tyrannical regime presently in power in Iran. According to these members of Congress, the MEK (PMOI) prevented the Iranian regime from obtaining nuclear weapons; provided information to the U.S. regarding Iran-sponsored bombing attacks on Israeli interests; and supports the Middle East peace process. Finally, members of Congress have stated that the MEK (PMOI) is not engaged in terrorist activities but, rather, in a legitimate struggle for an Iran of democracy, religious tolerance, human rights and non-violence.

International law

Established principles of international law recognize the legitimacy of the Iranian Resistance's conflict with the religious fascism ruling Iran, as distinct from terrorism. The Geneva Convention Relative to the Treatment of Prisoners of War of 12 August 1949, in Part I, Article 3, refers expressly to 'armed conflict not of an international character occurring in the territory of one of the High Contracting Parties'. The International Committee of the Red Cross's 1952 commentary on the Geneva Conventions states, 'It sometimes happens in a civil war that those who are regarded as rebels are in actual fact patriots struggling for the independence and dignity of their country,' and further, that in the debates on the convention, 'It was not possible to talk of "terrorism", "anarchy", or "disorders" in the case of rebels who complied with humanitarian principles.' The PMOI, as pointed out earlier, fully adheres to the Geneva Conventions.

Dr Jean-Marie Henckaerts, legal adviser to the ICRC, proposes a seven-point 'recipe' to armed opposition groups in order to ensure their compliance with international humanitarian law. These, based on the provisions of IHL and the ICRC's experience in the implementation of IHL, are as follows: 'Make a declaration of intent to respect IHL; take prisoners, rather than execute them; attack only military objectives and combatants; do not use terror tactics; issue instructions to fighters; install a system of command responsibility; punish violators of IHL in fair and regular trials.'

These 'recommendations' have been fully implemented by the PMOI. It has declared its full commitment to IHL both to the ICRC and to other international authorities. It has allowed ICRC registration of and regular access to all the prisoners it has taken and has released them under ICRC supervision. It has never targeted civilians and has in fact gone out of its way to ensure that no civilian is ever harmed as a result of its operations. It has never used terror tactics. Resistance combatants in the National Liberation Army are organized in a regular force wearing uniform at all times and with a recognizable chain of command. As for the punishment of IHL violators, Iranian Resistance leader Massoud Rajavi has publicly pledged that any combatant found guilty of targeting civilians would be handed over to an international court for trial and the Resistance would pay compensation to the victim's family. Clearly, the Iranian Resistance has, in theory and practice, satisfied all these criteria.

An international seminar on the 'Relevance of International Humanitarian Law to Non-State Actors', sponsored by the ICRC and the College of Europe and held in the Belgian town of Bruges in October 2002, heard the views of several leading experts on international humanitarian law on the subject of 'non-international conflicts'. Professor Eric David, a world authority on international humanitarian law, told the seminar,

> When it comes to armed groups, rebel groups or similar forces, international humanitarian law applies in cases of non-international armed conflicts, as demonstrated by Article 3 common to the four Geneva Conventions, the second Additional Protocol, and Article 8 paragraph 2 of the Statute of the International Criminal Court.
>
> Is it not strange that a group that did not participate in the elaboration of a rule can be bound by that rule? The legal answer is straightforward: the State is bound by the rule and the State includes not only the government, but also the entire population that is made up of individuals and groups.

He emphasizes that 'international humanitarian law as a whole applies to national liberation movements provided they accept it'.

In addressing the question of 'terrorism and international humanitarian law', Professor Yves Sandoz, then the Director for International Law and Communication for the International Committee of the Red Cross, said:

The most useful references [to terrorism in international humanitarian law] can probably be found under Article 51 paragraph 2 of Additional Protocol I and Article 13 paragraph 2 of Additional Protocol II. In identical terms, these two articles prohibit ' ... acts or threats of violence the primary purpose of which is to spread terror amongst the civilian populations ...' Within the framework of armed conflicts, the prohibition to terrorize applies thus only to the civilian population.

Professor Sandoz mentions 'blind violence directed against civilians or acts perpetrated against specific categories of persons because of their ethnic background or religious belief' as what international humanitarian law 'clearly defines as the hard core of terrorist acts'. He states that, according to IHL, 'the notion of terrorism applies, in case of conflict, only to acts directed against the civilian population', adding that in a global definition of terrorism, 'violence deliberately used against civilians as well as blind or indiscriminate violence can without hesitation be called "terrorist"'.

Professor Sandoz points out that even in situations outside 'the framework of an armed conflict', not all use of violence can be automatically categorized as 'terrorism'. He mentions that 'there is, for instance, reluctance to totally outlaw the use of violence against repressive regimes that do not allow the expression of dissenting views by the democratic opposition'.

The legitimacy of the Iranian Resistance in legal terms can also be approached from the point of view of the definition of 'terrorism'. The vast majority of definitions of terrorism, despite their remarkable divergence, would confirm the clear demarcation that separates PMOI's resistance from terrorism. While there is no universal definition of terrorism, they all point out that an underlying aspect of terrorism is the targeting of civilians and innocent people to create terror. James M. Poland, Professor of Criminal Justice at California State University, who has researched and written extensively on terrorism and hostage negotiations, put the emphasis on the 'innocent' by stating, 'Terrorism is the premeditated, deliberate, systematic murder, mayhem, and threatening of the innocent to create fear and intimidation in order to gain a political or tactical advantage, usually to influence an audience.' Walter Laqueur, the author of The Age of Terrorism, also emphasized the issue of 'innocent people' being targeted: 'Terrorism constitutes the illegitimate use of force to achieve a political objective when innocent people are targeted.'[13] Professor Donna Arzt, director of Syracuse University's Center for Global Law and Practice, has stressed two aspects of a terrorist act: 'The victims: the victims of terrorism are usually specified as civilians or non-combatants, in order to differentiate terrorism from attacks on military targets, which are outright acts of war ... The intent: the intent of terrorism is either to intimidate or coerce a civilian population.'[14]

Terrorism specialist Alex P. Schmid, from the UN International Terrorism Prevention Office, wrote, 'Terrorism is a method of combat in which random or symbolic victims serve as an instrumental target of violence.'[15]

Legitimate military targets

Much of the present-day discussion on the question of terrorism centres on the issue of legitimate military targets and how to define them. The recognized definition of legitimate military objectives comes in Article 52 of Additional Protocol I to the Geneva Conventions (1977), as one 'which by [its] nature, location, purpose, or use makes an effective contribution to military action and whose total or partial destruction, capture or neutralization, in the circumstances ruling at the time, offers a definite military advantage'.

Legitimate military targets thus include armed forces and persons who take part in the fighting; positions or installations occupied by armed forces as well as objectives that are directly contested in battle; military installations such as barracks, war ministries, munitions or fuel dumps, storage yards for vehicles, airfields, rocket launch ramps and naval bases. Military lawyers have also included as legitimate infrastructure targets things like lines and means of communication, command, and control – railway lines, roads, bridges, tunnels and canals – that are of fundamental military importance. The third category of targets regarded as legitimate communications targets include broadcasting and television stations, and telephone and telegraph exchanges of fundamental military importance.

On 25 March 2003, the USA launched air strikes against Iraqi television stations. This was repeated on several occasions during the hostilities. US military commanders, defending the attacks, described the Iraqi television and radio as legitimate military targets and British Defence Secretary Geoff Hoon said that Iraqi state television was part of the Iraqi government's control, command and communications network.[16] During the war in Kosovo, British Prime Minister Tony Blair told a press conference at NATO headquarters in Brussels that targets such as 'lines of communication, lines of supply, oil refineries and oil supplies' were regarded as legitimate.[17]

NATO Secretary General Lord Robertson told the British House of Lords, on 19 April 1999, that all NATO ministers agreed that military targets include 'strategic assets such as bridges, barracks and headquarters'. NATO Spokesman Dr Jamie Shea said on 21 April 1999: 'Any aspect of the power structure is considered as a legitimate target by NATO. In dictatorial societies it becomes progressively impossible to distinguish between the party and the state; as we all know, they become conflated with each other, and this is also the party headquarters which contains the propaganda of the ruling socialist party.' A senior NATO commander in the former Yugoslavia, Lieutenant General Michael Short, explained NATO's strategy of avoiding civilian casualties:

> I put out guidance saying that if you are working a target area and you're not sure call me, and I'll tell you whether to drop or not. Call me and describe the village and say, 'Boss, I see a village and I see tanks parked next to the houses in the village. What do you want me to do?' And I'll say, 'Tell them to hit the tanks.' And if he hits a house by mistake, that's my responsibility.'

Judging these statements by authoritative sources in NATO, as an example of the way conventional military outfits approach the issue of target selection, one can readily conclude that the PMOI has been far more restrained in its handling of target selection to ensure that no civilians ever get in harm's way as a result of its operations.

Victims of terrorism

While there is consensus among all experts that the clerical regime in Iran has been the main patron of international terrorism in the world for the past two decades, it is equally clear that the People's Mojahedin Organization of Iran and the Resistance movement have been the biggest victims of mullahs' terrorism. Some 300 members and activists of the Iranian Resistance have fallen victim to the mullahs' terrorist attacks outside Iran. Professor Kazem Rajavi, Iran's first post-revolutionary ambassador to the United Nations in Geneva and a renowned human rights activist, who was the representative of the National Council of Resistance of Iran in Switzerland, was assassinated in Geneva on 24 April 1990. Mohammad Hossein Naghdi, who defected to the NCRI when he was Iran's chargé d'affaires in Rome, was gunned down by the mullahs' terrorists in Rome in March 1993. Ms Zahra Rajabi, the Iranian Resistance's ambassador-at-large for refugees, was murdered in Istanbul in February 1996 by assassins who included officials of the mullahs' consulate in the city. Ali-Akbar Ghorbani, the PMOI's representative in Turkey, was abducted, tortured to death and his body dumped in a forest near Istanbul in 1992.[18] Other dissidents have been assassinated in countries as far apart as Switzerland, the United Arab Emirates, Turkey, Pakistan and Iraq by Tehran-dispatched hit squads. In some of these murders, the mullahs' 'diplomats' have been directly implicated in the planning and execution of the assassinations.

The mullahs' agents carried out 150 terrorist attacks against PMOI members in Iraq from 1993 to 2003, which included bombing a city bus in Baghdad, on 9 June 1999, which led to the death of six Mojahedin members and gravely wounded thirty others, use of car bombs to blow up Mojahedin offices, remote-controlled bombs to attack passing vehicles, as well as kidnappings and assassinations.

Antithesis to terrorism

The PMOI has played a significant role in exposing and thwarting many terrorist plots by the mullahs' regime and uncovering evidence of the Iranian regime's role in dozens of terrorist attacks across the world. *Time* magazine carried a report on 11 November 1996 titled, 'Terror Central, How Iran's Mullahs Run Their Secret Assassination Network'. The article described the PMOI as 'a key source of documentation on Iranian terrorism' and pointed out that members of the Iranian Resistance 'are the main targets of Tehran's death squads'.

Elton Gallegly, chairman of the sub-committee on international terrorism, non-proliferation and human rights of the International Relations Committee at the US House of Representatives, wrote in a letter to the US representative of the National Council of Resistance of Iran, Soona Samsami, on 24 September 1998:

> I have forwarded the materials on the Buenos Aires bombing (that you provided me) to the United States Department of State. We have been informed that they were able to verify some of the information and that it proved very helpful in the course of their investigation ... I would like to thank you and the People's Mojahedin of Iran, which put the lives of their members as well as their resources at risk in order to gather this valuable information.

As a final word in this chapter, one must reiterate that the crux of the issue is not terrorism or the means and methods of overthrowing the clerical regime. Rather, the heart of the problem is for outside powers to recognize the right of the Iranian people to resist the ruling religious tyranny and to establish democracy in their country and for them not to provide support for the illegitimate regime ruling Iran.

In a speech at a meeting on Capitol Hill to discuss the right policy on Iran, Iranian-born US historian and scholar Ali Parsa, Professor of History at California State University and lecturer on modern Middle East history at the University of California, Los Angeles (UCLA), warned of the danger of repeating past mistakes:

> In the post-Cold War world, U.S. needs not to repeat the same mistakes of 1953, when it replaced the moderate and liberal minded Mossadeq with the totally submissive shah for the fear of communist expansion. Now, that threat is gone. Today's global threat is fundamentalism in all forms, especially the Islamic fundamentalism which is the most aggressive and dangerous type. This danger to peace and security of the world could only be effectively remedied from inside the Islamic world. The only real choice that does not antagonize the Islamic world is transformation from within and by the progressive Muslims. Five centuries have passed since Christianity was transformed by the Reformation; and more than two centuries since the Enlightenment thinkers transformed Europe and the West into a rational, forward-looking society. Muslims are experiencing not an identical, but similar phase in their history, and they have to fight their own battle for reform and enlightenment. The very first, but important, step the West can take is to remove the obstacles from their path, and not add one to them.

The time has come for the Mojahedin to be taken off the terrorist list of the State Department. The Iraq war, once again, proved that the Mojahedin are no threat to America's national security, but are, in fact, strategic allies in combating Tehran's fundamentalism. It is both politically wise and morally right to take the Mojahedin off the list of 'foreign terrorist organizations'. They are not terrorists. They are democratic freedom fighters.

Notes

1. Speech by PMOI Secretary General at a gathering of PMOI personnel on the foundation anniversary of the organization, 13 September 2003.

2. United Nations website (<www.un.org>), Secretary General's speech at Tilburg University in the Netherlands, November 2002.

3. Hansard, House of Lords, col. 151, 27 March 2001.

4. Ibid., col. 183.

5. *L'Osservatore Romano*, the Vatican, 5 April 1986.

6. Thomas Jefferson, *Notes on Religion*, 1776, p. 548.

7. Kenneth Katzman, Congressional Research Service, the Library of Congress, 'Terrorism: Middle Eastern Groups and State Sponsors', 9 August 1999.

8. Nigel Brew, Parliament of Australia, Research Note no. 43, 2002–03. Foreign Affairs, Defence and Trade Group, June 2003.

9. Bruce McColm, Democratic Strategy Institute, Affidavit to Washington Appeal Court, Washington DC, 15 October 2001.

10. Khalid Doran, Orientalist and Middle East expert, Affidavit to Washington Appeal Court, 29 August 2001.

11. Professor Marius Deeb, speech on Capitol Hill, 'Does Washington Need a New Policy Towards Tehran?', 18 June 2003.

12. Central Intelligence Agency, 'CIA World Factbook: Iran', <http://www.cia.gov/cia/publications/factbook/geos/ir.html>.

13. Walter Laqueur, *The Age of Terrorism*, Boston: Little, Brown, 1987.

14. Donna Arzt, Preface to *Terrorism and Terrorists*, Center for Global Law and Practice, Syracuse University.

15. Alex P. Schmid, *Political Terrorism, a Research Guide on Concepts, Theories, Databases and Literature*, Amsterdam: North Editions, 1983, pp. 58–119.

16. Reuters, 26 March 2003.

17. BBC World Service, 20 April 1999.

18. The Turkish government arrested several agents of the Iranian regime and they were convicted of the abduction and murder of Ali-Akbar Ghorbani. The assassins were working on the orders of the Iranian embassy in Turkey. See Amnesty International Reports 1993 and 1997.

PART III
Battleground Iraq

6 | Iranian resistance and Iraq

War is the continuation of politics by other means. *Karl Von Clausewitz*[1]

The presence of a part of the Iranian Resistance's forces in Iraq has been a controversial issue, hotly debated not only in the context of Iranian politics, but also on the regional and international level. Critics say that the PMOI's presence in Iraq during the rule of Saddam Hussein means that it was a stooge of the Iraqi regime. Advocates say in defence of the PMOI that its presence in Iraq was and remains an unavoidable necessity of the campaign against the ruling religious dictatorship in Iran. It is obvious that a regime that has remained in power by relying on the most severe suppression inside Iran and the most active support for terrorism outside Iran can never be overthrown by exiles on the banks of the Thames, the Seine or the Potomac. Furthermore, they cite the organization's continuing presence in Iraq even after the fall of the Baghdad regime and its good ties with the Iraqi people as a clear exoneration of the PMOI from such charges.

With Iraq now in post-conflict trauma and Iran becoming the focus of international concern with regard to terrorism, weapons of mass destruction and 'rogue state' behaviour, the PMOI's presence in Iraq continues to generate much interest and differing views around the world. In the latest twist, the *Washington Post* reported on 11 September 2003 that there was a deep split over the issue between the US Departments of State and Defense. The *Post* article summed up the zigzag course of events since the months preceding the Iraq war:

> In January, before the war against Iraq was launched, U.S. officials held a secret meeting with Iranian officials and suggested the United States would target the People's Mujaheddin as a way of gaining Iran's cooperation to seal its border and provide assistance to search-and-rescue missions for downed U.S. pilots during the war. In early April, U.S. forces bombed the Mujaheddin camps, killing about 50 people, according to the group, before a cease-fire was arranged on April 15. That was during a period of growing alarm within the administration about spreading Iranian influence among Iraqi Shiites.
>
> The cease-fire convinced the Iranian government it had been double-

crossed on the issue of the Mujaheddin. But within weeks, Bush's senior policy advisers reversed course and ordered U.S. forces to disarm the group, secretly telling Iranian officials even before action was taken on May 9.

Since then, however, relations with Iran have soured over continuing revelations about its nuclear program and allegations that it harbors al Qaeda leaders implicated in the May 13 bombings of residential compounds in Saudi Arabia. After the bombings, U.S. officials suspended the secret talks with Iranian officials.[2]

The *Washington Post* article noted that in a recent letter to Defense Secretary Donald Rumsfeld on the PMOI presence in Iraq, Secretary of State Colin Powell stated that 'intercepts of Iranian government communications indicated the Mujaheddin continued to pose problems for the government in Tehran'.[3]

The US-led war in Iraq, how the Iranian Resistance and the mullahs' regime approached it, and its impact on Iranian politics, will be discussed in the following chapters. In this chapter, we shall review the political and historical background to the present situation and discuss the PMOI's relations with the Iraqi regime under Saddam Hussein.

Many politicians and political parties, who noted the threat of Islamic fundamentalism and terrorism stemming from it and considered the religious dictatorship ruling Iran as the source, found it quite understandable to see part of the Mojahedin forces based in Iraq. In an 8 June 1995 press conference on Capitol Hill, Senator Robert Torricelli said this in reply to a question on whether the presence of forces of the PMOI on Iraqi soil undermined the legitimacy and effectiveness of the Resistance:

> I think simply because the People's Mojahedin has forces located in Iraq does not make it less legitimate or effective. The People's Mojahedin is based in Iraq because there is no place else for it to go and it needs to be in the proximity of Iran. Its presence in Iraq is not a political statement in the confrontation between Iraq and the United States. It is a simple reflection of geographic and political realities. It would be unfair to hold that presence against the People's Mojahedin and their common intentions with the United States. They are acting in concert with the United States' objectives in ending this despotic government and creating a pluralistic democracy in Iran.

Torricelli added:

> No doubt the fact that they are in Iraq (because of its proximity to

Iran) is very helpful to them, but the world does not allow us to be so purist that we can resist identifying with people who share our objectives, simply because of their relationship with our adversaries. On that theory, we would have resisted support from the Russians against the Nazis and half our allies against the Soviet Union could not have met our test of purity. The United States also maintained military bases during the Cold War in Franco's Spain and in Marcos's Philippines. We used military bases because they were important to achieve a large national objective. If the People's Mojahedin needs to have military bases in Iraq, I think it is that same tradition.

Even if we agree that the presence of forces adjacent to Iranian territory is a necessity for a resistance which is serious in its resolve to overthrow the dictatorship in Iran, the question arises as to how an opposition movement like the People's Mojahedin could maintain an independent presence in Iraq under Saddam Hussein? This is a rational and legitimate question and must be answered regardless of the fact that it has been a favourite subject for the clerical regime's propaganda war against its opponents.

Whatever the reasons behind the PMOI's presence in Iraq, the unequivocal evidence of the Mojahedin's independence, according to many outside observers, is the fact that they stayed away from two major wars (the Persian Gulf War in 1991 and the recent one in 2003). In the recent war that led to the downfall of the Baathist regime, the Mojahedin not only refrained from firing a single shot in the conflict, but also remained in Iraq after the war was over. Ironically, the expression of support for the PMOI by Iraqis from all sections of society and ethnic and religious groups has been far greater than it was before. Evidence of this support is presented in the next chapter.

If the Mojahedin has been an independent force in Iraq, however, then the obvious question would be why Saddam Hussein's regime tolerated it? The answer lies in the geopolitical realities of the region: the religious regime in Iran is committed to the export of fundamentalism to other parts of the Islamic world. Iraq, for a host of reasons, has been number one on the Iranian regime's target list. The American scholar Professor Marius Deeb, of the School of Advanced International Studies at Johns Hopkins University, in an interview on 27 May 2003, believes that the presence of the Mojahedin in Iraq was 'a marriage of convenience'. He notes: 'The Mojahedin had no stake in the war. It is the location [Iraq] they are interested in, and they are not interested in who is in power. Their interest is to change the regime in Iran, which I think should be our interest too, because as long as the regime in Iran is there, terrorism is embedded in it.'

What Professor Deeb refers to is the reality of regional geopolitics: irrespective of the nature of the regime in Iraq, the Islamic Republic of Iran will continue to export fundamentalism into the country with the intention of installing a vassal clergy-dominated state in Iraq. Here are some of the reasons:

1. Export of terrorism and fundamentalism is an intrinsic and inseparable characteristic of the *velayat-e faqih* regime in Iran, which calls itself the 'Mother of All Islamic Lands' and sees its Supreme Leader as 'the leader of all Muslims in the world'. It is the engine that keeps the regime going in spite of all its contradictions.

2. Iraq has always been the top priority for the ruling mullahs' export of terrorism: six of Shiite Islam's Imams are buried there; more than 60 per cent of the population are Shiites; there is a 1,200-kilometre border between the two countries that the Iranian regime's agents have no difficulty in crossing, and many cultural and historical similarities with Iran. It was the obsession with setting up an 'Islamic Republic of Iraq' that provided the main incentive for Khomeini and his disciples to insist on continuing the war with Iraq for eight years with the slogan of 'liberating Qods [Jerusalem] via Karbala'.[4] For very much the same reason, the fundamentalist regime in Iran refused to sign a peace accord with Iraq for fifteen years after the 1988 cease-fire.

The geopolitical factor and the special nature of the fundamentalist regime in Iran clearly show that the independence of the Mojahedin in Iraq has a political and strategic basis. It is true that the Mojahedin and the NLA needed to use Iraqi soil to push forward their strategy of overthrowing the Iranian regime. It is equally true that it was with the permission and agreement of the Iraqi government that they were able to use this territory. But for the same geopolitical reasons mentioned above, any government in Iraq, as long as it is not a stooge of the mullahs' regime, would find itself threatened with expansionism and the export of fundamentalism by its eastern neighbour.

No Iraqi government, neither the previous one nor the one that will come to power in due course, can find a compromise with the fundamentalist regime in Iran to put an end to this meddling. For over a decade, between the first Gulf War in 1991 and its downfall in 2003, the Baathist regime in Iraq tried hard to arrive at such a compromise, but the deal fell through every time before its final conclusion. The reason was not that Baghdad was not prepared to accommodate the mullahs' demands and concerns, but the fact that the fundamentalist rulers in Iran never had the intention of abandoning their plans to export the 'Islamic revolution' to Iraq, as Khomeini demanded in his political will. This is the reality that forces any government in Baghdad that wants to withstand the ever-present threat from the mullahs' regime and safeguard Iraq's national interests, to recognize the independence of the Mojahedin and the Iranian Resistance.

The fratricidal war

In September 1980, after the start of the Iran–Iraq war, the PMOI strongly condemned the Iraqi regime's invasion of Iran and its forces rushed to the front to defend the Iranian people in the face of foreign aggression. Thousands of PMOI members and supporters went to the war fronts immediately. This principled policy against a foreign army entering the country was adopted despite the fact that the clerical regime's provocations and meddling in Iraq's internal affairs in the name of 'export of Islamic revolution' had played an important role in igniting the flames of war.

Many Mojahedin members and supporters, including Dr Ahmad Tabatabai, a veteran Mojahedin official, were killed in the war and many more taken prisoner by the Iraqi army. Some of these prisoners were freed ten years later and rejoined the ranks of the Mojahedin. Ironically, a considerable number of Mojahedin members, while fighting the Iraqi army at the front, were shot from behind or arrested and tortured by Revolutionary Guards. Some of them were executed.

A 1984 report by the US State Department to Congress acknowledged that after the Iraqi forces invaded Iran in September 1980, 'Mujahedin units went to the front immediately. They were tolerated by the fundamentalists only in the first hectic days of the war, and most were soon expelled.'

The war with Iraq was a true catastrophe for the Iranian people, who lost a million of their youths and suffered material losses estimated at over one trillion dollars. Worse still was the fact that Khomeini took advantage of the war to stifle all dissent within Iran, consolidate his grip on power, and turn Iran into the closed society he had envisaged from the outset. Islamic fundamentalism was undeniably the biggest winner of the war in its first few years. Exploiting Shiite Islam's traditional cult of martyrdom and elaborate mourning ceremonies, the mullahs turned the war into a hybrid culture of religious hysteria and jingoistic fervour. Teenagers, some as young as twelve, were press-ganged and shipped to the front, where they were sent to their deaths in their thousands in futile human wave attacks against the superior Iraqi armour. The Bassij, the Revolutionary Guards' notorious paramilitary agency, set up its branches in every school, factory, office and neighbourhood across the country. The war allowed the mullahs to set up and develop with startling speed a nationwide apparatus of social control, extending the reach of their inquisitorial powers to every household in the cities and even in the most remote villages. War became the staple food for television, radio and the print media, all in the hands of the clerical state. Even today, fifteen years after the guns fell silent, the eight-year war with Iraq continues to dominate much of the output of the official Iranian media.

Khomeini instantly recognized the advantage that his regime could derive from the war at a time when it was facing a growing challenge from the Mojahedin inside Iran. In his first public reaction to the war, Khomeini described the conflict as 'a divine blessing' and used it in every way to enhance his policy of 'export of revolution' and consolidate his grip on power by ruthlessly suppressing all dissent. The opposition forces, led by the Mojahedin, were quickly branded as 'fifth-columnists' and 'agents of the Baathist-Zionist regime'.

After June 1982, when the Iraqi forces retreated to international boundaries and Iranian towns and cities were no longer under Iraqi occupation, the National Council of Resistance of Iran declared that there was no longer any reason to continue the war and called for an immediate truce. The NCRI and all its members, including the PMOI, stated that Iran's national interests lay in a just and durable peace, which was then at hand. This position was supported by much of the international community. Khomeini and his regime, however, decided to continue the war and coined the motto 'liberate Qods [Jerusalem] via Karbala'. After the cease-fire agreement in 1988, which Khomeini likened to 'drinking a chalice of poison', several senior Iranian officials publicly admitted that the continuation of the war had been an extremely destructive policy, but placed the blame at Khomeini's door. Rafsanjani acknowledged that the war had left more than a million Iranians dead and inflicted economic damage in excess of 1,000 billion dollars.[5]

The peace campaign

With Iraqi forces out of Iranian territories by the middle of 1982, the National Council of Resistance of Iran and its members launched an extensive campaign for peace inside and outside Iran. Prior to that time, the NCRI and the PMOI had meticulously declined the numerous approaches made by the Iraqi government to establish contact with them.

On 9 January 1983, Deputy Prime Minister Tariq Aziz visited and held talks with NCRI President Massoud Rajavi at the latter's residence in Auvers-sur-Oise, north of Paris. In a joint 'peace declaration' at the end of the meeting, both sides called for an immediate end to the war and the establishment of a just and lasting peace between Iran and Iraq. Rajavi

explained the views of the just resistance of the Iranian people on the peaceful settlement of the dispute between the two countries, which could be achieved through direct negotiations between the two sides within the framework of sovereignty and territorial integrity of both countries and on the basis of observance by both countries of non-interference in the internal affairs of one another and good neighbourly relations.

Rajavi pointed out in the declaration that the mullahs' regime would not accept peace unless out of total desperation. Reiterating his condemnation of every sort of harassment of civilians, Rajavi asked the Iraqi government to observe the sanctity and security of Iranian cities, villages and defenceless civilians.

On 12 March the same year, the NCRI unanimously adopted a historic peace plan, which emphasized the 1975 Algiers Pact between Iran and Iraq. In the Algiers Pact, both sides agreed to set the borderline in Arvand Rud [Shatt al-Arab] waterway along the thalweg. The NCRI peace plan stated, 'The National Council of Resistance hereby declares that it considers the 1975 Algiers Treaty (preceded by the Algiers Pact of the same year) and the land and river borders stipulated in the aforementioned treaty, as the basis for a just and permanent peace between the two countries.' The plan called for an immediate cease-fire, formation of a cease-fire supervisory committee, withdrawal of all forces to the internationally recognized borders, exchange of all POWs within three months after the declaration of cease-fire and referral of war reparations claims to the International Court of Justice in The Hague.

On 21 March 1983, in an official response to the NCRI peace plan, the Iraqi government commented: 'We welcome the peace initiative expressed in the NCRI's statement and would like to express Iraq's desire to realize peace and to co-operate with the NCRI or any Iranian to that end, and to establish relations on firm grounds.'[6]

These developments opened a new chapter in the Iran–Iraq war and dealt a strategic blow to Khomeini's war-mongering policy. The Iranian Resistance launched an extensive campaign for peace inside and outside Iran between 1983 and 1988. Hundreds of demonstrations and other forms of protest were organized by supporters of the resistance movement in Iran in favour of the peace plan and against the war. In a statement on 1 April 1984, the NCRI declared: 'Consistent with its programme and that of the future provisional government, the National Council of Resistance, as the sole democratic alternative to the clerical regime, will do its utmost to pursue its plan on the basis of safeguarding the Iranian people's interests. The NCRI considers the policy of active promotion of peace as patriotic and humane.'

The NCRI peace plan received widespread international support. More than 6,000 members of parliaments and distinguished political and social figures, together with more than 220 political parties, organizations, associations and trade unions from fifty-seven countries around the world, signed an international declaration which supported the NCRI peace plan and condemned the 'war-mongering policies of Khomeini's medieval regime'. Among the signatories in 1986 were current British Prime Minister Tony Blair, Foreign Secretary Jack Straw, Home Secretary David Blunkett, Treasury Secretary Gordon Brown, former NATO General Secretary George Robertson and many other distinguished figures. The statement said, 'We urge the United Nations and all its member-states to back [the NCRI] peace plan as a basis for terminating the war.'

In the meantime, opposition to the war grew rapidly in Iran and people responded to the call for peace by boycotting the war and running away from the fronts. The war not only lost its jingoistic appeal, but became a despised conflict that was being dragged on only because the mullahs needed it.

The mullahs' response

As the peace movement spread with remarkable speed inside and outside Iran, the Iranian regime counter-attacked with a rising wave of terrorist attacks outside Iran, while at the same time using Western hostages in Lebanon as bargaining chips to extract major concessions from the United States and Europe. Tehran engaged in separate under-the-table deals with the USA, France, Britain and Germany over their nationals, who were being held hostage by the Iranian regime's agents in Lebanon. Of all these, one achieved international notoriety and became known as the Iran-Contra or Irangate affair.

Irangate, also known as the arms-for-hostages deal, was a secret arrangement between the US government and the mullahs' regime in 1985 for the release of American hostages in Lebanon in exchange for US arms for Iran. One of the key conditions set by the Iranian regime was that the US administration openly brand the PMOI as a terrorist and Marxist organization. The United States accepted and fulfilled this condition. Even before the world learnt about Irangate in 1986, the French government was forging ahead with its own secret deal with the mullahs. Flushed with success after their bargain deal with the Americans, the Iranian rulers raised the stakes in secret talks with Paris. They demanded the expulsion of Massoud Rajavi from France. Negotiations went on for more than a year and the mullahs raised the pressure on the French. After the hijacking of a Kuwaiti airliner by Iranian agents, which led to the death of two passengers, Le Monde wrote on 14 December 1984, 'In the view of [Khomeini's Prime Minister] Mr Mousavi, the extradition of the hijackers will not even be considered "as long as the leader of terrorists is not extradited". Without mentioning any names, the prime minister was alluding to Mr Massoud Rajavi, the leader of the People's Mojahedin, who has sought refuge in France.'

At the same time, the Majlis Speaker Hashemi Rafsanjani told the French chargé d'affaires in Tehran, Pierre Lafrance, 'Saying "we accept political refugees" is only an excuse ... These (Mojahedin) are criminals, not political refugees.'[7] According to the minutes of secret negotiations between Rafsanjani and the French chargé d'affaires on 30 March 1985, made public a year later by the PMOI, the French diplomat told Rafsanjani that Foreign Minister Roland Dumas wanted 'balanced and improved relations between Iran and France' and that 'people like Rajavi have contacts, not with the government, but with political parties in France, Italy, Britain and other places, as they see themselves as part of the Socialist movement'.[8]

The rapprochement between Paris and Tehran led the French government to impose increasing restrictions on the presence and activities of Massoud Rajavi in France. The Iranian regime precipitated the process by ordering the murder of a French hostage in Lebanon, which raised public pressure on Paris to do something for the remaining hostages, and by making new terrorist threats against France. As a result, the French government turned a blind eye on the overt activities of Iranian intelligence agents against the NCRI in France. The mullahs' regime organized an extensive campaign against Rajavi's presence in France. To stir up the residents of Auvers-sur-Oise against the Iranian Resistance's presence in their community, Iranian intelligence arranged a bomb blast near the NCRI office. It also mobilized its agents to demonstrate against the Mojahedin at Auvers-sur-Oise and spent extravagant sums to buy journalists who would write articles demonizing the Iranian Resistance in the eyes of the French public.

The NCRI approached several European countries to seek a temporary stay for Rajavi, but was turned away, as these governments dreaded terrorist reprisals by Tehran. Rajavi's attempt in June 1986 to stay temporarily at the home of his brother, Professor Kazem Rajavi, who lived in Switzerland, was equally unsuccessful, as the Swiss government refused him entry. In such circumstances, on 7 June 1986, Rajavi went to Iraq together with a thousand Mojahedin members. Paying back the French government, the mullahs duly released the French hostages in Lebanon.

Former journalist Eric Rouleau, the French ambassador to Tunisia at the time, later revealed that he had been sent to Tehran on a secret, four-day mission in 1986 to negotiate the release of French hostages in Lebanon and had discussed the matter with Mohsen Rafiqdoust, the Minister of Revolutionary Guards. Rouleau recounted how, after reaching an agreement with the mullahs' regime and only hours before flying to Lebanon to receive the hostages, who were supposed to be released, Rafiqdoust 'suddenly called off the agreement'. Rouleau was told that he was wasting his time negotiating with Rafiqdoust, because there were 'people from your opposition in the adjacent room busy negotiating and saying that they were prepared to release five prisoners (that the regime wanted from France) and instead of one billion, they would pay two billion dollars and expel the leaders of the Iranian opposition, or even arrest them ... Eventually it was the Chirac government which got the hostages released,' Rouleau averred.[9]

A precondition for moving to Iraq

Although the French government's pressures on the Iranian Resistance to quit France had been going on for over a year, Rajavi decided to move to Iraq only when he was assured of the Resistance's independence in Iraq and the non-interference of the Iraqi government in its affairs. In return, the Resistance would not intervene in Iraq's internal affairs under any circumstances.

The Resistance's move to Iraq in 1986 was taking place at a time when regional alignments were vastly different from the situation that arose after Iraq's invasion of Kuwait and the 1991 Gulf War. At the time, all European countries and the United States had warm relations with the Iraqi government and senior Iraqi officials were warmly welcomed by the White House and European leaders. With the very real spectre of the Iranian regime militarily defeating Iraq and occupying that country, Arab countries in the region and Western powers were doing their utmost to prevent such a disastrous outcome of the war, which clearly would have led to the rapid spread of Islamic fundamentalism and extremism across the Middle East and North Africa. In a clear sign of American worries about the Iranian regime's massive offensives into

Iraq, Secretary of State Alexander Haig warned that the United States would not stay neutral in face of any substantial changes in the Persian Gulf region due to the Iran–Iraq war. Henry Kissinger, for his part, classified the threats to US interests in the region into four groups: 'Shi'ite radicalism, Islamic fundamentalism, Iranian revolution and the Soviet imperialism'. He also emphasized, *New York Times*, 12 January 1987, the need to create 'a balance of power in the region'.

The United States removed Iraq from the list of state sponsors of terrorism in 1982 and diplomatic relations between two countries were restored two years later. President Reagan sent Donald Rumsfeld, his special emissary to the Middle East at the time, to meet with the Iraqi president.

Massoud Rajavi told the Iraqi president, on their first meeting on 15 June 1986,

> It is no secret that a few years ago, the Mojahedin fought against Iraqi forces, but after Iraq proved to Iranians and to the world its readiness for peace, we should all focus our attention on the mullahs' regime, for it is the only party which wants to continue the war. Today, the Iranian people are longing for peace, and the world public opinion is also in favour of peace in this war.[10]

For his part, the Iraqi president, whose remarks were made public by the Iraqi press, said, 'The Iraqi leadership respects the Iranian Resistance and its political and ideological independence and its freedom of action in its work and its movements to achieve its goals.' He added, 'The relations between Iraq and the Iranian Resistance are based on peace, respect for each other's national sovereignty and respect for ideological and political choice of both nations.'[11]

A new army is born

There is no doubt that the peace strategy was fraught with high political risks, because the mullahs were bound to accuse the Iranian Resistance of 'collaboration with the enemy' and 'acting as a fifth column'. The Resistance's logic, however, was that if the war was illegitimate and benefited only the mullahs' regime, and if it was against the best interests of the Iranian people, the clerics' propaganda would be thwarted in time and truth would ultimately prevail. As Abraham Lincoln once remarked, 'You can fool some of the people all of the time, and all of the people some of the time, but you cannot fool all of the people all of the time.'[12]

Within months after Rajavi's move to Iraq, the soundness of the

Resistance's logic seemed to prevail. Anti-war sentiments rose as Iranians grew weary of the exorbitant human and material cost of war. Draft-dodging, disobedience in the army and desertions took place with increasing frequency. Many Air Force pilots and personnel left the country to seek refuge abroad. The presence of Resistance forces along the Iran–Iraq border boosted the morale of Iranians opposed to the mullahs' rule and gave them a new hope. Thousands crossed the border to join the Resistance.

A nationwide poll in 1987 showed that 83 per cent of Iranians opposed the continuation of the war, while a mere 7 per cent supported it and 10 per cent expressed no views. The NCRI's peace initiative caught the imagination of millions, while the mullahs' deafening propaganda against the PMOI and the NCRI met with public apathy.

The anti-war movement received a boost in June 1987 with the formation of the National Liberation Army of Iran. The army became a magnet for disaffected youths who did not want to serve in the clerical regime's war machine. Drawing on the expertise of many officers of the Shah's or mullahs' armed forces who joined its ranks, the NLA rapidly established itself as a force to be reckoned with. Commenting on the NLA's five-hour military parade in the autumn of 1991, Reuters wrote on 18 October: 'By the standards of resistance groups the world over, it was an impressive display of might.'

Operating as a regular armed force and using armour and heavy artillery captured from the Iranian Army, the NLA carried out more than 100 operations against the clerical regime's armed forces until the cease-fire in July 1988. These attacks were a heavy military blow to the clerical regime's war machine, but of far greater importance was the political impact that the NLA operations were having. Hundreds of Iranian soldiers deserted their units to join the NLA, while those loyal to the clerical regime were demoralized by the mere presence of a standing army of Iranians across the border fighting against the fundamentalist government in Tehran.

In March 1988, NLA forces captured a battalion headquarters of the crack Seventy-seventh Division in Fakkeh in the oil-rich Khuzestan Province. It was the first warning to the clerical regime. In less than three months, the NLA captured the headquarters of the Sixteenth Armoured Division and seized the strategically located town of Mehran, taking 1,500 prisoners, including the chief of staff and several other senior commanders of the division, and capturing dozens of main battle tanks, armoured personnel carriers and heavy artillery with an estimated overall value of two billion dollars.

The clerical leaders clearly sensed the imminent threat posed by the NLA. After eight years of conflict, both the Iranian and the Iraqi regimes knew that neither side could pose an existential threat to the other one at that stage of the war. As for Iran, the Iraqi Army could not threaten the very existence of the clerical regime, even if it captured an entire province. But it was a whole different ballgame when it came to the NLA, and the mullahs knew it. When its forces seized Mehran, local people welcomed them with open arms, chanting, 'Today Mehran, tomorrow Tehran.' The mixture of a disenchanted and war-weary population and a powerful opposition army capable of conducting division-size operations was indeed a very serious threat and the mullahs had to do something about it, and fast.

Chalice of poison

The newscaster's sombre voice in the midday news bulletin on Tehran Radio on 18 July 1988 gave listeners an eerie premonition that they were about to hear an important announcement. Seconds later, the whole country was electrified as Khomeini announced that the Islamic Republic of Iran agreed to implement UN Security Council Resolution 598, adopted a year earlier to bring about a cease-fire in the Iran–Iraq conflict. In making the announcement, the man who had just recently vowed 'to continue the war until the last man alive and the last house standing in Tehran' said he was 'drinking a chalice of poison' to save his regime. He stressed that it was not possible at the time to reveal the reason why the Iranian regime had to end the war, but in the following years, particularly after Khomeini's death in June 1989, several senior officials divulged the fact that the clerical leadership was fearful of the Mojahedin and the NLA being part of a wider conspiracy to topple the religious regime in Tehran. Finally, the Iranian Resistance's peace strategy had prevailed and defeated the clerical regime's war-mongering policy and expansionist goals.

Days after the clerical regime's acceptance of Resolution 598, the NLA launched its biggest operation, codenamed the Eternal Light. The offensive began on 20 July and NLA forces thrust 180 kilometres deep into Iranian territory, seizing the cities of Kerend and Islam-Abad and a large swathe of strategic territory, cutting off the vital road link between the mullahs' armed forces in western and south-western Iran. Large-scale fighting, sometimes hand-to-hand, erupted across a long front. The clerical regime reacted with panic: Khomeini made a personal plea over the radio and television for young men to go to the front; all summer exams were cancelled; the Majlis and other key institutions were closed down; all sports events were called off, as the mullahs mobilized 200,000 Revolutionary Guards and other loyalists from across Iran to fight the NLA. Hashemi Rafsanjani, Acting Commander in Chief of the Armed Forces, moved his headquarters to Kermanshah to oversee personally the fighting. In the end, 55,000 Guards were killed or wounded, while 1,263 NLA fighters were slain or captured.

For the Iranian Resistance, however, Operation Eternal Light was far more than a large battle. For years after the battle, stories of the courage and dedication of Resistance fighters, particularly women combatants, were being recounted by local people in every tea-house and gathering place in western Iran. Songs and films were made and books written to commemorate NLA men and women who sacrificed their lives on the fertile plains of Kermanshah, encouraging many youths in Iran to join the Resistance.

Treason or patriotism?

The clerical regime has conducted a virulent campaign over the years to portray the NCRI and the PMOI as traitors for joining forces with Iran's enemy in a patriotic war. The mullahs accused the Iranian Resistance of being Iraq's 'fifth column', of providing Iraq with 'co-ordinates of residential areas in Iran to have them bombed', of 'torturing Iranian POWs in Iraq', and of 'selling Iran's secrets to the Iraqi regime'.

For two decades, these accusations have been repeated almost incessantly by the Iranian regime's propaganda apparatus inside and outside Iran. But where lies the truth? Ever since the 1988 cease-fire and the death of Khomeini a year later, the clerical rulers have come under increasing pressure to justify their decision in 1982 to continue the war until 1988, leaving behind on the Iranian side alone a million dead, two million wounded and maimed, three million homeless refugees, fifty demolished towns and cities, and more than 1,000 billion dollars' worth of material damage.

Hashemi Rafsanjani later conceded, 'The Italian military attaché told us that the oil-rich states in the region were ready to pay 60 billion dollars to Iran on behalf of Saddam Hussein, if Iran dropped its third condition for peace, which was that Saddam be punished.'[13]

The Iranian Resistance's peace strategy in the 1980s has been vindicated by later developments. After the cease-fire, all the leading clerical figures distanced themselves from the war policy and implicitly blamed Khomeini for the decision to prolong the war. Rafsanjani, who ran the war effort on behalf of Khomeini, blamed his mentor for the decision to continue the conflict after 1982: 'After the liberation of [the southern port city of] Khorramshahr, I was no longer responsible for the war. I was Imam Khomeini's representative in the Supreme Defence Council, but the Imam did not allow anyone to discuss with him whether to stop the war or agree to a cease-fire.'[14] Khomeini's son, Ahmad, responded by exonerating his father and blaming his aides for prolonging the war:

> As for the Khorramshahr affair, the Imam believed that it was better to end the war at that point, but eventually, those responsible for running the war said we had to cross the Arvand River [Shatt al-Arab] to be able to get war reparations from Iraq. The Imam did not at all agree and said that if you are going to continue the war, you should realize that this war is not going to end if you remain in the state you are in. He said the war should only continue up to a certain stage. Now that Khorramshahr is liberated, it is the best time to end the war.[15]

Mohsen Rezaii, the Commander in Chief of the Revolutionary Guards, gave his own version of the high-level meeting of clerical officials to decide on the course of the war. In a speech on 18 July 1998, he said:

> After the liberation of Khorramshahr, we had two meetings with Imam Khomeini. I was not in the first meeting, but attended the second one. Mr Hashemi [Rafsanjani], the Supreme Leader [Khamenei], Mr Ahmad (Khomeini's son), [Prime Minister] Mr Moussavi, and [Chief Justice] Mr Moussavi Ardabili were in that meeting. The Imam asked, 'Why do you want to go to the other side of the border?' Some gave political answers. We and our brothers in the Army gave our military reasons and said that if we crossed the Arvand River [and moved into Iraq], we would be in a much stronger position to defend ourselves. The politicians said we have reached this stage without gaining any concessions. The Imam listened to all views and said, 'We will get ready to cross the border.' Many say the Imam was against the continuation of the war after Khorramshahr was liberated, but he wanted to see how determined the officials were in their proposals. When the reasons were presented, the Imam made the decision himself.[16]

Public statements by clerical leaders make it clear that both factions of the mullahs' regime were united in the decision to continue the war in 1982. It is a telling sign of the Iranian people's anti-war sentiments that senior officials of the Islamic Republic are trying to rewrite history and distance themselves from the war-mongering policy they all fervently supported in the 1980s.

The 1991 Gulf War

In the annals of the Iranian Resistance, 2 August 1990 marks a black day, when Iraq's occupation of Kuwait brought about a sea-change in the region's political and strategic alignments. Overnight, old alliances and conflicts underwent a seismic shift, as countries in the region, and in the world at large, tried to adjust themselves to the shocking decision by the Iraqi government to invade Kuwait. Until then, most countries in the region, from Saudi Arabia, Kuwait and the United Arab Emirates to Jordan, Egypt and countries of the Arab Maghreb considered the fundamentalist regime in Iran as the most serious threat to regional peace and stability. But the occupation of Kuwait, on 2 August 1990, changed all that.

It was clear to the Iranian Resistance from the beginning that the clerical regime stood to gain the most from this crisis, while the main losers, outside Iraq, would be the Iranian people and the Resistance, which had nothing whatsoever to do with the conflict. The ramifications of the occupation of Kuwait and the ensuing Persian Gulf War in January 1991 were readily visible:

1. Executions, torture and human rights violations in Iran became overshadowed by the events in neighbouring Iraq. Western governments, eager to win the Iranian regime's co-operation against Baghdad, took an indulgent view of the Islamic theocracy's human rights record.
2. The clerical regime's clout in regional and international politics rose, as its historic regional counter-weight, Iraq, became significantly weakened. Tehran's rulers found themselves the target of simultaneous coveting by both Iraq and the West. In the run-up to the war in January 1991, the Coalition and the Baghdad regime competed in winning the mullahs to their side. One by one, countries which had severed or toned down their ties with the Iranian regime over Tehran's sponsorship of terrorism re-established or upgraded diplomatic relations.
3. The Kuwaiti crisis led to a sharp hike in oil prices, boosting the Iranian regime's revenues by at least 13 billion dollars a year. The extra foreign earning and the rush by foreign companies to sign up contracts with the Iranian government were a shot in the arm for the chronically mismanaged clerical state and provided at least temporary relief for the crisis-ridden economy.

The most important impact of the invasion of Kuwait, however, was political: for more than a decade, the threat of Islamic fundamentalism and the mullahs' regime as its principal state sponsor became secondary to the threat posed by Iraq and the Saddam Hussein regime. Warnings from the Iranian Resistance (including my book, *Islamic Fundamentalism: The New Global Threat* in 1993) fell on deaf ears. Islamic fundamentalism was appeased, not confronted, and allowed to penetrate the fabric of Islamic societies, leading large numbers of young people to set their feet on the trail of death and destruction.

In the months leading to the Persian Gulf War, the Khamenei–Rafsanjani duo tried to encourage the Iraqi regime to stay in Kuwait and reject any compromise solution. At the same time, they reassured the Coalition of their co-operation in a war against Iraq. Knowledgeable Iraqi sources admitted later that Iranian leaders told visiting Iraqi officials on the eve of the war that the USA and its allies would not attack if they saw the Iraqis were well dug in in Kuwait and determined to fight to the bloody end.[17]

The mullahs welcomed the war between their two enemies, Iraq and the USA, and in closed-door meetings, senior clerics were saying that 'Islam would profit from destruction wrought on either side of this war.' In the meantime, they were getting ready to launch an offensive against the Iranian Resistance in Iraq and to use the power vacuum in the aftermath of the predictable fall of the Baathist regime to instal an Iranian-style theocracy in that country. As President George H. W. Bush addressed a joint session of Congress on 6 March 1991, to declare the end of the Persian Gulf War, tens of thousands of Revolutionary Guards were making the final preparations to cross the border into Iraq. In a few days, they would be heading for the PMOI's main camps in the Iran–Iraq border region.

'Not my war'

The invasion of Kuwait and the subsequent Persian Gulf War in January 1991 put the Iranian Resistance and the PMOI on the spot, for it was not their war and yet they were one of the biggest victims of the conflict. From day one, the Mojahedin and the NLA had only one reason for being in Iraq, and that was to fight the clerical regime in Iran. Their policy was to stay away from Iraq's internal affairs and the Baghdad government's domestic and foreign policies. Conversely, they did not allow any country, including Iraq, to interfere in their policies and positions.

From 2 August 1990, until the end of the US war in Iraq the following March, the PMOI and the NLA stayed away from every aspect of the conflict. At the time, some Palestinian factions and other Middle Eastern groups based in Iraq openly supported the Baghdad regime's stance.

In many countries, particularly in the region and in Muslim countries, major demonstrations were taking place in support of Iraq and against the USA and its Coalition allies. The Iranian Resistance, however, did not take any position in support of Iraq or against the other side, even though it was based in Iraq. The PMOI closed down its radio and television broadcasts and its weekly publication from the beginning of the Kuwaiti crisis, when Iraq's olive branch to Tehran raised the chances of a peace accord between Iraq and the Iranian regime. In the months prior to the conflict, the Resistance closed down all its bases in the north and south of Iraq – a total of sixteen bases and headquarters built and maintained entirely by the Resistance using its independent financial means – to avoid any clashes, even unwanted ones, with Iraqi people and groups during or after the war.

The mullahs, whose goal was to root out the presence of the PMOI and the NLA in Iraq in the immediate aftermath of the conflict, were angered by the fact that the Resistance forces survived the war and remained politically and militarily unscathed by the storm that surrounded them. The clerical rulers decided to make their own move by taking advantage of the chaos and disarray that dominated Iraq's domestic scene immediately after the war.

In March 1991, six brigades and divisions of the Revolutionary Guards, numbering 60,000 men, crossed the international border and attacked PMOI and NLA bases and positions. Although the NLA deployed only 20 per cent of its forces to confront the onslaught, in two weeks it succeeded in beating back the Revolutionary Guards' attacks, inflicting 5,000 casualties on them and taking several hundred prisoners. Those who were not immediately released were registered and regularly visited by the International Committee of the Red Cross, until they, too, were released. The ICRC formally expressed its satisfaction over the treatment of these POWs to the PMOI.[18]

The clerical regime tried hard to use Iraqi Kurds in addition to its own forces against the NLA. The PMOI, through its sources inside the regime, was able to obtain several secret memoranda of the Revolutionary Guards, which unveiled the Iranian regime's ploy. In one such document, dated 4 March 1991, Brigadier General Kamal Hedayat, commander of the Guards' headquarters in north-west Iran, ordered 'commanders of all subordinate units' to provide the 'necessary facilities for movements' of the Guards' Iraqi Kurdish agents 'under the control of Ramezan Headquarters of the Revolutionary Guards'. Ramezan Headquarters is the largest command centre of the Revolutionary Guards in western Iran and attacks on PMOI forces in Iraq are planned and commanded by it.

In another memorandum, dated 26 March 1991, 'the command headquarters of the Revolutionary Guards' [paramilitary] Bassij Force' ordered the Regional Commands of the Bassij across the country to 'dispatch Iraqi volunteers to Qods garrisons for deployment'.

Unbridled terror

The world remembers Iraq in the inter-war period (1991–2003) as the scene of a crippling economic embargo and continuing strife between successive US administrations and the Baathist government. But Iran also loomed large in this smorgasbord of conflict and violence. Iranian intelligence agents and Revolutionary Guards conducted some 150 terrorist attacks on PMOI personnel in Iraq from 1993 to 2003. The attacks killed dozens of Mojahedin members and hundreds of Iraqi civilians, the 'collateral damage' of these indiscriminate attacks.

The attacks included, for example, the assassination of three PMOI members as they drove in a car along a causeway in Baghdad on 10 July 1995. One of the gunmen was arrested and admitted that he had been sent by the Iranian Intelligence Ministry along with two others to carry out the attack. On 10 July 1995, the mullahs' regime used three 320 mm 'super guns' mounted on a lorry carrying bricks as cover to attack the Mojahedin's central office in Baghdad. The shells exploded at the heart of Baghdad and wounded dozens of Iraqi civilians, maimed two and wrecked the building housing the Iraqi Union of Writers and Poets. On 9 June 1999, a roadside truck bomb destroyed a civilian bus carrying members of the Mojahedin on a highway north of Baghdad, killing six PMOI members and wounding more than twenty passengers. Several Iraqi civilians were killed in a separate bus that was also blown away by the force of the blast. A state-run Iranian daily tacitly acknowledged that the clerical regime's agents were behind the attack: 'The show of force against the Mojahedin in Baghdad demonstrated that the Islamic Republic has stood by its serious responsibilities.'[19] On 18 April 2001, the clerical regime launched seventy-seven surface-to-surface Scud missiles at seven NLA camps along the Iran–Iraq border, killing one and wounding dozens of PMOI members. Nine Iraqi civilians were killed and twenty-five more wounded, as some of the missiles hit residential areas in the towns of Jalawla, Kut and Al-Amarah.

One would normally expect that so many terrorist attacks claiming so many civilian lives would arouse worldwide condemnation and protests against the perpetrators. Western governments' policies on Iran and Iraq in the 1990s, however, were anything but normal. The terrorist attacks were often overlooked as 'a bilateral issue' and barely got a mention in annual government reports on terrorism. This only emboldened the fundamentalist regime to step up its terror attacks inside Iraq and boast of them. Ali Younessi, Minister of Intelligence and Security, declared, 'We will take our revenge on the Mojahedin through the Iraqi people.'[20]

Independence, the red line

During extensive investigations by UNMOVIC, the United Nations Monitoring, Verification and Inspection Commission, in Iraq in autumn 2002, the inspectors of this UN body visited the Iranian Resistance's camps on several occasions and witnessed the independent status of the PMOI and the NLA in Iraq. In my capacity as chairman of the NCRI's foreign affairs committee, I met and volunteered for a formal interview with the head of an UNMOVIC team responsible for chemical weapons in Baghdad on 11 January 2003. Minutes of the interviews are kept in the UNMOVIC archives in New York and NCRI archives also have a copy. The UNMOVIC official asked me, 'If the Iraqi government ever asked the Iranian Resistance to conceal Iraq's proscribed weapons in its bases, what would be your response?'

I replied: 'Although we have never received such a request from the Iraqi government, our reply would definitely be negative.' The official, a top expert from Britain, then asked: 'What if the Iraqi government insisted?'

My response: 'If that situation arose, we would leave Iraq rather than submit to such a request. For our movement, the most important principle and the red line not to cross from the day we came to Iraq has been our independence. This remains the same today.'

In their discussions with the representatives of the Iranian Resistance following their visits to NLA camps, UNMOVIC officials reiterated the same positions made by their UNSCOM predecessors. They were surprised by the degree of independence that the camps enjoyed and the fact that there were no Iraqis in the camps. Equally interesting to them was the fact that NLA camps were the only locations in Iraq where inspectors could visit the site without the presence of Iraqi 'minders'. They also appreciated the transparency and openness of the Iranian Resistance in dealing with UNMOVIC inspectors.

The independence of the Iranian Resistance's camps in Iraq was the result of an open and official agreement between the Iraqi government and the Iranian Resistance. The Iranian Resistance's camps in Iraq were treated as foreign embassies and the Resistance's sovereignty within its own camps was recognized; the Iraqi government exercised no authority over them.

In his report to the UN Security Council on 12 December 1998, Richard Butler, the Executive Director of UNSCOM, wrote:

During the reporting period, teams conducted no-notice inspections at a number of sites that had not been declared by Iraq. Access to these sites was provided and inspections took place with one exception, which was at a facility occupied by the People's Mojahedin Organization of Iraq (PMOI). The site of this facility was declared as being not under the authority of Iraq. Discussions over access were left to the Commission and the organization. A dialogue has begun on this matter and the PMOI has accepted, in principle, that its sites are subject to access by the Commission.

Prior to this, on 3 December 1998, UNSCOM Deputy Chairman Charles Duelfer had written in his report to the Security Council on PMOI locations in Iraq, 'In subsequent discussions with representatives of the Iranian Mojahedin it has been recognized that inspection teams have the right to visit any site in Iraq.'

On 5 December 1998, the Iraqi government notified UNSCOM that the Mojahedin camps 'belong to a foreign party over which Iraq has no control' and that 'according to rules agreed with the Special Commission, sites belonging to foreign agencies must have agreement between the head of the inspection team and the foreign agency'.[21] The same day, the Iraqi news agency quoted Hessam Muhammad Amin, director of Iraq's liaison office with the arms inspectors, as saying, 'They wanted to enter a location which belonged to a foreign party in Iraq and Iraq has no control over that location.' Amin said that according to operational procedures mutually worked out by Iraq and UNSCOM, when inspectors want to visit a site belonging to a foreign party, Iraq could not officially intervene and the inspection teams would gain access to the premises through direct talks with the officials of the foreign party in question.

During UNMOVIC inspections in Iraq, the Iraqi government again reiterated its respect for the Iranian Resistance's independence in its camps and the representative of the Iraqi government wrote in an official letter: 'Sites belonging to the People's Mojahedin Organization of Iran are sites that the Government of Iraq has allowed this organization to use without any interference.'[22]

The Resistance has shown its independence on numerous occasions in the years it has maintained a presence in Iraq. In a speech on 2 July 1988, Iraq's president said that the PMOI was 'fully independent' and added: 'For record, let me say that we once asked the Mojahedin some questions about their home country, Iran, but as they thought their response might contain information on their country that might be harmful to their people, they flatly refused our request and we, of course, respect their position as an independent political force.'[23]

Even the clerical regime, despite all its propaganda aimed at portraying the Resistance as a tool in the hands of Saddam Hussein's government, has been compelled on occasions to acknowledge the PMOI's independence. The state-run weekly *Kayhan Havaii* wrote on 15 April 1992, 'Iraqi dignitaries talking in private circles admit that Baghdad did not have an open hand to deal with the Mojahedin.' The paper added: 'It is certainly true that exerting control over an armed group which has incredible co-ordination with powers outside Iraq does not appear to be so easy for the Iraqi government.'

Wafiq Sameraii, a former head of Iraq's military intelligence who sought refuge in Britain after fleeing Iraq, commented on the PMOI in a 13 December 2000 interview with Al-Jazeera television,

> If we say that the Mojahedin are completely dependent on the Iraqi regime, we would be making a mistake, and if we say that this group is ready to listen to whatever the officials say in Baghdad, we are again making a mistake. But it is natural to be affected in one way or another by the official position of Iraq and the security necessities for that country.

Notes

1. Karl Von Clausewitz, *On War*, Harmondsworth: Penguin, 1968 (1832).

2. Glenn Kessler, 'State Questions Military Tolerance of Iranian Dissidents', *Washington Post*, 11 September 2003, p. A19.

3. Ibid.

4. In spite of the former government in Iraq's preparedness to sign a total peace agreement between the two countries, e.g. in August 1990 on the basis of the 1975 Algiers treaty, no peace accord has been signed to this date (August 2003) with Iraq by the mullahs ruling Iran.

5. Rafsanjani, Tehran Friday Prayers sermon, 9 August 1991.

6. 'Iraqi Official Welcomes Iranian Resistance Peace Initiative', *Baghdad Observer, 21 March 1983*.

7. Rafsanjani, Tehran Radio, 31 March 1985.

8. *Mojahed* weekly, no. 285, 11 April 1986.

9. Eric Rouleau, interview, Al-Jazeera television, 22 December 1999.

10. *Unita*, Rome, 15 June 1986. See also Statement by the PMOI, 15 June 1986.

11. *Baghdad Observer*, 16 June 1986.

12. Abraham Lincoln (1809–65), US president, quoted in 'Abe' Lincoln's Yarns and Stories, ed. Alexander McClure (1904), p. 184.

13. Ayatollah Hashemi Rafsanjani, Memoirs, Tehran, 2001.

14. Ali Akbar Velayati, Political History of the War Imposed on Iran by Iraq, Tehran.

15. Jomhouri Islami, Tehran, 3 April 1995.

16. Jameeh, Tehran, 20 July 1998.

17. Editorial, Al-Jomhourriah, Baghdad, 20 January 1992. Saad Albazaz, editor of the daily, revealed that throughout the crisis in the Gulf, Rafsanjani encouraged Baghdad to take a hard-line position. Quoting a senior Iranian official, he wrote: 'I have far more than what you have requested ... we were with you in the Kuwaiti affair. We ask you not to consider our official statements as a reflection of our positions only. We are on your side and fully understand your conditions.'

18. Letter of Michel Ducreaux, head of ICRC delegation in Iraq, to the PMOI, 20 October 1994.

19. Ressalat, Tehran, 26 June 1999.

20. Ali Younessi, state television, 23 August 2000.

21. Associated Press, 5 December 1998.

22. Hessam Mohammad Amin, letter dated 9 December 2002, Appendix.

23. Al-Jomhourriah, Baghdad, 3 July 1988.

7 | US-led war in Iraq: the Iranian factor

Even though the United States has a physical presence in the countries that surround us, the reality is that the United States is in fact surrounded by Iran. *Ali-Akbar Hashemi Rafsanjani*[1]

Around 5.30 a.m., Thursday, 20 March 2003, shortly after US President George W. Bush's forty-eight-hour ultimatum to Iraq ended, the United States began the first air attacks in a war that would end the thirty-five-year rule of the Baath Party over Iraq. On Monday, 7 April, US tanks entered the Presidential Palace in Baghdad and on 10 April, Kirkuk fell. Finally, on 14 April, Tikrit, the last major Iraqi city, surrendered.

Thus, in less than a month, one of the most important wars in contemporary history ended, although its consequences and repercussions have just begun. But while Iraq has been under the spotlight of the international media, particularly since the war began, a great deal of mystery and ambiguity still surrounds the 'Iranian' factor in the war and its aftermath. What was the secret deal between the US-led Coalition and the Iranian regime on the eve of the war? How extensive was the clerical regime's intervention in Iraq in the wake of the fall of the Saddam Hussein regime? And what was the position of the Iraq-based Iranian Resistance in the war and the post-conflict situation in Iraq? What will be the role of the Iranian 'factor' in Iraq's immediate and short-term future? These are significant issues that form the subject of the next three chapters.

Setting the stage

Several weeks before the war began, the clerical regime put the Revolutionary Guards, the regular Army and the Qods Force on full alert. Altogether, thirty-eight brigades were stationed across the entire border with Iraq.[2] Arrangements had been made for the deployment of 350 combat battalions in a matter of twenty-four hours by incorporating internal security forces and the paramilitary Bassij in to these forces. The Iranian armed forces stepped up combat engineering and highway construction in the border regions, such as Kermanshah, in December 2002. They moved different types of weapons systems and missiles to the region, including Sarpol-Zahab and Kenesht Pass. The objective was to preposition these forces for rapid deployment into Iraq once the opportunity arose. In January, a senior military commander, Brigadier General Ali-Asghar Karizi, announced in western Iran, 'We have thought of necessary arrangements to confront the Mojahedin forces in the event of a US attack on Iraq.'[3]

For months prior to the war, the Iranian regime's leaders had been saying privately, and sometimes even publicly, that the war between the USA and Iraq represented the best opportunity to establish 'the rule of Islam' in Iraq and eliminate PMOI forces in that country. In an article entitled 'The Best Chance to Close the File on the Monafeqin', the pro-Khamenei daily *Afarinesh* wrote on 2 March 2003, 'The Iraqi crisis offers the best opportunity to get rid of the PMOI for ever, if the opportunities that present themselves are fully exploited.' To achieve their goal, Tehran's rulers launched a misinformation campaign against the PMOI presence in Iraq. This would alienate the Iraqi people from the PMOI and provide a useful excuse for the Islamic Republic to attack the Mojahedin forces in Iraq. The ruling ayatollahs were also trying to arouse the hostility of the United States and its allies against the PMOI and the NLA, to induce the Coalition to see the Iranian Resistance as an integral part of the Iraqi regime and, therefore, a legitimate military target in the coming war.

It was in this context that the Ministry of Intelligence and Security sharply escalated its anti-Mojahedin propaganda in the months leading up to the war. MOIS claimed, for example, that the PMOI had been entrusted with 'controlling Kirkuk and other towns bordering Iran' and 'guarding Kirkuk's oil fields in northern Iraq'. It also said that the PMOI was 'training in urban warfare under the supervision of Iraqi officers so that if need be, it would be used in the war against the US'. The mullahs also claimed that the PMOI and Al-Qaeda carried out joint training and that the PMOI was hiding Iraq's weapons of mass destruction. These are a few out of several hundred pieces of 'news' in the run-up to the war that were fed to the state-controlled media or put out through other news outlets that have ties with the Iranian intelligence:

- IRNA, 18 June 2002: 'The Baghdad regime has sent a group of [Mojahedin] members along with some Palestinian groups to the Kurdish city of Khaneqin. Forces belonging to the terrorist [Mojahedin] group are the Baghdad regime's main instrument for repressing popular uprisings and are now controlling security in some sensitive areas and centres in Iraq.'
- Iranian state-run television, 20 June 2002: 'Following Iraq's efforts to deploy forces of the [Mojahedin] terrorist group in northern Iraq,

elements from this group have been stationed along the contact line with Iraqi Kurdistan and oil pipelines.'

- *Siasat-e Rouz*, state-owned daily, 16 July 2002: 'The Mojahedin forces in Iraq are to be used for the suppression of any internal plot and chaos and for rapid guerrilla-type operations inside Iraq.'
- Official Iranian news agency, IRNA, 22 September 2002: 'The Iraqi regime has given the task of guarding Kirkuk oil field in northern Iraq to the Mojahedin.'
- 'Islamic Revolution in Iraq' TV, broadcast from Tehran, 21 November 2002: 'A large number of members of the Iranian opposition terrorist gang, the Mojahedin, have been deployed throughout Iraq, including Baghdad, Kirkuk, Mosul, Khaneqin and Ramadi, and their task is to put down any popular uprising that may happen during a US attack on Iraq. It must be noted that the Mojahedin participated alongside the Republican Guards in the suppression of the historic uprising in the north and south of the country in 1991 after the liberation of Kuwait.'
- Tehran radio, 27 January 2003: 'The Iraqi regime handed over the control of some regions near Khaneqin to the Monafeqin terrorist group. A number of Mojahedin forces took control of Kirkuk and several towns bordering Iran.'

In dozens of statements in the months leading up to the war, the PMOI refuted these 'reports' as baseless fabrications of the Iranian regime's Ministry of Intelligence and Security. After the war, it became clear that all these claims had been false, as the US military acknowledged that the PMOI did not participate in any way in the conflict.[4]

Iranian Resistance's position

The presence of the PMOI and the NLA in Iraq, as discussed in the previous chapter, has always been based on two principles: independence and non-interference in Iraq's internal affairs. The PMOI, therefore, had no reason to take part in the US-led war in 2003, just as it stayed away from the 1991 war. Months before the start of the war, the Iranian Resistance made its position known and formally informed the different parties, particularly the United States.

More than a month before the start of the war, in February 2003, NCRI President Massoud Rajavi issued a message addressed to the Iranian people, which was beamed into Iran by satellite radio and television networks and published in *Mojahed* weekly, the PMOI's journal. In this message, Rajavi also emphasized that the PMOI has not been and is not involved in Iraq's internal affairs; its only objective in being present in Iraq is to pursue its struggle against the clerical regime in Iran. He emphasized that the PMOI's only enemy is the clerical regime in Iran. Rajavi's message read in part:

> Our war, from the first day until the very end has been, is, and will be with the inhuman mullahs' regime and with no one else ... Our goal in coming to Iraq and establishing a presence alongside our homeland has been, remains, and will be this and none other. Everyone knows that the Mojahedin and the Iranian Resistance have not interfered and do not interfere in Iraq's internal affairs, just as the Iraqi government has never interfered in our Resistance's affairs.
>
> The Iranian Resistance has no enemy other than the religious, terrorist dictatorship ruling Iran. Thus, as has been proven in the past two decades, any enmity or hostility toward, and slander against, the People's Mojahedin and the Iranian Resistance, domestically or internationally, are designed to placate and appease the ruling mullahs or one of their factions.[5]

In a letter sent to US Secretary of State Colin Powell on 4 February, I explained to him, in my capacity as NCRI's foreign affairs committee chairman, the Iranian Resistance's position. Here are excerpts of the letter:

> The presence of a part of the forces of the People's Mojahedin of Iran on Iraqi soil is only for the sake of the struggle against the religious, terrorist dictatorship ruling Iran. The full and all-round independence of this Resistance from Iraq, which the mullahs deliberately ignore and strive to vilify, is a well-known fact for all informed sources and observers and can be readily proven at any time. This Resistance has never interfered in Iraq's internal affairs and is not doing so now. Conversely, the Iraqi government has not meddled in the affairs related to this Resistance.
>
> The mullahs' regime has imposed the resistance against this religious, terrorist dictatorship on us and on our people since June 20, 1981. To this day, the clerical regime has executed more than 120,000 of the best sons and daughters of Iran. The UN General Assembly and the Human Rights Commission have condemned this regime in 49 separate resolutions for its violation of fundamental freedoms and the most rudimentary rights of the Iranian people. The Resistance has repeated time and again that our preference is for the mullahs' regime to give way to free elections under United Nations supervision, rather than impose on the Iranian nation a struggle that has to be waged, in the words of President Bush, at the risk of 'intimidation and death'.

The Iranian Mojahedin's struggle and war are directed only at the blood-thirsty mullahs ruling their country. It is also true that around the world, no one has shown the least hostility towards the Mojahedin and the Iranian Resistance, unless he is currying favours with the mullahs or doing their bidding. Throughout the 17 years the Mojahedin have spent alongside their country's borders on Iraqi territory, they have never participated in any other conflict. Even the Mojahedin's routine military exercises have never had, and do not have, any objective other than deterring or repulsing the military and terrorist attacks and aggression by the mullahs' regime.

Contrary to the mullahs' lies, for the past 12 years the Mojahedin have not had any presence in Kirkuk or in any other region in northern Iraq or Iraqi Kurdistan. The Iranian Mojahedin have never been engaged, and are not engaged now, in any clashes or conflict with Iraqi Shiites in any of the Shiite cities or regions in southern Iraq and all the rumours and lies pertaining to such fictitious clashes are part of a dirty psychological war being waged by the mullahs against the Iranian Resistance.

In the face of ludicrous lies by the mullahs' regime, whose weapons of mass destruction programmes and facilities, including secret nuclear sites, have been revealed by the Iranian Resistance on a number of occasions, we have always welcomed throughout the past decade UNSCOM's visits to all our sites at any time and continue the same attitude toward UNMOVIC. We consider such visits to be greatly advantageous to us, for they refute and further discredit mullahs' lies.

The letter also highlighted the dangers and threats posed by the fundamentalist regime in Iran to peace and tranquillity in the region. I sent similar letters to British Foreign Secretary Jack Straw on 24 February, German Deputy Chancellor and Foreign Minister Joschka Fischer on 23 February and the French Foreign Minister Dominique de Villepin in late February 2003.

Staying out of the fray

From the summer of 2002 onwards, as the Iraq crisis began to escalate, the PMOI and the NLA undertook several actions in order to distance themselves from the conflict and the battle zones, and not impede the advancing US/Coalition forces. The PMOI and NLA evacuated Camp Habib (north of Basra), Camp Homayoun (Al-Amara), Camp Mouzarmi (Al-Amara) and Camp Fa'eza (Al-Kut) in August 2002. The NLA and PMOI have had no presence in southern Iraq since then. In November 2002 and in January 2003, the PMOI gave the co-ordinates of its camps and centres to UNMOVIC officials in Baghdad and it in turn conveyed the information to New York. Additionally, two PMOI main camps, Camp Ashraf north of the Iraqi town of Al-Khalis and Camp Badizadegan, west of Baghdad, were visited by UNMOVIC in January and several news outlets reported the visits. In the visits, inspectors emphasized that there was nothing suspicious in these camps. In a 16 January dispatch on the visit, Reuters wrote:

U.N. arms experts launched an aerial and ground inspection of a military base of exiled Iranian rebels Thursday, a day after raising Iraqi ire for pouncing on a presidential complex in Baghdad. On the eve of the 12th anniversary of the 1991 Gulf War, Iraqi officials said a team of experts from the U.N. Monitoring, Verification and Inspection Commission (UNMOVIC) drove to Mujahideen Khalq base in Karkh some 12 miles from Baghdad. Another team flew helicopters over the site as the inspection proceeded on the ground. It was the second Mujahideen position to be scrutinized by the experts this week ... A Mujahideen spokesman had welcomed the first visit and said the group was ready for more to dispel once and for all Iranian charges that it was hiding banned weapons.

Before and during the war, the NCRI's representative in the UK conveyed the positions of the Iranian Resistance and the locations of its bases to British Defence Secretary Geoff Hoon and his deputy through Bruce George, chairman of the Parliamentary Defence Committee, Stephen MacCabe, Win Griffiths and Lord Corbett. NCRI's representatives in the USA and Europe informed the US government of the positions of the Iranian Resistance on the USA–Iraq war. Several members of the US House of Representatives and the Senate conveyed the position of the Iranian Resistance to the Pentagon and the State Department. US government sources used the same channels to assure the PMOI and the NLA that US forces would not engage the forces of the Iranian Resistance. On 17 April 2003, the New York Times quoted NCRI officials as saying they 'had been assured by "proper U.S. authorities" that their other camps would not be targets'.

Regrettably, during the war and particularly in April, Coalition forces bombed PMOI bases repeatedly, inflicting a large number of casualties, including fifty dead, among them several women.

Months before the war, the clerical regime was working to convince the Coalition forces to bomb the PMOI bases. Besides direct and indirect behind-the-scenes negotiations, the State Exigency Council Secretary and former Islamic Revolutionary Guards Commander in Chief Major General Mohsen Rezaii, said: 'If the Americans spare the Mojahedin's bases in Iraq during their general attack on Iraq, then it shows a clear bias in their approach towards terrorism, a bias which would further worsen their past record against the Iranian people. On the other hand, if the Americans attack the Mojahedin bases, this would in turn be considered as a goodwill gesture towards us.'⁶ An article in the *Wall Street Journal* divulged what was behind these attacks:

> The dismantling of the Iranian opposition force in Iraq ... fulfils a private U.S. assurance conveyed to Iranian officials before the start of hostilities that the group would be targeted by British and American forces if Iran stayed out of the fight, according to U.S. officials ...
>
> But National Security Adviser Condoleezza Rice and Secretary of State Colin Powell contended that Tehran could be persuaded to remain neutral toward U.S. invasion next door, especially if it knew the MEK [PMOI] would be attacked and prevented from harassing Iran in the future, the official said.
>
> That message was conveyed by British officials before hostilities began. Foreign Minister Jack Straw informed his Iranian counterpart Foreign Minister Kamal Kharrazi in a meeting in London in February.
>
> Britain's Iranian Ambassador Richard Dalton repeated the message in March in a meeting with Hassan Rowhani, the cleric who heads the Supreme National Security Council, Iran's chief foreign policy making body.⁷

The *Washington Post* wrote on 18 April 2003:

> Two senior U.S. officials – Zalmay Khalilzad from the White House and Ryan C. Crocker from the State Department – met secretly in January with Iranian officials to discuss potential cooperation. U.S. officials asked that Iran seal its border to prevent escape of Iraqi officials among other requests, and suggested that the United States would target the Iraq-based camps of the Mujaheddin-e Khalq Organization, or People's Mujaheddin, a U.S. official said. A more concrete commitment to attack the camps was later relayed to Tehran through British officials.

In another article (25 May) on secret negotiations between the United States and the Iranian regime before the war, the *Post* wrote: 'At one of the meetings, in early January, the United States signalled that it would target the Iraq-based camps of the Mujaheddin-e Khalq (MEK), or People's Mujaheddin, a major group opposing the Iranian government.'

Quoting informed sources within the Iranian regime, the *Lebanese Daily Star* wrote, on 2 April, that in a special and direct fifteen-minute conversation between British Foreign Secretary Jack Straw and mullahs' Foreign Minister Kamal Kharrazi in the early-morning hours of 20 March, as the war was about to begin, 'Straw told Kharrazi that Mojahedin bases would be considered legitimate military targets and bombed by the coalition forces.' The attack on PMOI bases came while all PMOI and NLA personnel had received specific instructions from their commanders that under no circumstances should they fire upon US/Coalition forces, even if attacked. As a result, the PMOI and NLA did not fire a single shot at US/Coalition forces during the entire conflict. During the course of the war, neither the PMOI nor the NLA used any anti-aircraft weaponry. The PMOI and NLA had removed all their anti-aircraft batteries to prevent any misunderstanding.

The cease-fire agreement

When the scope of the Iranian regime's interference in Iraq became somewhat clear, US/Coalition forces signed an agreement of 'mutual understanding and co-ordination' with the PMOI and NLA in Iraq in mid-April. This accord was originally announced by Brigadier General Vincent Brooks, spokesman for the United States Central Command (USCENTCOM) in Doha and later confirmed by other US officials. The introduction to the agreement noted: 'NLA/PMOI state that they have not fired even a single bullet against U.S./Coalition forces in this war because their only enemy is the religious dictatorship ruling Iran. NLA/PMOI also state that they have never been involved in the war or any act of hostility with U.S./Coalition forces.'

In a report on the agreement, the *New York Times* wrote on 29 April:

American forces in Iraq have signed a cease-fire with an Iranian opposition group the United States has designated a terrorist organization, and expect it to surrender soon with some of its arms, American military officials said today.

Under the deal, signed on April 15 but confirmed by the United States Central Command only today, United States forces agreed not to damage any of the group's vehicles, equipment or any of its property in its camps in Iraq, and not to commit any hostile act toward the Iranian opposition forces covered by the agreement.

In return, the group, the People's Mujahedeen, which will be allowed to keep its weapons for now, agreed not to fire on or commit other hostile acts against American forces, not to destroy private or government property, and to place its artillery and anti-aircraft guns in non-threatening positions.

The cease-fire agreement clearly noted that it 'does not constitute an act of surrender' and it emphasized that the agreement 'does not surrender or capitulate troops under command of the NLA Commander'. The agreement also recognized the right of the PMOI to defend themselves against the clerical regime's attacks. Article 11 stated:

NLA reserves the right to self-defence against the Iranian regime's attacks and to prevent and confront theft, looting and abduction. The NLA agrees, if it becomes necessary, to leave the designated geographical limits established in Article 2 above in order to protect itself in self-defence. It will inform the Coalition Forces prior to doing so, in order that the Coalition Forces can avoid engaging the NLA unit.

Article 7 stipulated: 'For mutual protection of forces, the undersigned U.S./Coalition and NLA Unit Commanders will provide each other with the location of all known land mines in and around the geographic vicinity as described in Article 2. NLA emphasizes it has never planted any mines anywhere.' Article 8 said that all parties 'shall cooperate in complying with the provisions of this agreement'.

Victims of raids

In their attacks on the Mojahedin after the war, the clerical regime's Revolutionary Guards and terrorists murdered or abducted several dozen PMOI members and wounded more than fifty. They beheaded Javid Hosseini, cut off the lower arms of Farhad Mostowfi and the sixty-five-year-old Iraj Karim, and poured dirt on their bodies. They also abandoned the bodies of Ahmad Falahatgar, Bijan Mohiti, Omar Dehghani, Mohammad-Ali Malai and Mehdi Khorashadi near Kani Massi and Seyyed Narein, east of the town of As-Saadia. Local people buried them there and later transferred them to Camp Ashraf. In the course of these attacks and Coalition bombings, several members of the PMOI Leadership Council, including Ms Massoumeh Pour-Eshraq, Ms Marzieh Ali-Ahmadi, Ms Shahin Hatami, Ms Nezhat Arzbeigi and Ms Mahboobeh Soufaf, were killed. Hossein Mosharzadeh and Sadeq Seyyedi, veteran PMOI officials and political prisoners under the Shah's regime, were among those killed by Revolutionary Guards and terrorists dispatched from Iran. Each one had been campaigning against the regimes of the Shah and the mullahs for more than thirty years.

Tehran's terrified reaction

The announcement of the cease-fire agreement between the Coalition forces and the PMOI caused shock and anger among the ruling mullahs in Tehran. Khamenei, Khatami, Rafsanjani and other officials vehemently denounced it. The Associated Press wrote on 30 April 2003:

> Iran's top leader on Wednesday said that by striking a ceasefire with an Iranian armed opposition group, America was demonstrating it believed the only bad terrorists were those who were not its 'servants'.
>
> 'The world (including the United States) has recognized them (People's Mujahedeen) as terrorists. Now, America supports them. It shows terrorism is bad if terrorists are not America's servants,' the radio quoted Ayatollah Ali Khamenei as saying.
>
> The ceasefire appears to be a way for the United States to increase pressure on Iran, which Washington has accused of meddling in Iraq after the collapse of Saddam Hussein's regime.

During his visit to Beirut, Khatami said: 'As regards the Iranian terrorist group in Iraq I must say that we lodged some protests to the United States. Unfortunately, after occupying Iraq, America has reached some agreement with this terrorist group. However, we are hoping that the US would think more about this issue.' He added: 'This terrorist group is one of the biggest terrorist groups in the world and the US agreement with it clarifies that country's approach to terrorism.'[8]

In a joint press conference with the French Foreign Minister in Tehran, Foreign Minister Kamal Kharrazi said, 'If an agreement has been reached between the United States and this terrorist group which would allow the group to remain in Iraq and keep its weapons, it would show America's ill intentions and violate international law.'[9] Intelligence Minister Ali Younessi added: 'If the US would hand over PMOI members to the Islamic Republic, it has acted on its responsibility. Otherwise, it must send them to another country. The Americans intend to use the Monafeqin as a tool against this state. But the Islamic Republic would never allow that to happen.'[10]

Radio Liberty's Middle East political analyst noted, 'Washington–Mojahedin talks have angered the Islamic Republic. Tehran accuses the U.S. of duplicity in the war against terrorism. Nonetheless, a U.S. commander in Iraq said that cooperation between the Mojahedin and U.S. forces and its commitment to democracy means that its status as a terrorist group must be reviewed.'[11] The pro-Khamenei *Islamic Republic* daily wrote on 29 May:

> The United States has for more than a decade looked to the Monafeqin as an alternative to the Islamic Republic. It provided vast overt and covert support to the Monafeqin's unbridled terrorism and closed its

eye to their crimes against Iranian people and officials ... Even now, while the Monafeqin are still blacklisted in the United States, American officials, especially in the Congress, are aware of Monafeqin's contacts and engage in dialogue and understanding with them ... Moreover, after developments in Iraq, this terrorist grouplet received new missions from the US to create national security problems for the Islamic Republic. We cannot simply overlook this issue.

The state-run *Kayhan* daily had already stated on 2 May:

Iraqi sources confirm that the Monafeqin terrorist grouplet had emerged as the fifth column since the start of the US/UK attacks on Iraq. In recent days, several anti-Monafeqin demonstrations were held in Baghdad. Under the direction of Iraq's Baathist army, the PMOI committed genocide in Iraq. People in that country hate them. A State Department official says that this deal does not contradict the wider effort to combat terrorism.

The clerical rulers' frenzied reaction was due to their knowledge that the continuing presence of the PMOI in Iraq after the fall of the Iraqi regime provided more decisive evidence of the Resistance's independence and viability. It was common knowledge that if the PMOI had a single dark page during its seventeen-year presence in Iraq or that if it was a lackey of the former regime, it would not have stayed in Iraq in circumstances where the war had become inevitable, nor would it have escaped reprisal attacks by Iraqis after the fall of the Baathist regime. Immediately after the news of agreement was made public, the Iranian regime asked the United States in direct, secret talks, and indirectly through various intermediaries such as the Blair government, why there had been a ceasefire with the Mojahedin? And why the Coalition had failed to continue the bombing of the PMOI until it was completely annihilated?

Tehran's volte-face

Aware of the fact that the public announcement of a US–PMOI ceasefire discredited Tehran's long-standing accusation that the PMOI was an Iraqi proxy, the clerical leaders quickly abandoned the boisterous propaganda attacks on the Iranian Resistance for being 'Saddam's agents' and, instead, opted for a new line. Suddenly, Iran's state-run media took up the claim that the PMOI and the NLA were US proxies and part of its armed forces. They charged that the PMOI had put on US uniforms, acquired its weapons and was suppressing Iraqis from the north to the south and from the east to the west under the command of the US forces.

In an article entitled, 'US Equips Mojahedin with Heavy Weapons', the pro-Khatami *Yass-e No* daily wrote on 5 May:

At present, Mojahedin forces are prepared alongside US soldiers to suppress popular uprisings in the cities of Mosul and Falluja. Sources say a number of Kurdish leaders and forces as well as people in northern Iraq are angry because the Mojahedin have returned to these regions. Some of them have told their leaders: 'They would kill the Mojahedin even if the Mojahedin wear US uniforms.' ... Informed Iraqi sources say: 'Americans are preparing to use the Mojahedin in southern Iraq as well. Earlier, there were reports on the presence of Mojahedin in a number of Iraqi cities, including Mosul and Falluja, where anti-American demonstrations broke out.' The Mojahedin have reportedly been transferred to Baquba under the direction and orders of the Americans who have already put in place training courses for the Mojahedin.

In an article, 'US Co-operates with Mojahedin Terrorist Group', another government-sponsored paper, *Mardomsalari* daily, wrote on 1 May:

Americans have pursued a double standard in dealing with the Mojahedin grouplet. Amid the Iraq war, it bombed its bases and after the war, it protected them. Some believe that the Zionist lobby in the US has prevented America from getting close to Iran and has exerted political pressure on Iran on their agenda. They are using this grouplet as an instrument of pressure. Some others also believe that Iran's actions in Iraq in the context of support for the Supreme Council of Islamic Revolution in Iraq and actions by the Shiites against US military presence have prompted the US government to support this grouplet. Conversely, others emphasize that the bombing of Mojahedin bases in Iraq was a tactic to coerce Iran into co-operating with the USA on the situation in Iraq ... Iran must use proper means to change the US decision to support the Mojahedin.

The daily's editor in chief, Mostafa Kavakebian, wrote on 30 April that the 'Zionist lobby' had pushed the Mojahedin to become mercenaries of the USA:

Zionists view taking advantage of the Mojahedin as an instrument to realize their interests. While the Americans may justify their co-operation with the Mojahedin under the pretext of challenging the 9th Badr Corps, in reality, the Zionist lobby is very strong, because the Zionists want to step up violent relations between Iran and the United States. Through various intermediaries, Americans said they were not going to co-operate with the Mojahedin and would attack their bases. But they did the opposite and now are using this group to exert pressure on Iran.

Jam-e Jam daily claimed on 5 May that the PMOI had received new equipment from the US forces:

> Some Iraqi sources in Khorramshahr are saying: 'The US army is equipping the Mojahedin with advance weaponry in order to suppress Iraq's Muslim people and obtain information.' These sources added: 'In the latest round of cooperation between the Mojahedin and the USA, American army has given bullet-proof vests, M-16 rifles and special boots to the members of the Mojahedin to join the invading forces in suppressing anti-American moves in Iran.' On the basis of this report, at present, the Mojahedin are standing next to US forces in the cities of Mosul and Falluja ready to suppress popular uprisings in these regions.

The daily *Kayhan* had already, on 3 May, added its own fantastic charges to the collection:

> US servicemen have set up a new base for the Monafeqin grouplet 20 km north west of Mosul. The Central News Unit reported that the US move came after agreements reached with the Monafeqin leader and the US military. The CNU reported from Abadan that US forces transferred thirty Monafeqin to the town of Falluja to suppress local residents. Informed sources say that two helicopters transferred Monafeqin forces from north-west Baghdad to Falluja.

Three days later, the daily *Khorassan* wrote: 'An eyewitness who recently returned from Iraq said that Mojahedin members have been stationed at border crossings with Iran, wearing US uniforms and co-operating directly with the Americans in controlling incoming and outgoing traffic. The Mojahedin carry no weapons at these checkpoints. However, in some towns such as Samara, they carry weapons.' The state-run Sahar television channel reported on 4 May:

> The official news agency, IRNA, reported that some Iraqi sources say the US Army is arming the Mojahedin with advanced weapons to suppress Iraq's Muslim people and obtain information.
>
> The US is supporting the terrorist Mojahedin at a time when Washington attacked Afghanistan and Iraq on the pretext of combating terrorism.
>
> The US has also given special equipment to the Mojahedin to enable it to work in unison with the invading forces to suppress anti-American uprisings in Iraq. Today, in Mosul and Falluja, Mojahedin forces are

ready, alongside US soldiers, to suppress popular movement against the occupiers.

These false reports, after years of propaganda that the PMOI was dependent on Iraq, demonstrated the hollow nature of earlier claims about the organization relying on Iraq and about its involvement in 'suppressing the Iraqi people'.

Terror tag questioned

After the signing of 'the mutual understanding and co-ordination' agreement, discussions between the PMOI and US/Coalition forces continued. It was ultimately announced on 10 May 2003 that the PMOI had agreed voluntarily to have 'its personnel and equipment consolidated'. Announcing the agreement, Major General Raymond Odierno, commander of the US Army's Fourth Infantry Division, said that the PMOI personnel would gather at one camp while its equipment would be consolidated at another. It was also agreed that both camps would be protected by US/Coalition forces. Speaking to the press at a PMOI base near the Iranian border, General Odierno took the unusual step for a military officer of saying that the PMOI appeared to be committed to democracy in Iran and that their co-operation with the United States should prompt a 'review of their terrorist status'. He added, 'I would say that any organization that has given up their equipment to the Coalition clearly is co-operating with us, and I believe that should lead to a review of whether they are still a terrorist organization or not.' Further, when he was asked what role the PMOI and NLA could play in the future of Iraq, General Odierno said only that they shared similar goals to the United States in 'forming democracy and fighting oppression' and that they had been 'extremely co-operative'.

The *Los Angeles Times*, reporting on this second agreement on 12 May, quoted Captain Josh Felker, a US Army spokesman, as saying, '[t]his is not a surrender, it's a disarmament process. The MEK was never fighting coalition forces.' Captain Felker further stated: 'They are a very respected fighting force, and as such we are treating them courteously ... basically we don't want to disrespect them.' In a press release, the US Central Command stated on 17 May:

Coalition forces have consolidated 2,139 tanks, armored personnel carriers, artillery pieces, air defense artillery pieces and miscellaneous vehicles formerly in the possession of the Mujahedin-e Khalq (MEK) forces. The Fourth Infantry Division also reports they have destroyed most of the MEK munitions and caches. The voluntary, peaceful resolution of this process by the MEK and the Coalition significantly contributes to the Coalition's mission to establish a safe and secure environment for the people of Iraq.

In a press conference on 18 June 2003, from his headquarters in Iraq, Fourth Division Commander Major General Ray Odierno told the Pentagon press corps that the consolidation of the PMOI's weapons had been completed. Of the quantity of weapons involved, the general said, 'They had about 10,000 small arms, and they had about 2,200 pieces of equipment, to include about 300 tanks, about 250 armored personnel carriers and about 250 artillery pieces.' The Fourth Infantry Division said, on its official website on 22 May, that 'the latest status of the Mujahedin-e Khalq' at the end of the implementation of the agreement was as follows:

> The Mujahedin-e-Khalq (MEK) have completed their voluntary consolidation of equipment and forces in agreement with the April 16th cease-fire agreement with U.S. forces. 'The consolidation is complete as agreed and has gone very well, with excellent cooperation of the PMOI (People's Mujahedin of Iran or MEK),' said Lt. Col. Mark Young, commander of 3/67 Armor Battalion, 2nd Brigade, Fourth Infantry Division out of Fort Hood, Texas ... According to the agreement entered upon by Maj. Gen. Raymond Odierno, Task Force Ironhorse and Fourth Infantry Division Commander, Brig. Gen. David Rodriguez, Assistant Division Commander (Maneuver) and Mojgan Parsaii, Secretary General of the MEK, all personnel will be consolidated in Ashraf Camp, and all equipment will be stored at Alevi Camp.
>
> Young couldn't speak of the volume of equipment turned in but said it contained everything you would associate with a military force, from small arms to armored vehicles. He said there had been a large amount of ammunition turned in along with everything you would need to equip and maintain a small army.
>
> The 3/67's biggest challenge at Ashraf Camp is learning how to interact with the paramilitary organization that has been operating out of Iraq for the past 20 years. 'We are really acting as guests on their compound,' said Young. 'We have had to work very closely with them and in close cooperation. We are not running this compound, so we've had to come to a common understanding of what it is we're trying to accomplish.'
>
> Only about five percent of the battalion lives on the compound. The rest live in a nearby camp in the middle of the desert. Others occupy defensive positions the MEK once manned, as well as two permanent checkpoints along Highway 2. 'We basically have two primary missions,'

said Young. 'One is to ensure that the agreements we have made with the PMOI are carried out and secondly, provide a defense posture to the individuals on the compound. The primary goal is a stable Iraq. That is the goal. The MEK-PMOI understands the long term goal and that is what the coalition is working for,' said Young.

Michael Gordon of the *New York Times* wrote on 6 June that the US/ Coalition forces approached the PMOI with the request that the former could set up base at another camp, Baqerzadeh, which was empty at the time:

> The American soldiers who advanced into the heart of the Iraqi capital in April soon found themselves face to face with an Iranian resistance movement as they sought to sort out living arrangements for the soldiers in this dirt-poor and looted region. By the end of my first day here, I had meandered through an underground bunker complex, enjoyed a fine Iranian meal and heard a lecture on repression in Iran from a member of the resistance movement who had earned a university degree in Wichita, Kansas.
>
> But what were the new quarters? As the brigade arrived, it turned out that it would be setting up camp in a compound built by the Mujahadeen Khalq, an Iranian resistance group that the Clinton administration put on its terrorist list but that asserts it does not support terror attacks against the United States and wants to make common cause against the Iranian government.
>
> This group had quite a story to tell. I heard it from Amir Ghassemi, who had received the university degree, in mechanical engineering, in Wichita. He said his brothers and a sister had been arrested and executed by the Khomeini regime for handing out leaflets after the shah was ousted. He has been a member of the Iranian resistance movement for 16 years.
>
> The resistance movement assumed that it could stay on the sidelines during the American-led attack on Iraq and had sent a letter to Secretary of State Colin L. Powell indicating that it had no intention of opposing the American invasion. The United States bombed their bases anyway ...
>
> But at the sprawling compound here, where the Spartan Brigade was setting up Camp, the American military presence was their immediate concern. The compound was the resistance movement's rear logistics base and includes a 100-bed hospital for women, including female fighters, that had been stripped bare by looters after the war. It also has an underground bunker system that is outfitted with a filtration system, a precaution that they say is against an Iranian missile attack.

The movement says it spent $15 million building the complex, using funds donated by Iranian business people within Iran and in exile ... but now the Iranians want to move hundreds of its women here.

The Spartan Brigade's commander, Col. David Perkins, met with a woman who is one of the Iranian group's military commanders to discuss arrangements for using the compound. The Iranians surprised the Americans by serving a chicken dinner. The resistance movement seemed prepared to accept the Americans, but made the point that it was their compound and that they eventually expected to get it back.

The mullahs' continuing agitation

The theocratic regime in Iran continued to view the presence of PMOI personnel in Iraq, even after the consolidation of their weapons, as a grave threat to itself. Foreign Minister Kharrazi and other senior figures mentioned the issue of the Mojahedin's presence in Iraq in almost every meeting with his foreign counterparts. In a trip to South Africa, Kharrazi told the press, 'The American administration is harbouring terrorists, because right now in Iraq there is an organization called MKO, which are Iranian terrorists.' Kharrazi said the USA was 'safeguarding' the PMOI personnel in Iraq, who, he alleged, 'are pretty active'.[12]

The mullahs' regime went out of its way to secure Washington's agreement for more moves against the Iranian Resistance. For several months, the ruling mullahs held out the tantalizing prospect of extradition to the USA or its allies of a number of Al-Qaeda operatives it was harbouring in Iran. In return, the clerical regime was asking for PMOI members who were in Iraq as refugees. The *New York Times* reported on 2 August 2003: 'American and Middle Eastern officials said Iran had signalled that any surrender of Qaeda figures to the United States should be matched by a surrender to Tehran of members of the Mujahedeen Khalq.' The *New York Times* quoted well-placed US officials as saying that Al-Qaeda's number three, Seif al-Adel, was among al-Qaeda elements in Iran, and added: 'A senior Bush administration official said the administration would reject any kind of swap. There will be "no quid pro quo", this official said.'[13] Other news outlets reported that 'a senior Bush administration official denied a report that it was in talks with Iran on a possible exchange of senior al Qaeda members for members of the Iranian opposition group, Mojahedin-e Khalq Organization'. The official was quoted as saying that the USA has 'communicated to Iran the importance of turning over senior members of al Qaeda. No quid pro quo, no negotiations, no exchange.'[14] Patrick Clawson, deputy director of the Washington Institute for Near East Policy, told the news media that any such exchange would have caused legal problems, as the USA is a signatory of the United Nations Convention Against Torture and is thus required not to hand over to the Iranian regime persons who might face torture in that country, which is clearly the case with PMOI members and supporters.[15]

The Iranian regime continued to press Washington on the issue of the PMOI presence in Iraq, using both incentives and threats. When the State Department shut down the Washington offices of the National Council of Resistance of Iran and the PMOI in August 2003, the clerical regime conferred rare praise on the USA and Kharrazi welcomed the move to gag the mullahs' opponents, but in the same breath he demanded further US action against the Iranian Resistance in Iraq. The Associated Press reported:

> Iranian Foreign Minister Kamal Kharrazi called the U.S. action 'a positive step that conforms to its international responsibilities', the official Islamic Republic News Agency reported.
>
> Kharrazi said Washington should have acted sooner against the dissidents as they had long been on the terrorism list, the agency said.
>
> 'The onus is on the United States to confront the provocations by the group,' the minister said.[16]

To achieve its goal and raise the pressure for action against the PMOI, the clerical regime once again resorted to misinformation tactics. In one instance, it used the services of its agents in the Patriotic Union of Kurdistan, whose special ties with the fundamentalist regime in Iran have long been known, to claim that some 1,000 PMOI 'renegades' were fighting the 'Americans, the Kurds and the Iranians' in the mountains of northern Iraq. An Agence France Presse reporter in the Iraqi town of Jalawla, close to the Iranian border, quoted 'deputy chief of the PUK branch in nearby Saadia, Abdul al-Karim Mahmud', as saying that 'more than 1,000 of the [PMOI fighters] have kept their arms and headed into the mountains. Now they are fighting the Americans, the Kurds and the Iranians.'[17] The news agency also carried the PMOI's strong denial of this new allegation:

> 'This report is a sheer lie and fabricated in its entirety by the mullahs' intelligence ministry' in Iran, the Mujahedeen protested in a statement sent to AFP in Nicosia, referring to the good ties between the PUK and Tehran.
>
> 'In this way, Tehran is setting the stage for terrorist and criminal plots in Iraq and attributing them to the Mujahedeen,' it said.

'By spreading these lies, the clerical regime is trying to pave the way for greater intervention in Iraq and terrorist operations against the Mujahedeen in Iraqi territory,' the group charged.[18]

The Iranian regime was at the same time actively courting those in the US State Department who advocated rapprochement with the fundamentalist state and clung to the failed memories of the Irangate era. The *Washington Post*, on 11 September, quoting 'administration officials', wrote that the 'U.S. military appears to have allowed an Iraq-based Iranian opposition group ... to retain its weapons'. The same sources told the *Post* that the Mojahedin were 'crossing into Iran to conduct attacks' and 'enjoyed wide freedom to continue their operations'. They said 'intercepts of Iranian government communications indicated the Mujaheddin continued to pose problems for the government in Tehran'.[19]

While it is true that the Iranian Resistance poses problems for the government in Tehran, this has nothing to do with the presence of some of its members in Iraq. The origin of many of these false claims, such as the PMOI members' crossing of the border to conduct attacks in Iran, is clearly Iranian intelligence, which has a long record of manipulating information and distorting facts to influence other countries' views of the Iranian Resistance. The top US commander in Iraq, Lieutenant General Ricardo Sanchez, denied these allegations and emphasized, 'There is no problem with the MEK [PMOI] that we are having today.' 'Are they continuing to enter Iran? I can guarantee you that is not happening,' General Sanchez told reporters in Iraq.[20]

In a separate report, on 13 September Agence France Presse quoted the US military commander on the scene, Lieutenant Colonel Thomas Cantwell, as denying the claims that PMOI personnel were crossing into Iran from Iraq to conduct attacks. 'These claims were non-existent by June when troops from the 324 Military Police took control of Camp Ashraf and the MEK was consolidated,' he reportedly told AFP.

Ex-president and strongman Hashemi Rafsanjani's speech in the Assembly of Experts on 11 September 2003, reported by the IRNA, reflected a growing confidence among the ruling clerics in Iran that their chances of defeating US policy in Iraq have improved with the turn of events. Rafsanjani told his clerical peers, 'Even though the United States has a physical presence in the countries that surround us, the reality is that the United States is in fact surrounded by Iran.' He then added, 'Our enemies such as Saddam, the Taliban and the [Mojahedin] have been swept out of our way, and soon the USA will be too.'

Notes

1. Rafsanjani, IRNA, 11 September 2003.
2. Press release by the PMOI, 'Mullahs' Regime Positions Surface-to-Surface Missiles Close to Iraq Border', 23 January 2003.
3. IRNA, 28 December 2002.
4. *Los Angeles Times*, 12 May 2003.
5. *House Magazine*, London, 31 March 2003.
6. Mohsen Rezaii, ISNA news agency, 6 August 2002.
7. David Claude, *Wall Street Journal*, 17 April 2003.
8. IRNA press agency, 15 May 2003.
9. Radio Liberty, 12 May 2003.
10. Ibid.
11. Ibid.
12. South African News Agency (SAPA), 22 July 2003.
13. Doug Jehl, 'Iran Said to Hold Qaeda's No. 3, but to Resist Giving Him Up', *New York Times*, 2 August 2003.
14. Radio Farda, 1 August 2003.
15. Ibid.
16. 'Iran Confers Rare Praise on the U.S.', Associated Press, 17 August 2003.
17. 'Mujahedeen Fighters Regroup in Mountains on Iraq–Iran Border', Agence France Presse, 13 September 2003.
18. Ibid.
19. Glenn Kessler, 'State Questions Military Tolerance of Iranian Dissidents', *Washington Post*, 11 September 2003.
20. Andrew Cawthorne, Reuters, 11 September 2003.

8 | Iraq and the spectre of Islamic fundamentalism

I'm getting the impression that America fought Saddam Hussein
and the Islamic fundamentalists won. *Nicholas Kristof*

The no-words-minced comment by the *New York Times*'s prominent columnist from Basra at the end of the US-led war that ousted the Iraqi
regime was among the early alarms coming from ancient Mesopotamia,
now under the rule of the world's youngest great power. Kristof warned,
on 25 June 2003, that 'an iron curtain of fundamentalism risks falling
over Iraq, with particularly grievous implications for girls and women'.
He recounted a chilling story to drive home his point:

> For a glimpse of the Islamic state that Iraq may be evolving into, consider
> the street execution of an infidel named Sabah Ghazali.
>
> Under Saddam Hussein, Christians like Ghazali, 41, were allowed
> to sell alcohol and were protected from Muslim extremists. But lately
> extremists have been threatening to kill anyone selling alcohol. One day
> last month, two men walked over to Ghazali as he was unlocking his
> shop door and shot him in the head – the second liquor store owner
> they had killed that morning.
>
> President George W. Bush hopes that Iraq will turn into a shining
> model of democracy, and that could still happen. But for now it's the
> Shiite fundamentalists who are gaining ground ... Here in Basra, Islam-
> ists have asked Basra University (unsuccessfully) to separate male and
> female students, and shopkeepers have put up signs like: 'Sister, cover
> your hair.' Many more women are giving in to the pressure and wearing
> the hijab head covering. 'Every woman is afraid,' said Sarah Alak, 22, a
> computer engineering student at Basra University. Alak never used to
> wear a hijab, but after Saddam fell her father asked her to wear one on
> the university campus, 'just to avoid trouble'.

Kristof's unnerving conclusion: 'We may just have to get used to the
idea that Americans have been midwives to growing Islamic fundamentalism in Iraq.'

Like their fellow Christians in post-revolutionary Iran, Iraq's Christians
are dreading the rise of fundamentalism among the country's tradition-

ally tolerant Muslims. An American reporter recounted his observations after the war:

Two weeks ago, Raad Karim Essa arrived home from work to find his furniture on the street. His Muslim landlord wasn't renting to Christians anymore.
'He told us not to argue and threatened us,' said Essa, 42, a father of four. 'He said the government was no longer here to protect us. What could we do? We feared for our lives.'
'The Muslims want to destroy us,' said Amira Nisan, 38, Essa's wife. 'I think we were better off under Saddam.'
Such a sentiment is voiced increasingly today among Iraq's 800,000 Christians.
Like most of their countrymen, Christians greeted the fall of Iraqi President Saddam Hussein with celebration and hope. But in little more than a month, their desire for greater religious freedom has been replaced by fear of the fundamentalism rippling through Iraq's Shiite Muslim majority, which has moved quickly to exert its influence after decades of violent repression.[1]

These articles and hundreds of similar reports by Western observers and journalists visiting Iraq reflected the dilemma confronting the United States over Iraq's future. The war unleashed forces in Iraq that raised serious questions over whether the nation would be able, indeed ready, to embrace democracy. The *Chicago Tribune's* correspondent, Liz Sly, on 27 August 2003, quoted a young Shiite cleric, Sheikh Abbas Zubaidi, as saying, 'The new government will be ruled in the name of God in heaven, whose light shines into all walks of life ... You can tell America: Islam is back.' Glenn Kessler and Donna Priest wrote in the *Washington Post* on 23 April, 'As the administration plotted to overthrow Hussein's government, U.S. officials said, it failed to fully appreciate the force of Shiite aspirations and is now concerned that those sentiments could coalesce into a fundamentalist government. "It is a complex equation, and the U.S. government is ill-equipped to figure out how this is going to shake out," a State Department official said.' *Newsweek's* Farid Zakaria wrote, 'It would be a tragedy if in the search for quick legitimacy, America ended up empowering the kinds of forces it is currently battling all over the Arab world,' calling these forces 'extremist, illiberal and intolerant'.[2]

It is an undeniable fact that the war and the overthrow of Iraq's secular Baathist regime let the genie of fundamentalism out of the Iraqi bottle. Fundamentalism is not an indigenous and deeply rooted phenomenon in Iraq. The country's history shows clearly that in the past centuries, different ethnic groupings and religions have lived together in harmony on the historic land of Mesopotamia. Today, fundamentalism in Iraq, particularly Shiite fundamentalism, is imported from its eastern neighbour, Iran. Examples such as the murder of Christians or imposing the veil on women, which have no precedents in Iraq, show that fundamentalists in Iran have exported this behaviour to Iraq.

Middle East experts mostly concur that the issues that dominate the international news media's reporting on Iraq at present are likely to be transient: the real, longer-term problem will definitely be the Iran-backed Shiite fundamentalism. As Zakaria noted, 'The news out of Iraq sounds grim – killings, chaos, instability. But these problems are likely to be temporary.' Confusion reigns in the search for a resolution to deal with this problem. Zakaria offers a theory:

> What is called democracy in the West is really liberal democracy, a political system marked not only by free elections but also the rule of law, the separation of powers and basic human rights, including private property, free speech and religious tolerance. In the West, this tradition of liberty and law developed over centuries, long before democracy took hold. It was produced by a series of forces – the separation of church and state, the Renaissance, the Enlightenment, the Reformation, capitalism and the development of an independent middle class. England and the United States were considered free societies 200 years ago – when under 5 percent of their populations voted.

Here is his solution: 'In Iraq today, first establish a stable security environment and create the institutions of limited government – a constitution with a bill of rights, an independent judiciary, a sound central bank. Then and only then, move to full-fledged democracy.'[3]

The problem with theories put forward by Zakaria and like-minded observers of the region is that they tend to offer temporary relief rather than lasting solutions. Delaying elections or the handover of power to Iraqis can work, but only for a relatively short span of time. The experience of Algeria and other societies shows that this approach does not serve as a solution and may in fact contribute to the rise in fundamentalism as the public becomes more sympathetic to the fundamentalists' ranting and violence against the foreign occupiers or even the indigenous tyrant.

There are those who offer long-term solutions, but in such generalized, vague and abstract forms that they can only infuriate the policy-makers and planners dealing with the grim day-to-day realities of the situation. In the immediate wake of the conflict on 23 April, the *Washing-*

ton Post quoted a Bush administration official as saying, 'The most radical aspects of Islam are in places with no education at all but the Koran ...There is no math, no culture. You counter that [fundamentalism] by doing something with the education system.' While the important and long-term role of education cannot be overstated, the official forgets that in its recent history, Iraq has always had secular education, rated among the best in the Middle East prior to the 1990s. Furthermore, a change in the educational system would need at least ten years or more to produce any palpable impact on society. In the meantime, what should be done about the current state of affairs?

Fanning the flames of fundamentalism

The biggest illusion in analysing the current situation in Iraq is to view the growing phenomenon of fundamentalism in that country as a home-grown and inherently 'Iraqi' problem. It is not. Stop Iran's ruling ayatollahs fanning the flames of fundamentalism in Iraq and you will find Iraq as fertile a ground for fundamentalism as the Arabian desert. Unfortunately, many observers are too oblivious of recent history to recall that in the 1980s, the Iraqi people in general rejected Khomeini's strenuous efforts to win them over to the side of his fundamentalist 'Islamic revolution' and, instead, defended their homeland in the face of the clerical regime's aggression.

The Iranian theocracy's failure to export its brand of extremism to Iraq was due in no part to lack of effort. Shortly after Khomeini took power in Iran, he began to call openly for the 'export of Islamic Revolution to Iraq'. Not a day went by without mullahs calling on the people of Iraq, particularly the Shiites, to overthrow the government and set up an 'Islamic Republic'. A historian wrote at the time:

Beginning in 1980, Iran actively promoted its own revolutionary vision for Iraq. All anti-Iraqi Islamic organizations, including Ad Dawah al Islamiyah, commonly called Ad Dawah, and the Organization of Islamic Action were based in Tehran, where they came under the political, religious, and financial influence of the ruling clergy. To control rivalry and infighting among the different groups, Iran helped to set up the Supreme Council for the Islamic Revolution in Iraq (SCIRI) on November 17, 1982. It was headed by Iraqi cleric Hujjat al Islam Muhammad Baqeir al Hakim. Establishing SCIRI was viewed as a step toward unifying the political and military work of all groups and as an attempt to unite them under a single command directly supervised by their Iranian counterparts. In return, SCIRI acknowledged the leadership of Khomeini as the supreme commander of the Islamic nation. Nevertheless, the majority of Iraqi Shias resisted Tehran's control and remained loyal to Iraq.[4]

In a report entitled 'Iraq: U.S. Regime Change Efforts and Post-War Governance', the Congressional Research Service wrote:

> The Supreme Council for the Islamic Revolution in Iraq (SCIRI), was set up in 1982 to increase Iranian control over Shiite opposition groups in Iraq and the Persian Gulf States. SCIRI's leader, Ayatollah Muhammad Baqer al Hakim, was the late Ayatollah Khomeini's choice to head an Islamic Republic of Iraq, a vision that, if realized, might conflict with U.S. plans to forge a democratic Iraq ... In addition to its agents and activists in the Shiite areas of Iraq, SCIRI has about 10,000–15,000 fighters/activists organized into a 'Badr Corps' that, during the 1980s and 1990s, conducted forays from Iran into southern Iraq to attack Baath Party officials there ... Iran's Revolutionary Guard, which is politically aligned with Iran's hard line civilian officials, has been the key patron of the Badr Corps. Providing it with weapons, funds, and other assistance. The Badr Corps fought alongside the Guard against Iraqi forces during the Iran–Iraq war. However, many Iraqi Shiites view SCIRI as an Iranian creation and SCIRI/Badr Corps operations in southern Iraq prior to Operation Iraqi Freedom did not spark broad popular unrest against the Iraqi regime.[5]

Ayatollahs' caliphate ambitions

Ayatollah Ahmad Jannati, head of the powerful Guardian Council, is one of the most influential figures in the Islamic Republic and a close confidant of the regime's Supreme Leader. Shortly after the fall of the Iraqi regime, Jannati told Tehran's Friday prayers congregation on 2 May: 'The Iraqi people have reached the conclusion that they have no option but to launch an *intifada* and resort to martyrdom operations to eject America from Iraq ... I urge the Iraqi people to remain united, follow the *ulema*, make ceaseless efforts to expel the enemy from Iraq's pure land and establish an Islamic government ... This is the way. They (Iraqis) should learn from Iran's Islamic revolution.' Three months later, ex-president and Expediency Council chairman Hashemi Rafsanjani told a group of Revolutionary Guards, 'the unfavourable state of US occupiers in Iraq set a good example of divine justice'. Already claiming the moral high ground, Rafsanjani said, 'God punishes tyrants by tyrants; enemies of the Islamic Republic were punished by each other but the Islamic Republic of Iran is now firm and stable, being concerned about the condition of Muslim Iraqi people.'[6]

The mullahs' intervention in post-conflict Iraq was in contravention of their pledge to the US–UK Coalition prior to the war not to interfere in Iraq's internal affairs. It was not the first time that the mullahs were not living up to their part of the deal in a secret agreement with Washington and London. Back in 1986, Irangate insiders in Washington were reportedly livid when they heard Rafsanjani giving a disingenuous account of events that became known as the 'arms-for-hostages' deal during the Friday prayers in Tehran. This time, the deal was, as we saw in the previous chapter, for the Iranian regime to refrain from any meddling in Iraq during and after the war. In return, Tehran received assurances that the Iranian Resistance's bases in Iraq would be bombed.

As the US-led war in Iraq was still in progress, however, the clerical regime took advantage of the power vacuum and sent thousands of its Revolutionary Guards and agents to attack the bases of the National Liberation Army of Iran in Iraq. The attacks began on 9 April and left more than fifty Mojahedin killed and a greater number wounded. A number of the wounded were abducted and taken to Iran. Emboldened by the bombing of PMOI bases in Iraq and eager to 'finish off the job', Iran's clerical rulers broke their promises to the USA and the British. The mullahs had long been planning what to do in case of another war in Iraq. For Iran's clerical rulers, Iraq was far too important to leave in a stable, prospering situation under American rule. A secret meeting of the Supreme National Security Council, held on 22 December 2001, and attended by Khamenei and Khatami, concluded: 'The possible attack by the USA against Iraq will create crisis in the region for some time and poses many dangers to us. The only way out for us is to take the upper hand in the future government of Iraq through the Supreme Council of Islamic Revolution in Iraq.'

In early July 2002, the regime's leaders again discussed the Iraq–USA crisis. Hashemi Rafsanjani said: 'If we could bring the USA to the position to attack the Mojahedin, we would guarantee our survival. After that, we could easily confront the USA with the help of Iraqi groups and form an Islamic Republic in Iraq.' In September 2002, Khamenei summoned the commanders of the Qods [Jerusalem] Force and the Nasr terrorist headquarters to instruct them to prepare quickly the Ninth Badr Corps mercenaries for intervention in Iraq. The regime's leaders decided to send sufficient weapons into Iraq and prepare safe houses and weapons warehouses to hide weaponry. They also decided to form rapid reaction armed cells.

In late February 2003, Revolutionary Guards Corps Qods Force commander Brigadier General Qassem Soleimani, Ramazan Garrison commander Brigadier General Iraj Masjedi, Ramazan Garrison operations commander Brigadier General Hamid Taqavi and Fajr Garrison commander Brigadier General Obeidavi were entrusted with directing the operational plan in Iraq. Soleimani personally followed up this plan. Ramazan Garrison deputy commander Brigadier General Ahmad Forouzandeh implemented plans to infiltrate Iraqi towns and popularize the slogan of 'no East, no West, only an Islamic Republic'. This was intended to gain a bigger share of power in the future Iraqi government. He held many meetings with the Ninth Badr Corps commanders, including Hazrat Rassul Division commander Ahmad Rashed, Imam Hussein Division commander Montazer, Heidar Karar Division commander Ahmad Badran.

In early February, Badr Corps commanders had been briefed about their missions in Iraq:

- Heidar Karar Division's mission was to control the town of Al-Amara through the Howeiza axis;
- Imam Hussein Division's mission was to control the city of Basra through the Khorramshahr axis;
- Hazrat Rassul Division's mission was to control the town of Al-Kut through the Mehran axis;
- Imam Ali Division's mission was to control Baghdad and Diyala Province through Marivan and Khaneqin axes.

The Command Headquarters of the Armed Forces and the Joint Command Headquarters of the Revolutionary Guards Corps in Tehran took control of and monitored the activities of the Ninth Badr Corps divisions. On 28 March 2003, the Badr Corps intelligence and reconnaissance units secretly entered Iraq in small groups.

On 6 April, Ramazan Garrison commander Brigadier General Iraj Masjedi announced in a meeting with Iraqi groups affiliated with the regime that southern cities had fallen and the borders were wide open, making it ideal for military forces and groups to enter Iraq's cities in the south. The Ramazan Garrison commander co-ordinated the entry into Iraqi territory. They gave everyone entering Iraq a Kalashnikov, a cartridge belt and some cash in US dollars. The Guard's commanders emphasized that 'we must infiltrate as many Iraqi forces as possible to fill the future power vacuum in Iraq'. Forces of the Fajr Garrison and the Badr Corps positioned themselves around the town of Al-Qorna on 7 April. They began registering agents and distributed weapons among them. A number of agents affiliated with the Fajr Garrison went to

Nasseriya, Al-Kut, Al-Hay and Al-Muqyia to organize their forces and co-ordinate with tribal leaders to set up their networks.

On 9 April, when there were no longer any doubts about the fall of the Iraqi government, the Qods Force and its affiliated garrisons sent the Ninth Badr Corps commanders and forces to the already specified locations in Iraq through five axes. In addition to the Ninth Badr Corps, Iraqi clerics working under Khamenei and political advisers to Baqer Hakim entered Iraq in large and small groups under the command of Fajr and Zafar garrisons to take control of Iraqi cities. All commanders of Ramazan Garrison and intelligence commanders as well as personnel of the garrison's First Corps entered Iraq on 9 and 10 April. The garrison's operations commander Hamid Taqavi and Abu Mojtaba, Intelligence Commander of the Hezbollah movement affiliated with the Fajr Garrison in Ahwaz, as well as all Iraqi personnel of the Ramazan Garrison, entered Iraq.

The Crisis Headquarters Chief Ahmad Forouzandeh had organized the First Corps in groups, allocating each group to a different city. He personally took command of dispatching the forces. The commanders of the Ramazan Garrison were:

- Abu Mojtaba, head of the Hezbollah movement from the Fajr Garrison in Ahwaz;
- Abu Zeinab Khalesi, commander of terrorist groups affiliated with the Intelligence Ministry and the Ramazan Garrison;
- Abu Fallah, an intelligence commander of the Fajr Garrison;
- Abu Hatam, in charge of a terrorist group who went to Al-Amara;
- Abu Zeinab Helli, commander of a terrorist group;
- Abu Hanna Baghdadi, in charge of the mission in Baghdad. Ramazan Garrison commander Iraj Masjedi put him in charge of several terrorist groups in the town of Al-Kut as well.

On 10 April, the Ninth Badr Corps forces entered the border town of Khaneqin and captured half the city. US forces, however, clashed with them a few days later and forced them to withdraw. When the commanders of the joint operational headquarters of the Qods Force entered Iraq on 10 April, they formed a tactical command headquarters in the Maydan region near the Iraqi town of Sulaimaniya. On 13 April, Tehran opened all borders to Iraqis living in Iran and issued a memorandum based on which Iraqis in Iran could return to Iraq with permission from the Nasr and Ramazan garrisons or the MOIS. The mullahs were concentrating the dispatch of forces from Qom to Najaf and Karbala. Some 14,000 Revolutionary Guards Corps personnel, forces of the Ninth Badr Corps and 2,000 clerics entered Iraq in a relatively short period. Imam Ali Division forces set up their headquarters in a location called Qal'eh in the Maydan region in Iraqi Kurdistan. Its commanders, including Abu Majed Basari and Abu Aqil, its deputy commander, went to that headquarters. The Badr Corps also set up bases in Sulaimaniya and Penjwin. The Badr Corps and Imam Ali Division entered Iraq through the Nowsoud axis. Imam Ali Division, Mostafa and Malek Ashtar brigades took control of Diyala Province in central Iraq. Parts of those forces took up positions in Maydan, Kelar, Khaneqin, Mandali and Naftkhaneh. Part of the Imam Ali Division was stationed in Baquba on their way to Baghdad.

On 15 April, forces of Imam Ali Division and Malek Ashtar and Mostafa brigades started descending on Baghdad. To reinforce the regime's strength in the central region, Mahmoud Farhadi, an intelligence commander of the Ramazan Garrison and Abu Leqa, the Ninth Badr Corps commander and other commanders were based in Baquba. Large amounts of US dollars were brought by the Ramazan Garrison for the forces based in different Iraqi cities. The next day, Mostafa brigade forces and the intelligence brigade of the Ninth Badr Corps were stationed in different parts of Diyala Province, especially in Baquba and Khalis. This brigade was responsible for the province and its commander Abuzar Khalesi was stationed in Baquba. All of the brigade's forces were transferred to Diyala Province by 17 April.

When the war began, the forces were dispatched at night, according to the plan by the Ramazan Garrison, whose intelligence commanders warned the ninth Badr Corps that people in Khuzistan Province supported the PMOI and would report movements to the organization. The Guards commanders used ambulances, equipped with command communication systems, to cross the border.

Strategy: 'slow expansion of influence'

After US forces expanded their control over different parts of Iraq, the clerical regime's leaders reached the conclusion that they could not directly face the Americans in Iraq. They therefore embarked on a two-pronged strategy. The first was to expand public activities by setting up charity, assistance, medical help and other civil networks, similar to those of the Hezbollah in Lebanon. They also expanded clandestine armed cells to conduct military operations against US forces and Iraqis opposed to the presence of the Iranian regime and its affiliated forces. This strategy derived from the analysis that time was against the Americans in Iraq: the US public would not tolerate a lengthy presence of US forces in the country. The best approach, therefore, was to expand the organization of the regime's affiliated forces in Iraq so as to have the upper hand in any development. At the same time, the thinking was that, with the use of secret armed cells, the secure and stable environment the USA was after had to be disrupted. Tehran leaders believed that Iraq 'would be a ripe apple, which it could pluck up sooner or later'.

In a private meeting of the regime's leaders on 21 April, Hashemi Rafsanjani said: 'We can invest in Iraqi Shiites. The situation could not be better. There is no time in détente, which calls for passive action. We must activate Iraq and the region's full forces. The British had prepared the situation for us for expansion in the south.' This view is reflected in the clerics' public comments as well. Rafsanjani said, 'The fight against blasphemy and arrogance has surpassed geographical borders. Islam was never restricted to a particular border.' 'Referring to the many problems the US has in Iraq, he said money, military force and strong propaganda are not impediments in confronting the US,' the state-run news agency, ISNA, reported on 25 May.

Arbaeen demonstration, a springboard

In a meeting between Khamenei, the Revolutionary Guards commanders and those responsible for Iraqi affairs on 20 April, it was decided that Arbaeen (commemorating the fortieth day marking the anniversary of the martyrdom of Hussein, the third Shiite Imam) should be made a show of force against the Americans. Subsequently, in a private meeting with Hakim, Khamenei said: 'The US wanted to set up an American brand of Shia in Iraq through Majid Kho'i. However, it no longer has a pawn. The situation is ripe to solidify our position.' He added: 'Try to demonstrate maximum show of power by exploiting the religious sentiments of the Shiites in Karbala. At the time when popular support is on the rise, try to go to Iraq. Given the presence of Shiites in the south, you much achieve maximum expansion and control the power in the cities.'

The Arbaeen ceremony was a springboard and the first phase of the regime's plan to set up its own alternative in Iraq. Tehran had three specific objectives:

- slogans against the US presence in Iraq and in support of the Islamic Republic;
- establishing the position of Mohammad Baqer Hakim as the *vali-e faqih* (Supreme Leader) of Shiites in Iraq. Khamenei said this must be accomplished even if it entailed 5,000 casualties; and
- popularizing the slogan of 'no East, no West, only an Islamic Republic'.

The Ramazan Garrison was assigned to implement this plan with Khamenei's personal financial help. The regime had planned to bring millions of people as supporters of Baqer Hakim. To this end, Revolutionary Guards commanders in Karbala held a meeting with 200 Iraqi oppositionists, all on Tehran's payroll, and briefed them about the objectives of this ceremony. Sheikh Hassan Hashemi Golpaygani, Khamenei's representative in SCIRI, carried Khamenei's message to the leading clerics in Karbala and Najaf. He called on them to put up a united front and invited the people to stand united under the banner of Hakim.

The Revolutionary Guards have divided their activities in Iraq into two main regions. The Zafar Garrison is responsible for Baghdad and Diyala Province and the Fajr Garrison is responsible for other Iranian cities. Thousands of mullahs' agents are present as military and paramilitary forces as well as religious preachers in different Iraqi towns, including Baghdad, Al-Amara, Baquba, Al-Kut, Najaf, Karbala and parts of Basra and continue their work in the framework of 'expanding influence'. In smaller towns and regions, Tehran-affiliated forces and groupings run the administrative affairs through which they intend to institutionalize and at the same time expand their influence and control.

Reacting to Tehran's meddling

So extensive was the Iranian regime's meddling in Iraq that it prompted US and British officials openly to warn the mullahs about their actions. On 25 April US Defense Secretary Donald Rumsfeld, reported by AFP, said that the United States would not allow a pro-Iranian regime to be established in Iraq, in a strong warning to Tehran not to interfere: 'A vocal minority claiming to transform Iraq into Iran will not be permitted to do so ... We will not allow the Iraqi people's democratic transition to be hijacked by those who might wish to install another form of dictatorship ... There is no question that the government of Iran has encouraged people to go into the country and that they have people in the country attempting to influence the country.' In a speech to the Council on Foreign Relations in New York on 28 May, Rumsfeld again issued a stern warning to Tehran, reiterating that 'interference' in Iraq by its neighbours or their proxies 'will not be permitted'. Rumsfeld particularly warned Iran against 'seeking to mold the future path of Iraq's social and political development'. He said: 'Indeed, Iran should be on notice: efforts to try to remake Iraq in Iran's image will be aggressively put down.' Rumsfeld added there had been discussion in Washington on whether to deal with Iranian President Mohammad Khatami, a moderate, or deal with the clerics, or not deal with either.

He said the argument for dealing with Khatami was that it would encourage moderate forces:

> The argument against that is that he clearly is there at the whim of the clerics, and each time he moves toward very much reform, he gets his leash, the chain, pulled on him and he is stopped from doing that. For that reason, [US policy in recent years has been] not to engage the top two layers of that country in the hope that the people of Iran would find ways to persuade the leadership in that country that they are going down the wrong road.

The White House also warned Tehran that its meddling in Iraq was unacceptable. The *Los Angeles Times* wrote on 24 April: 'As Shiite Muslims in Iraq flexed their political muscle, the Bush administration said Wednesday that it had warned Iran's fundamentalist Shiite government against interfering with its neighbour's "road to democracy" … In a message to Tehran, the Bush administration "made clear to Iran that we would oppose any outside organization's interference in Iraq", White House Press Secretary Ari Fleischer said.' Another US daily, *USA Today*, added on the same day:

> The United States has warned Iran in recent days not to interfere as Iraq seeks to map out its political future, White House spokesman Ari Fleischer said Wednesday.
>
> 'Infiltration of agents to destabilize the Shiite population would clearly fall into that category,' Fleischer said. There have been reports that Iranian-backed clerics have been behind anti-American rhetoric at Shiite Muslim rallies, including this week's mass pilgrimage to the Iraqi city of Karbala.

An initial assessment in Tehran

A month after the fall of the Iraqi regime, the clerical regime summoned all Ninth Badr Corps commanders and leaders of the Supreme Council for Revolution in Iraq (SCIRI) to Iran to assess the progress of its policy in Iraq and determine the future course of action. These meetings were held on Wednesday and Thursday, 21 and 22 May 2003 at the Qods Forces' headquarters at the former US embassy in Tehran. A number of Badr commanders also attended special meetings with the commanders of the Qods Force and the Ramazan Garrison. After an initial assessment, Khamenei received all Ninth Badr Corps commanders at his residential quarters to finalize the discussions. Some of those taking part in this meeting included:

- Abu Hassan Ameri, the Ninth Badr Corps commander;
- Abu Ali Basari, former Ninth Badr Corps commander and current commander of the southern axis based in Basra and Baghdad;
- Abu Hessam, the Ninth Badr Corps Counter-Intelligence commander of the southern axis, based in Basra;
- Abu Morteza Mashadi, the Ninth Badr Crops Personnel Directorate chief;
- Abuzar Khalesi, Mostafa Brigade commander in Diyala Province;
- Seyyed Abu Legha', the Ninth Badr Corps operations commander and current commander of Baghdad operations;
- Abu Zolfaqar, Imam Ali Division commander who was originally arrested by the US forces. After his release, he went to Iran to take part in these meetings;
- Abu Ahmad Badran, commander of the Heidar Karar Division;
- Abu Ahmad Rashed, commander of Hazrat Rassul Division;
- Abu Montazer Hussayni, commander of Imam Hussein Division;
- Abu Mojtaba Sari [Savari], commander of the Hezbollah movement in Al-Amara Province;
- Abu Jaafar Moussavi, deputy commander of Seyyed ol-Shohada movement, and three other commanders of this movement;
- Three commanders of the 15th of Sha'ban movement.

In the meeting it was decided that the Ninth Badr Corps be organized based on the Revolutionary Guards Corps Bassij format. Accordingly, the Ninth Badr forces will set up cells in mosques in their regions and begin to recruit young and new forces from all regions. In light of problems raised by the Badr Corps commanders, the Qods Force pledged to provide logistic support to it. Salaries for all Ninth Badr personnel were approved for two years and no personnel would be forced in to early retirement. The Revolutionary Guards and the Bassij pledged to share their experiences with the Ninth Badr Corps in a series of political briefings. Other issues discussed included problems with receiving wages from the Guards Corps, anti-US demonstrations, US attacks on the SCIRI and the Ninth Badr Corps headquarters and the arrest of a number of their leaders.

A week later, towards the end of May, officials of the SCIRI held a meeting in Tehran, attended by senior officials of the council. SCIRI leaders met senior regime officials on 20 and 30 May 2003. They included:

- Abu Islam Sa'di, Chief of SCIRI's Budget and Credits;
- Abu Ali Mowla, Executive Chairman of SCIRI and a top deputy to Mohammad Baqer Hakim;

- Two other SCIRI officials, who came through the Mehran border and went to Tehran from Ilam Province;
- Seyyed Mohsen Hakim, SCIRI spokesman and son of Abdul Aziz Hakim. He took part in several meetings with officials of the Iranian Armed Forces Command Headquarters and the Nasr Headquarters.

The continuing meddling of Tehran, several weeks after the disarming of the PMOI on 10 May 2003, again irritated US officials. On 28 May US administrator Paul Bremer complained of 'troubling' Iranian activity in Iraq and said it could result in serious problems if it went too far. Reuters quoted him as saying:

> We have seen a rather steady increase in Iranian activity here, which is troubling ... What you see at the most benign end of it is Iranian efforts to sort of repeat the formula which was used by Hizbollah in Lebanon. [That] is to send in people who are effectively guerrillas and have them get in the country and try to set up social services and decide that these social services are their ticket to popularity. And then they start to arm themselves and you wind up with a serious problem if you let it go too far.

Two weeks later, US National Security Adviser, Dr Condoleezza Rice, warned the Iranian regime 'not to meddle in the formation of new power structures in Iraq'. In a 12 June report from Los Angeles, Agence France Presse wrote:

> US national security adviser Condoleezza Rice took tough aim at Iran on Thursday, warning them to halt any illicit weapons programs. 'We cannot tolerate circumstances in which Iran, with a different vision of what Iraq ought to look like, tries to stir trouble in southern Iraq,' she told the Town Hall speakers' forum in Los Angeles. Rice also cautioned Tehran to crack down on any international terrorists and stop them from passing through Iran.
>
> We ... have to make very clear to the Iranian government that we cannot tolerate circumstances in which al-Qaeda operatives come in and out of Iran,' she said. She said the elected Iranian government had not managed to deliver on its promise of democracy and had instead allowed an unelected regime to 'frustrate the efforts of democracy'.
>
> 'We have to stand with the aspirations of the Iranian people which have been clearly expressed,' Rice said.

Rice's concerns were echoed by Bremer during a visit to Washington in June. He said Iranian meddling was 'not playing a helpful role in Iraq.

They are active there. They appear to be working against the interests of the Iraqi people, which is also against our interests.'[7]

Even in the south of Iraq, where the British had offered major concessions to Tehran to dissuade it from interfering in Iraq's internal affairs, the top British official in that country, John Sawers, voiced dismay over the mullahs' meddling. The *Guardian* wrote on 3 June:

> Britain's most senior official in Baghdad warned yesterday that Iran was still giving 'unwelcome' support to fundamentalist Shia groups in Iraq.
>
> John Sawers, the prime minister's special envoy to Baghdad, accused Iran of backing religious militias vying for power in post-war Iraq. 'We have seen signs of and attempts to exercise undue and unwelcome influence in support of fundamentalist groupings,' he said in an interview.
>
> He said Iran was still supporting the Badr corps, the armed unit of the powerful Supreme Council for Islamic Revolution in Iraq. The Party, and much of the Badr corps, spent most of Saddam Hussein's reign in exile in Tehran. It has been ordered, like other political militias, to disarm.
>
> 'There is traffic across the border of people and goods which at the moment is very difficult to keep track of,' Mr. Sawers said. 'But it's clearly not done with purely humanitarian intent.' Although there were some extremist Shia clerics in Iraq, few Iraqis supported an Iranian-style theocracy. 'It's not in anybody's interest in this country,' he said.

The independent Inter Press Service reported on 4 July that Tehran had offered US$200 to 300 to young Iraqi clerics to go on six- to nine-month missions to Iraq and promote its policies:

> Iran has officially denied U.S. allegations that it is meddling in Iraq's internal affairs. But a visit earlier in June to the Iran–Iraq border post near Khaneqin indicated otherwise. Ali Behbehani, an Iraqi Shiite who fled with his family to Iran in the 1980s and returned to Iraq last month, said religious leaders in Iran's holy city Qom were offering Iraqi religious students money to return home and preach Islam.
>
> 'The program was started a month ago by the International Centre for Islamic Studies,' he said. 'They have offered 200 to 300 dollars to Iraqis who volunteer to return to their city of origin and preach Islam for a period of six to nine weeks. After that we can either return to Qom or continue to live in Iraq and earn our living.'
>
> Behbehani said the Qom centre is home to about 500 Iraqi students and about 2,000 international pupils from Afghanistan, Pakistan, India, Europe, and the United States. It is not clear whether the Qom centre has similar return programs for other countries.

Notes

1. Mark Mueller, 'Iraqi Christians Fear Rise of Shiite Fundamentalism', *Charlotte Observer*, 19 May 2003.

2. Farid Zakaria, 'How to Make Friends in Iran', *Newsweek*, 23 June 2003.

3. Farid Zakaria, 'How to Make Peace', *Newsweek*, 21 April 2003.

4. 1Up Info – Iraq – Impact of the Iranian Revolution on Iraqi Shias/Iraqi Information Resource.

5. 'Iraq: U.S. Regime Change Efforts and Post-War Governance', updated 4 August 2003, Congressional Research Service, Order Code RL31339.

6. Hashemi Rafsanjani, IRNA, 18 August 2003.

7. Paul Bremer, *Washington Times*, 24 June 2003.

9 | An anti-fundamentalist front

> We must unite with the Iranian Mojahedin and support their
> democratic stance against fundamentalism. *Declaration of Iraqi
> tribal chiefs*

Of all the rallies and demonstrations in some twenty cities worldwide in
June 2003 to protest against the detention of the Resistance's President-
elect Maryam Rajavi and more than 160 Iranian refugees in France, the
rally by 20,000 Iraqis at the PMOI's Camp Ashraf, 100 km north east of
Baghdad, was the biggest surprise. In a report on the event, in which
Iraqi Shiites, Sunnis and Kurds all took part, the French News Agency
wrote: 'Thousands of men and women fighters paraded in the largest
camp, some 100 kilometres (65 miles) north of Baghdad, 700 of them
each carrying a picture of one of the group's "martyrs", as they called
for the release of one of their top leaders from French custody. They
were joined by several thousand members of tribes from three provinces
to commemorate June 20, 1981.'[1] AFP added,

> On Thursday their allies among the tribesmen joined them in calling
> for the release of Maryam Rajavi, the wife of the commander of the
> Mujahedeen's military wing, from French custody.[2] 'We have lived with
> the Mujahedeen for 20 years, and they are like friends and brothers,'
> said Matalk Hamad of the Juburi tribe. 'They are not terrorists and we
> ask the United Nations to intervene to have the detainees freed by the
> French government, and particularly Mrs. Rajavi.' He was backed by
> Adnan Maimed of the Somaidai, Abdullah Ibrahim of Al-Janabi, and
> other speakers, who later issued a joint statement condemning the
> French police action.[3]

Tribal and clan leaders in Diyala Province issued a resolution and
declared their complete support for the People's Mojahedin and the
Iranian Resistance. Signed by fifty tribal leaders and elders on behalf of
the participants in the rally, the resolution read in part,

> We the leaders and the 'Sheikhs' of tribes residing in Diyala province
> who have participated in the festivities marking the anniversary of the
> Prophet Muhammad (may peace be upon him) hereby express our
> thanks and respect for the PMOI in Iraq for having held such a felici-

tous occasion. Expressing our sincere feelings towards this organization which is a freedom-loving, humanistic and Islamic organization with no ties whatsoever to fundamentalism or terrorism, we confirm that what has been said in satellite TV programmes about this organization to be a terrorist organization is not true, as we have not witnessed any wrongdoing on their part nor even heard of one, and have further noticed no misdemeanour or maltreatment on their part towards anybody. The reality is that they have a clear goal. This is an independent organization looking forward to free Iran from the clutches of the ruling mullahs' regime, the same mullahs who have never grasped any sense of Islam. So we hereby announce it for the whole world to know that this organization deserves to be backed in order to materialize a new world order far from the terrorist or religious fundamentalist trend.

In a report from Camp Ashraf, France's state-owned television channel FR3 reported on 1 July,

This morning, Diyala Province's tribal leaders came to declare their support for the Mojahedin. Of course, they know the Mojahedin well because their army has been based in their country for seventeen years. One tribal leader says, 'Mojahedin have been with us for seventeen years. They are fighting for their goals but have not harassed anybody. For this reason, they are closer to us as ever before. They are part of our family, they are our brothers.'

A Baghdad rally against fundamentalism

A large meeting was organized in Baghdad by the Iranian Resistance on 21 July 2003, to commemorate the twenty-second anniversary of the founding of the National Council of Resistance of Iran. Many Iraqi parties and dignitaries took part in the 22 July meeting to declare their support for the Iranian Resistance. The attendance far exceeded the organizers' expectations and the meeting turned into a rally against a common enemy, Islamic fundamentalism, as one by one Iraqis from all sectors of society took the podium to express their solidarity with the Iranian people and their resistance movement against the fundamentalist regime in Iran.

Representatives of a number of parties and political groups in Iraq, political, social and cultural dignitaries, scientists, as well as the sheikhs and leaders of various tribes across Iraq condemned the Iranian regime's meddling in Iraq and declared their support for the Mojahedin. They included representatives from the Iraqi National Accord, Iraqi National Coalition Party, the Constitutional Monarchist Movement and the

Assyrian National Party. Dr Khalid Mirza, head of Baghdad's City Council, and Professor Tariq Jaburi, Baghdad's senior judge, were among the distinguished political dignitaries who addressed the meeting. Leading sheikhs from the tribes of Baghdad, Diyala and Anbar provinces, as well as physicians and professors of the University of Baghdad, a number of Shiite and Sunni clerics, religious figures and Christian priests also attended the meeting.

Dr Mirza said,

I am utterly surprised why the Mojahedin have been labelled terrorist. On the contrary, I have seen them as a force dedicated to democracy and freedom. They are open to dialogue. In one word, they are patriots seeking the interests of their own country, good neighbourly relations and fraternal relations with Iraq. Some time ago, Mrs Maryam Rajavi and a large number of the Resistance's activists were arrested in France in a very surprising manner and without any legal justification. We condemn the behaviour of the government of France. The Mojahedin enjoy respect and admiration in public opinion. I wish success for all of them and I hope that their hopes and aspirations for democracy and freedom are realized.

A distinguished Iraqi physician, Dr S. Sabooh, told the participants:

The Mojahedin believe deeply in their goal. With the highest degree of determination and selflessness, they have sacrificed all their personal interests. They live only for their country. Some of them were very well off, but gave that up. Some others had the best jobs and best educational degrees from the world's top universities. However, they have given those up, as well.

In another part of her speech, Dr Sabooh said,

When you talk about the Mojahedin, you should include the issue of women. Women have been oppressed, sometimes under the name of religion and other times under the name of traditions. Women are described as the source of sin, who should be hidden from the public's eyes. This is a catastrophe. The Mojahedin responded to this problem. They endeavoured so much to emancipate women and break their chains. They chose a woman, Maryam Rajavi, as their political symbol. Her biography represents an ideal example of the role of women in Iran's nationalist movement. For millions of Iranians, she is the source of hope for realization of democracy and human rights in their country.

Dr Sarmad Khondeh and Dr Hassan Samir, two prominent specialists and professors at the University of Baghdad, were among the speakers at the meeting. Sheikh Imad, a distinguished Iraqi cleric, condemned the mullahs' tyranny in the name of Islam in Iran. Sheikh Tariq Jaburi, the senior judge of Baghdad, called for the removal of the Mojahedin from the list of terrorist organizations. He said this measure only makes the mullahs happy. Sheikh Barakat, leader of the Zobaa Tribe in Abu-Ghraib, west of Baghdad, celebrated the founding anniversary of the National Council of Resistance of Iran and prayed for the victory of the Iranian Resistance over the clerical regime in Iran. Mr Abbas Davari, a senior PMOI official, expressed gratitude for the extensive support and solidarity of Iraqi political, social and religious forces for the PMOI. He said that the Iranian regime's meddling in Iraq continues regardless of who governs the country. Tehran is interested only in establishing a satellite Islamic Republic in the country.

A failed ploy

No one is more keenly aware of the impact of the Iranian Resistance's presence in Iraq on both Iranian and Iraqi societies than the ayatollahs who rule Iran. Their frantic efforts to remove this presence through political or military means, which have intensified significantly since the fall of the Baathist regime, clearly show the mullahs' deep-seated fear of the PMOI's presence in Iraq. The removal of the Mojahedin, as a democratic, Muslim organization, from Iraq would serve a short- and a long-term purpose for the clerical rulers of Iran. In the short run, it will relieve the clerical regime of a major threat lying in the wings on its border, at a time when the theocratic state finds itself increasingly entangled in a tightening web of crises. In a more strategic sense, the mullahs would rid themselves of a serious obstacle to their plans for the export of Islamic fundamentalism and extremism to Iraq and beyond, as the PMOI, with its tolerant and democratic interpretation of Islam, represents a genuine and viable counterweight to the ominous phenomenon of fundamentalism.

With Iraq increasingly mired in uncertainty, the clerical regime continues to exploit the situation to expand its influence, pressing the Coalition for more action against the PMOI and, at the same time, paving the way for direct attacks by the Revolutionary Guards and MOIS agents on Iranian dissidents in Iraq. The Iranian regime even tried to use the bombing that killed Mohammad Baqer al Hakim and dozens of his followers in the city of Najaf on 29 August 2003, to whip up the sentiments of ordinary Iraqi Shiites against the Mojahedin by pointing its fingers at the PMOI, even though the accusation only met with ridicule on the part of Iraqis. The state-owned daily, *Tehran Times*, wrote on 1 September:

> An Iraqi analyst said traces of Mossad agents were found at the Najaf blast site where Ayatollah Seyed Mohammad Baqer al Hakim, the leader of the Supreme Assembly for the Islamic Revolution in Iraq (SAIRI), and more than eighty others were martyred on Friday ... According to some reports ... members of the terrorist Mojahedin-e Khalq organization (MeK) have helped Zionist operatives in this mission.

The Ministry of Intelligence and Security (MOIS) has been particularly active since the end of the war to turn the Iraqi people against the PMOI. The plan was to incite the Iraqi people to voice opposition to the presence of the PMOI in that country and thus make it politically impossible for the organization to remain in Iraq. This would have also helped Tehran to isolate the PMOI and portray it as an enemy of Iraq to justify military and terrorist attacks on the organization. To this end, the mullahs' operatives offered considerable sums of money to some tribes along the border and elsewhere in Iraq to use their services against the PMOI. The efforts failed because the tribes refused to be drawn in, forcing the regime to carry out its terrorist operations under the name of the so-called 'Iraqi Kurdish fighters' or 'Iraqi Muslim fighters'. It is common knowledge that these were pseudonyms for the Iranian regime's operatives.

In May 2003, Tehran dispatched a commander of the Ninth Badr Corps, Abu-Zeinab Khalesi, to organize anti-Mojahedin demonstrations in the town of Al-Khalis, near PMOI's Camp Ashraf. It also sent Sheikh Mohammad Al-Allaq to Baghdad. Iraqis and local tribesmen stayed away from these showcase demonstrations. Having arrived in Baghdad from the Iranian city of Qom a week earlier, Mullah Al-Allaq staged a protest demonstration on 27 April 2003 against the Mojahedin outside the Palestine Hotel in Baghdad, where US forces had their headquarters. The several dozen protesters demanded that the PMOI be expelled from Iraq. The regime had planned to attract several thousand Iraqis to the demonstration, but the effort failed miserably. The Arab satellite TV Al-Jazeera reported that only scores of Iraqis took part in the rally.

At the same time, Intelligence Minister Ali Younessi told a press conference in Orumieh, north-west Iran,

> If it was possible for terrorist grouplets to escape to Iraq previously, today they can no longer do so, given the recent developments in Iraq. In light of the Monafeqin's record in collaboration with Saddam in

killing the Kurds and the Shiites, the people of Iraq would no longer tolerate this group on their soil. Iraq would, therefore, not be safe for the Monafeqin.[4]

Three days later, Al-Jazeera television reported a false story, given to it by Tehran's operatives, which said that an Iraqi civilian had been killed and several more wounded in Diyala Province by the PMOI. It also quoted some people in the province as demanding that the organization leave Iraq. Reacting to this false report, twenty tribal leaders in Diyala Province signed a letter that read:

> We, the sheikhs of Diyala tribesmen, deny the contents of the statement broadcast on Al-Jazeera television on Wednesday, 30 April 2003. We have never signed this statement, which is essentially false. We say that this organization has been active in Iraq for twenty years and its objectives have been clear to everyone. We do not want this organization expelled from Iraq because Iraq is its home. No one can expel the owner of the house from his house. We know our friends ... The Mojahedin organization is not after taking advantage of the situation.

In another show of solidarity with the Iranian Resistance by Iraqi tribesmen and people, particularly in Diyala Province – which borders Iran and where the PMOI has stayed for seventeen years – three major tribal leaders, Sheikh Ibrahim Taha Fiehan, head of the Al-Hamed tribe; Sheikh Faisal Houm Al Alivi, head of the Al-Neda tribe; and Sheikh Sa'dun Awad As-Soltan, head of the Jordiani tribe, wrote an open letter, dated 23 May 2003:

> We the undersigned testify sincerely that [members of] the People's Mojahedin are freedom-seeking and democratic intellectuals who respect human rights, women and children's rights. Their slogan is fighting for the realization of freedom and democracy and the abandonment of divisiveness, sectarianism, racism and fundamentalism. Since the presence of the organization in Iraq, it has not perpetrated any offence against anyone. On the contrary, it has contributed to law and order in Iraq. It has taken part in all religious ceremonies and respects Islam and Muslims, Arabs, Kurds and Turkmens. It even respects non-Muslim religions. It is opposed to all forms of terrorism. We must unite with it and support its humanitarian and democratic positions. We pray for security and humanity.

Twenty leaders of the powerful Al-Azzah tribe in Diyala Province also wrote a letter voicing support for the PMOI:

We, the leaders and elders of Al-Azzah tribe in the Azim dam region testify that the members of the People's Mojahedin are cultured people who have freedom-seeking and democratic ideals that herald freedom, democracy and human rights. We also testify that the Mojahedin's slogan is to fight for the realization of freedom and democracy and the negation of divisiveness, tribalism, racism and religious fundamentalism. This explains the need for the Mojahedin's presence in Iraq. So far, the Mojahedin has not committed any crimes against its friends and participated in providing security. It has also taken part in all religious ceremonies against the interference of the clerical regime. It respects Islam, Muslims, Kurds, Arabs, Turkmen and other ethnic groups. The Mojahedin has always acted against terrorism in all its forms. We ask God almighty for the success of the Mojahedin in safeguarding the security and honour of all human beings.

United against a common enemy

Deep bonds of friendship between the PMOI and a large cross-section of Iraqi society are based on the trust that has developed during the Iranian Resistance's seventeen-year presence in Iraq. Many Iraqis have first-hand and personal experience of dealing with the Mojahedin and have seen the movement's adherence to its principles and beliefs, as well as its honest approach to Iraqis in its daily contacts with the people.

The Iraqi people's extensive support for the PMOI after the fall of the former regime made it abundantly clear that the Iranian regime's propaganda against the PMOI, portraying the organization as the enemy of the Iraqi people, failed miserably.

If the PMOI had in fact engaged in any action against the people of Iraq, whether Arabs, Kurds, Shiites or Sunnis, they could not have stayed in Iraq after the fall of the regime. They might even have been forced to leave Iraq due to retaliatory attacks by the population had the organization been involved in Iraq's internal affairs or taken part in the suppression of the populace. This would have been particularly the case after 10 May 2003, when all the weapons of the PMOI and the National Liberation Army of Iran were consolidated under the monitoring of US forces, rendering them completely unarmed.

Today, history has totally discredited the clerical regime's false claims concerning the PMOI presence in Iraq. In a message on Voice of Mojahed radio, on 22 April 2003, the Iranian Resistance's Leader Massoud Rajavi reiterated the policy of the PMOI and the Iranian Resistance concerning Iraq's internal affairs:

We have said and repeat that we have not interfered in Iraq's internal affairs. The only concern of ours has been, is and will be the illegitimate, suppressive regime ruling our homeland, Iran. Thus, we have never had, nor do we have any enmity or hostility towards any group, whether Shiite, Sunni, Kurd or Arab in Iraq. Indeed, we welcome any understanding and friendship.

The Iraqi people saw for themselves that after Iraqi forces withdrew from Iranian territory in 1982, the PMOI worked relentlessly to bring peace between the two countries. While shedding crocodile tears for the Iraqi people, Khomeini and his aides continued the war pointlessly for seven more years, using human wave attacks and the slogan of 'liberate Qods (Jerusalem) via Karbala'. Their refusal to agree to peace meant that millions of young Iranians and Iraqis were sent to the inferno of war. Even after the cease-fire, virtually every Iraqi family had a relative held as a prisoner of war in Iran. For fifteen years after the hostilities, the clerical regime held thousands of Iraqi prisoners of war as hostages. Iraqi families were told of the torture and mistreatment of their loved ones by the Revolutionary Guards when Iraqi POWs returned from POW camps in Iran.

While it was impossible under the former regime for Iraqi parties and groups openly to express support or issue statements in solidarity with the PMOI, as has been possible in recent months, the vast support of the Iraqi people demonstrated itself in other forms. Iraqis living near PMOI bases and centres vigilantly informed the organization of suspicious movements by terrorists and agents dispatched by Tehran to carry out terrorist assaults on the PMOI. They also played an important role in uncovering and thwarting the mullahs' terrorist plots against the PMOI in Iraq.

Iraqis, including many Shiites, who have consistently resisted efforts by Khomeini and his clique to woo them, saw in the PMOI a phenomenon diametrically opposed to Khomeinism. The Mojahedin were Shiites, but unlike Khomeini, they viewed 'export of revolution' as contradictory to the true teachings of Islam and as a reactionary ploy to overshadow the Khomeini regime's domestic crises. The PMOI condemned the clerical regime's efforts to establish an Ottoman-style Islamic caliphate. It also denounced the continuation of the Iran–Iraq war and the use of human wave tactics. It, therefore, played an active role in breaking Khomeini's war-mongering spell. For millions of Iraqis, including Shiites, who every day received the bodies of their loved ones from the battle fronts, the PMOI's message of peace offered the hope of soothing the historic strife and bloodshed between the two nations, imposed on the two neighbours for centuries under the banner of 'Arabs versus Persians' and 'Shiites versus Sunnis'.

Moreover, the people of Iraq learned about the situation in Iran through the PMOI's Simay-e Moghavemat (Vision of the Resistance) television programme, also received in Iraq. They learned about the execution of 120,000 Mojahedin, who were Muslim and Shiites, the torture and execution of pregnant women, girls in their teens and mothers in their seventies, the massacre of 30,000 political prisoners in 1988 upon Khomeini's fatwa, and forty-nine UN censure resolutions against the regime for its gross human rights abuses.

In the Islamic world today, the international situation and the relative economic and social backwardness of Muslim communities have created a suitable setting for the rise of fundamentalism and for those who promote the clash of civilizations and religions. In these circumstances, no stronger antidote against so-called Islamic fundamentalism could be found than depicting the real horror of the ayatollahs' rule in Iran. The former regime in Iraq was fully cognizant of this fact and of the impact of the PMOI presence in Iraq as a bulwark against fundamentalism and 'Islamic revolution', which the clerics were trying to export to Iraq. They believed that the mere presence of an anti-fundamentalist force in Iraq informed and, at the same time, immunized, particularly younger Iraqis from this phenomenon. Many foreign observers would ask how Saddam Hussein's government could accept the complete independence of the PMOI in Iraq. The answer lies in the organization's anti-fundamentalist role. This reality has nothing to do with the nature and the identity of a government in power in Iraq. So long as the clerical regime remains in power in Iran, Iraq will remain the chief target for its export of fundamentalism.

An anti-fundamentalist front

It would not be difficult to recognize that so long as the clerical dictatorship rules in Iran, it will not allow a secular democracy to take shape in Iraq. This realization has led a growing number of Iraqis to feel the need to express their support for the anti-fundamentalist PMOI as a safeguard for their own society's future. What seems to have developed in a de facto fashion in Iraq is the seeds of a united anti-fundamentalist front, consisting of political, social and popular forces in Iran. Like their fellow Iranians and a large part of the Islamic world, Iraqis reject fundamentalism and retrogression. This is the basis of the message of solidarity and support from Iraqi political parties, personalities, intellectuals and experts for the Iranian Resistance. Today, anti-fundamentalist girls and women in Iraq use every opportunity to demonstrate their support for the PMOI. When the news of the freedom of the Iranian Resistance's leader Mrs Maryam Rajavi was made public, many Iraqi citizens went to the PMOI office in Baghdad to offer their congratulations. The reason was that nowhere do the people have a day-to-day, concrete understanding of fundamentalism as clear-eyed as it is in Iraq and Iran. Thus, for a common problem, they search and find a common cure. Iraqi intellectuals, drawing on their knowledge of the clerics' quarter-century rule next door, know full well that the coming to power of fundamentalists in Iraq would have disastrous consequences for science, civilization, progress and knowledge in Iraq. Iraqi women recognize that if they have to change their conduct and clothing out of fear of fundamentalist gangs today, if the fundamentalists were to rule in Iraq, the punishment for 'mal-veiling' would be flogging in public and that their social standing would plummet to that of second-class citizens.

Notes

1. 20 June 1981 marks the day when Islamic Revolutionary Guards opened fire on a 500,000-strong peaceful demonstration in Tehran organized by the PMOI. It is honoured every year as the national day of the resistance movement.

2. On 17 June 2003, Maryam Rajavi and more than 160 members and supporters of the Iranian Resistance were arrested by the French police. Most of them were released the same day, and Mrs Rajavi was released on 3 July by the Paris Appeals Court. The arrests were widely condemned by French political parties and human rights organizations.

3. AFP, 20 June 2003.

4. Ali Younessi, *Hamshahri* daily, Tehran, 11 May 2003.

10 | Iraqi Kurds and Iran

> We have not come across any evidence to suggest that the Mujahedin [PMOI] have exercised any hostility towards the people of Iraqi Kurdistan. *Statement by senior Iraqi Kurdish official*

Iraqi Kurdistan has been the scene of regional rivalry between at least four countries for almost half a century. It is not surprising, therefore, to find the long arm of the Iranian intelligence extending deep into this strife-ridden territory. The clerical regime had an extensive presence in this region during the Iran–Iraq war and particularly after the 1991 Persian Gulf War. It has used not only its economic and political leverage to spread its influence – given the long borders with Iraqi Kurdistan – but has also set up many headquarters and centres for Revolutionary Guards and Intelligence Ministry agents throughout Kurdistan. In the turbulent Iraq of the 1990s, Tehran took maximum advantage of the circumstance and garnered the co-operation of some indigenous forces, especially the PUK. Two Middle East experts, Hans-Heino Kopietz and Karen Dubrowska, wrote in an article in 1996:

> Ever since Jalal Talebani's PUK recaptured the town of Sulaimaniya on October 11, it has denied collaboration with Iran. But Barzani's KDP has circulated throughout Europe and North America a number of compromising letters allegedly written by Talebani, including one to the head of Iran's Revolutionary Guard Corps Intelligence Service and another to the Iranian foreign minister. The KDP claims the secret documents were seized on September 1 at Talebani's headquarters in Arbil, the capital of Kurdistan. The KDP also circulated a report it claims was written by the PUK on co-operation between the Zanyari Service (PUK intelligence) and the Iranian Information (intelligence) Ministry, and a report on co-operation with the Tehran-based Iraqi Islamic opposition umbrella organisation SCIRI (Supreme Council of the Islamic Revolution in Iraq).
>
> Iraqi opposition parties and personalities in London are embarrassed by the disclosure of the correspondence but few doubt that the documents are genuine ... In the letter allegedly written to Iran's foreign minister, Dr Ali Akbar Velayati, in the first week of August, Talebani states that there is a tripartite conspiracy 'composed of Saddam, Barzani

and Turkey, aimed at destroying the democratic experiment in Iraqi Kurdistan in general and the PUK in particular. This conspiracy has been sharpened after the clear co-operation between the PUK and the Islamic Republic (of Iran) after the latest operation' (i.e. the Iranian incursion into northern Iraq on July 26–29) ...

In a letter dated September 28 to one of his senior deputies, Talebani describes an agreement between SCIRI and the PUK. He emphasises that through this agreement the PUK has appeased Iran. 'By satisfying the Islamic Republic they will co-operate with PUK and SCIRI for bringing down the Baghdad regime and restructuring the future of Iraq according to our agreement with SCIRI which includes self-determination for the Kurds within the framework of Iraq.' Talebani then claims Iran regards the PUK and SCIRI as 'the locomotive for liberating Iraq ... that is we, the three of us (PUK, SCIRI and Iran) will carry out the main work'.

In an unsigned report describing co-operation between the PUK and Iranian intelligence (MOIS), it is stated that MOIS established a station in Sulaimaniya headed by a Mr Panahi. The PUK ostensibly exchanged intelligence on the Iraqi regime's apparatus, the Baath party, the Iraqi army and parties and groups within Kurdistan, and the Iraqi opposition. Most of the report is taken up with examples of PUK co-operation on Iranian border security which is focused on preventing members of Iranian opposition groups (and specifically the KDP of Iran) from approaching the Iran–Iraq border under the control of the PUK. On December 3 last year, for instance, an eight-man armed KDPI group was arrested near Penjwin. Their arms and belongings were confiscated and they were held in prison.

In a letter to Sardar Mohammad Jaafari, the head of the Iranian Revolutionary Guard Intelligence Service, Talebani allegedly accuses the KDP and the KDPI of taking part in anti-Iranian demonstrations in front of the White House and the Iranian embassy in London. He asks for military assistance, including weapons, ammunition and logistical and financial help, the opening of the border and a supply of weapons, ammunition, clothes and shoes for the PUK peshmerga fighters. The captured documents also include a two-page letter, allegedly in Talebani's hand-writing, dated August 14, 1996 to two of his close associates, named as Kosrat and Jebbar, giving details of PUK military planning with Iran to attack the KDP and violate a year-long ceasefire brokered by the US at Dublin ... Iraqi opposition sources pointed out that Talebani made an agreement to co-operate with SCIRI as early as October 1994 when Iran increased the presence of its intelligence services in northern Iraq.[1]

Massoud Barzani's KDP, despite the good relations it has tried to maintain with the clerical regime over the years, has at times been left with no choice but to take a public position against the theocratic state. A statement on 17 March 1998 by the spokesman for the KDP's politburo explicitly referred to the terrorist activities of the Intelligence Ministry in Iraqi Kurdistan. Rejecting the Iranian regime's accusation of espionage against several KDP members, the statement noted:

> In recent days several Iranian newspapers claimed that the KDP members recently arrested by the Iranian authorities were spies working for Israel and Turkey. The KDP strongly denies these unfounded allegations against members of our party who have dedicated all their lives to the struggle for the just cause of the Kurdish people. The detainees were refugees residing in Iran since the 1970s and 1980s. Their activities among Iraqi Kurdish refugees were overt and agreed to by the Iranian authorities. It seems that these unfounded allegations were made by the Iranian intelligence services to justify its murder of the KDP official Tahsin Argushi and the continued detention of others. It also comes in response to the strong protests shown inside and outside Kurdistan, especially by UN organisations, against the continued detention of the KDP members in Iran. The real reason behind these arrests is that we in the KDP did not give the Iranian Intelligence organisation the freedom it demanded to commit acts of terror and assassinations inside Iraqi Kurdistan.

In a report on the Iranian regime's influence on Iraqi opposition groups prior to the ousting of the Baathist regime, the *Middle East Intelligence Bulletin* wrote:

> The Kurdish factions in the north are also influenced by Iran. The PUK has always maintained excellent relations with the Islamic Republic and has even offered assistance with security and intelligence. Furthermore the PUK has not had any aversion to enabling Iran to launch military strikes into Iraqi Kurdistan. The last major offensive of this type occurred in July 1996 when Iran targeted the KDPI in PUK-controlled territories of Iraqi Kurdistan. The KDP has traditionally been more wary of Iranian influence. The Barzanis enjoyed good relations with the Shah, but their relations with the Islamic Republic have been strained. However, the KDP no longer shelters the Democratic Party of Iranian Kurdistan (DPIK) and largely severed its links to it after the assassination of DPIK leader Sadegh Sharafkandi in Berlin in 1992.[2]

Psy-ops against PMOI

In the aftermath of the 1991 Persian Gulf War, the clerical regime launched an extensive propaganda campaign against the PMOI's alleged role in the suppression of Iraqi Kurds. The propaganda blitz pursued particular objectives: it overshadowed Tehran's sending of tens of thousands of troops into Iraq in March and April 1991 to destroy PMOI bases. It also gave the impression that the mullahs supported the Kurdish cause. The ruling ayatollahs' passionate defence of Iraqi Kurds looked somewhat suspicious, considering the fact that ever since the first weeks of coming to power in 1979, they had been implementing a policy of suppression and ethnic cleansing of Iranian Kurds. In fact, one of the Iranian regime's top military commanders, General Ali Sayyad Shirazi, was notoriously known as the 'Butcher of Kurdistan' for his violent, genocidal offensives against Kurdish villages and towns in Iran.

In the immediate wake of the 1991 Persian Gulf War, however, Iran's clerical rulers had a different agenda. They wanted to extend their influence in Iraqi Kurdistan as much as possible, first in order to prevent it from becoming a launching pad for activities against the Islamic Republic, and second to use it as a card in the high-stake game over Iraq's destiny. Tehran also attempted to enlist Iraqi Kurds to its side in the confrontation against the PMOI and the Iranian Resistance.

PMOI detractors made extensive use of false allegations by MOIS that the Iranian Resistance was involved in the suppression of Iraqi Kurds. For their part, many of the Kurds flatly rejected these charges. In a report from Washington about the allegations, Reuters wrote, 'Reuters separately obtained a copy of a 1999 legal document signed by a senior official of a major Iraqi Kurdish group that said there was no evidence the Mujahideen took part in the Iraqi government's 1991 campaign against the Kurds.' Reuters quoted the document, proffered as evidence to a court in the Netherlands, as saying, '(We) can confirm that the Mujahedin [sic] were not involved in suppressing the Kurdish people neither during the uprising nor in its aftermath. We have not come across any evidence to suggest that the Mujahedin have exercised any hostility towards the people of Iraqi Kurdistan.'[3]

In the US-led war in Iraq in 2003, the clerical regime repeated similar allegations, including that attributing the presence of the PMOI in Iraqi Kurdistan to a plan to confront Iraqi Kurds or to 'patrol Kirkuk's oil wells'. In a press conference in Arbil on 23 March Hoshyar Zibari, a member of the Politburo and the foreign affairs chief of the Kurdish Democratic Party (KDP), who later became the interim foreign minister of Iraq, denied that the PMOI had any presence in Iraqi Kurdistan.

Developments since the war and the fall of the Iraqi regime proved the allegations false. Despite Tehran's efforts, Kurdish parties and people in Iraq have had no clashes with the PMOI and have lived side by side in harmony and peace.

The same holds true for the Shiites in southern Iraq. Despite Tehran's propaganda, designed to provoke the Shiites against the PMOI, once the war ended, it became obvious that the PMOI had never taken any actions against Iraqi Shiites. On the contrary, it enjoys credibility and popularity among a large sector of Iraqi Shiites who detest Tehran's meddling in the internal affairs of their country. Iraq's independent opposition, part of the transitional administration, has also acknowledged this reality. When published abroad as the most credible Iraqi opposition, the daily *Az-Zaman*, whose editor in chief, the distinguished Iraqi intellectual Sa'ad Al-Bazzaz is a member of Iraq's governing council, wrote:

> Independent sources described allegations against People's Mojahedin members that they would be part of the paramilitary forces that Iraqi President Saddam Hussein will use in a probable war as leaked by Iran's intelligence service and inaccurate. They added that relying on and promoting these leaked remarks distort the reality. Iranian intelligence service is used to leak such information through its Iraqi surrogates. They advised against mixing Iraqi affairs with other conflicts in the region.[4]

PMOI and the Kurdish question

With the start of PMOI's open political activities after the fall of the Shah, the organization stressed the rights of ethnic minorities, particularly the autonomy of Iranian Kurdistan. In autumn 1980, on the eve of the first presidential election, the PMOI nominated Massoud Rajavi as its candidate. He quickly garnered the support of the democratic opposition to Khomeini and emerged as the 'alternative candidate'. All Kurdish parties, political and social forces endorsed his candidacy. Two decades later, the clerical regime still considers the PMOI's support for the legitimate demands of Iranian Kurds as 'treason'. It tried very hard to arouse the chauvinistic sentiments of Iranians against the PMOI.

On 8 November 1983, the NCRI unanimously adopted the plan for the autonomy of Iranian Kurdistan. The party's Secretary General Abdol Rahman Qassemlou described the plan as 'the most advanced autonomy plan relative to similar plans around the world'. In the same way that it respected the autonomy of Iranian Kurds within Iran's territorial integrity, the PMOI supported recognition of the rights of Kurds in Iraq. Iraqi Kurdish parties and personalities welcomed that position. Head of the Patriotic Union of Iraqi Kurdistan, Jalal Talebani, for example, wrote a letter to Massoud Rajavi on 2 March 1984:

Honourable and dear brother Massoud Rajavi, on behalf of the Patriotic Union of Iraqi Kurdistan (PUK) politburo, I would like to express my greetings and very best wishes to you and other Mojahedin brothers in your just struggle against the reactionary gang of zealots who rule Iran ... We are therefore always ready to strengthen our good relationship with the People's Mojahedin Organization of Iran.

Regrettably, in time, bowing to pressure by the clerical regime and to secure its support, Jalal Talebani changed his stance and the PUK went so far as to launch armed attacks against the PMOI and Iranian dissidents. Dozens of PMOI members were killed.

The NLA's Counter-Intelligence Directorate issued a detailed report in July 2002 on an extensive MOIS scheme to infiltrate the ranks of the army. Under the heading 'What is Happening in Sulaimaniya', the report also exposed parts of the activities against the PMOI in Sulaimaniya, where the MOIS has set up a permanent headquarters. The report contains the text of interrogations of two persons, Farhang Esma'eelzadeh and Massoud Nasser Assefian, by PUK intelligence officers. The interrogators focus almost exclusively on information about the PMOI, which indicates that the intelligence service's task is to engage in constant intelligence gathering about the PMOI and the Iranian Resistance.[5]

Despite all these acts by the PUK, the PMOI never reciprocated and focused its attention on its only enemy, the religious dictatorship in Iran.

Massoud Barzani's Kurdish Democratic Party of Iraq has maintained close relations with the Khomeini regime since the first days of its rule. Barzani's group had bases inside Iran, but it did not collaborate with the Khomeini regime against the Mojahedin and never challenged them. Despite encounters in the border region, both in Iran and in Iraq, Barzani's forces and the Mojahedin combatants never opened fire on one another and maintained an amicable relationship.

During its stay in Iraq, the PMOI has repeatedly demonstrated its goodwill to Iraqi Kurds. During the Persian Gulf War, the PMOI and NLA evacuated all of their bases in the Kurdish areas in the north of Iraq. The move reduced the possibility of being caught up in the hostilities. Once the war ended, the PMOI sent of a number of messages in early March through the Kurdistan Democratic Party of Iran – Revolutionary Leadership, to the leaders of the Iraqi Kurds, explaining the regime's designs on the Iranian Resistance. The PMOI stressed that it did not seek to engage the Iraqi Kurds unless attacked. It reiterated that the Resistance's sole aim was to topple the mullahs' regime, which explained its presence in the central region of the Iran–Iraq border, the Iranian Resistance's only passage into Iran. It also specified that they had evacuated all their bases in other regions, including Iraqi Kurdistan.

As defectors from the MOIS have testified, the propaganda campaign concerning 'the suppression of the Kurds' was one of the ministry's top priorities. In an affidavit to the United States Court of Appeals for the District of Columbia in 2001, one such defector, Jamshid Tafrishi, wrote:

> My mission was to tell international organizations and foreign governments that the PMOI crushed the Kurdish uprising in Iraq. The plot was conducted under the supervision of Nasser Khajenoori, the regime's agent in the USA. He arranged for me and other agents to be interviewed by an Iranian radio broadcast in Los Angeles so we could air our stories on how the PMOI had oppressed the Kurdish people alongside Iraqi forces. Khajenoori further prepared a written brief on the subject on my behalf and sent it to the US intelligence and government agencies and the United Nations.[6]

A non-governmental organization with consultative status with the United Nations, the International Educational Development, launched an extensive investigation about these allegations. It published the results on 22 August 1995 as a United Nations official document. It said:

> We have been distressed because of certain misrepresentations of events in the area, in particular allegations made that the NLA has collaborated with the armed forces of the Government of Iraq, *inter alia* by participation in attacks against Kurdish people in Kirkuk, Qara Hanjeer, Kifri and Altun Kopir in April 1991 ...
>
> From our independent investigation and discussion with parties involved, we find these allegations false. Accordingly, we wish to set out the facts as we believe them to be.
>
> During the Gulf War, the NLA evacuated the military bases they had in Kurdish areas along the Iran–Iraq border – some in the north and some in the south. They relocated to the middle border area away from Kurdish settlements. The key reason for this costly relocation was to remove themselves from Iraq's internal affairs.
>
> After the defeat of the Iraqi forces in the Gulf War, the Iranian regime began a two-pronged initiative to annihilate the NLA and to establish an Iranian-controlled Islamic government in Iraq. In March 1991, Iran sent

seven Guards Corps divisions and brigades to attack NLA base camps on the border. However, these were heavily defeated by NLA fighters. Six of the Iranian soldiers captured by the NLA wore Kurdish dress. At the same time, the Iranian regime sought to hire Iraqi Kurds to fight against the NLA, and in the Kurdish areas demolished the abandoned NLA camps.

The Kurdish prisoners of war (who were in fact Iranians) held by the NLA were subsequently presented to the International Committee of the Red Cross, and they conceded that the Iranian regime was trying to recruit Kurds to fight the NLA. The prisoners were released by order of M. Rajavi, Commander-in-Chief of the NLA and extensive documentation as well as film footage and photographs were also made available to the public about these events.

Most of the allegations made against the NLA regarding the Kurdish people come from a man named Jamshid Tafrishi-Enginee, who was cited by people at this session of the Sub-Commission as a former leader of the Iranian resistance. Our investigation indicates that Mr. Tafrishi-Enginee joined the resistance in 1988, but left after 19 months with a low rank ... He then travelled to Europe where he began to campaign publicly against the NLA. There is compelling evidence that he is in fact an agent of the Khomeini regime's Ministry of Intelligence.

The Islamic Culture and Communications Organization, ICCO, a key agency involved in the export of fundamentalism and terrorism as well as in the psychological warfare against the PMOI outside Iran, had invested heavily in the allegation of PMOI suppression of the Kurds. In 1997, NCRI's Counterterrorism Committee unveiled the ICCO's internal documents, which showed how the organization fabricated reports on PMOI's involvement in Iraqi Kurdistan, then fed them to the state-run media and ultimately published them through its paid operatives in the foreign media.[7]

The decade-long history of the clerical regime's psychological warfare against the PMOI's presence in Iraq and the lie about 'taking part in the suppression of the Kurds or Shiites in Iraq' was discredited completely by virtue of the support for the PMOI by the people and political forces in post-conflict Iraq.

Notes

1. Hans-Heino Kopietz and Karen Dubrowska, 'KDP Fans Kurdish Propaganda War', *Tower Magazine*, 12 October 1996.

2. 'Iranian Views on Regime Change in Iraq', *Middle East Intelligence Bulletin*, vol. 4, no. 11, November–December 2002.

3. Jonathan Wright, US State Department, Reuters, 22 May 2002.

4. Independent sources: 'The People's Mojahedin are not Part of Para-military Forces of the Iraqi Regime', *Az-Zaman*, London, 11 January 2003.

5. Report on MOIS infiltration plots, Counter Intelligence Department of the NLA, Iran Ketab, August 2002.

6. Jamshid Tafrishi, official affidavit to US Appeals Court, Washington, June 2001.

7. Documents concerning plans and conspiracies by the 'Organization of Islamic Culture and Communications' of the Iranian regime, Iran Ketab, February 1999.

**PART IV
The Secret War**

11 | Spies who came in from the dark

> Thanks to its dedicated, pious and experienced personnel, our
> country's Ministry of Intelligence and Security (MOIS) is one of the
> most powerful intelligence organizations in the world. *Ali Younessi*[1]

Every government has its own intelligence and spy agencies. Organized
crime gangs operate in almost every corner of the world. Terrorists
are also active in many countries. In only one country, however, do all
three operate under one government agency: Iran's Ministry of Intelligence and Security.

According to insiders and defectors, the MOIS is a notorious mafia
of terror, murder, espionage and organized crime. Much has been said
about this agency, whose huge budget and unrestrained power have
turned it into one of the key pillars of the mullahs' regime, but the
most shocking accounts have come from those who worked inside the
MOIS and collaborated with it for years.

Defector's chilling revelations

For many years, the MOIS used the services of Jamshid Tafrishi, bill-
ing him as a 'senior PMOI member'. Over a period of ten years, Tafrishi
played a key role in Tehran's anti-Mojahedin propaganda, publishing
reports and giving lectures on 'the imprisonment, torture and harassment of former PMOI members', accusing the PMOI of involvement
in the suppression of Iraqi Kurds and alleging that the Mojahedin had
been entrusted by Saddam Hussein with storing his weapons of mass
destruction in their camps. The MOIS also used Tafrishi to establish
contact with activists and artists who were co-operating with the National
Council of Resistance of Iran in a bid to encourage them to withdraw
their support for the Resistance.

Contrary to Tehran's propaganda, Tafrishi was not a PMOI member, let alone a senior official. He left Iran to go to Turkey in 1988 and
contacted the local association of PMOI supporters. He wrote to the
Iraq-based National Liberation Army of Iran and asked to join its ranks.
He went to Iraq in May 1989, but a year later, he wrote in a letter to
NLA officials: 'I am unable to continue my stay in the NLA, because of
personal problems and preoccupations.' A few days later, Tafrishi asked
to be sent to a refugee camp run by the office of the United Nations

High Commissioner for Refugees. His request was granted. In January 1991, he approached the PMOI office in Baghdad and requested financial help to leave Iraq. He was given the equivalent of US$1,800 and left Iraq to go first to Jordan and Turkey, before finally settling in Europe.

Tafrishi revealed, after his defection in the year 2000, that after arriving in Turkey in 1991, he was approached by Iranian intelligence agents, who recruited him. This was the beginning of an under-cover career in the Ministry of Intelligence and Security that went on for a decade. In an affidavit to the Federal Appeals Court in the District of Columbia in 2001, Tafrishi wrote:

> Until last year, I pretended that I was an opponent of the Iranian regime, while I was in fact carrying out assignments given by the Iranian regime's Ministry of Intelligence and Security. In those years, I actively participated in the Iranian regime conspiracy to accuse the PMOI of human rights violations. I was also involved in other plans, such as giving false information about the PMOI to foreign governments and alleging that the PMOI was supported by the Iraqi government, to tarnish the image of the organization.
>
> In those years, the Intelligence Ministry summoned me to Singapore four times to meet the most senior MOIS officials. Singapore is one of the locations the Intelligence Ministry uses to meet its agents. I later traveled secretly to Iran in a trip arranged by the MOIS and met with the Ministry's senior officials in Tehran and Shiraz. From 1995 until 1999, I received a total of 72,000 dollars from the Intelligence Ministry as payment for my work.
>
> I met Saeed Emami (a.k.a. Shamshiri), the number two man in the Intelligence Ministry for eight years, who was behind the murder of at least 100 dissidents in Iran. The latest of these serial killings was exposed in November 1998, when Dariush Forouhar and his wife Parvaneh were brutally murdered in their home in Tehran. Emami was also responsible for the assassination of dozens of dissidents abroad. I also met Mostafa Kazemi (a.k.a. Sanjari, Emami's deputy), Amir Hossein Taqavi (responsible for counter-PMOI operations in the Intelligence Ministry) and Hossein Shariatmadari (a Revolutionary Guards brigadier and Supreme Leader Ali Khamenei's representative at the government-owned *Kayhan* newspaper). My contact with the Ministry was a man by the name of Reza who was an assistant to Saeed Emami. It was revealed later that his name was Morteza Qobbeh. He was Emami's deputy and had the task of recruiting those who had left the Mojahedin Organization.
>
> The Ministry assigned me to carry out several tasks:

1. To draw up reports and articles for propaganda use against the PMOI as someone who had previously worked with the organization, accusing it of human rights violations and other crimes.
2. To recruit disaffected members and lure non-PMOI members of the NCRI away from that coalition.
3. To provide false information to European governments on the PMOI and the NCRI. I was also aware that other agents are engaged in similar activities in other countries.

Alleging human rights abuses against the PMOI was one of the most serious projects the Ministry was pursuing outside Iran with me and a number of its other agents. The Ministry was convinced that if it were successful in neutralizing the PMOI and the NCRI in their actions that exposed human rights abuses in Iran, the United Nations would no longer condemn the Iranian regime. They felt that the only way to achieve this was to accuse the PMOI of human rights abuses. Thus, acting as disaffected members of the PMOI, our responsibility was to accuse the organization of human rights abuses in order to disarm them of the human rights weapon.

In 1994, we were engaged in an extensive campaign to convince Human Rights Watch that PMOI is engaged in human rights abuses and encouraged them to prepare a report in this regard. The information was also being sent to the United States Department of State who was preparing a report on the Mojahedin at the time.

In 1996, using the same story against the PMOI, we met in Geneva with Professor Maurice Danby Copithorne, UN Human Rights Commission's Special Representative on the human rights situation in Iran. The Intelligence Ministry organized everything regarding this meeting. The contact person with Professor Copithorne was Nasser Khajeh-nouri, who operated from the USA but regularly visited Europe.

A similar attempt was made at Amnesty International in 1996, when a number of Intelligence Ministry agents met with the representative of the human rights organization in Germany.

One of our tasks was to discredit the PMOI among members of parliaments and governments in Europe and the United States. In this respect we were asked to claim that the PMOI is cooperating with, or being helped by, the Iraqi government.

As part of this plan, I was assigned to inform international organizations as well as foreign governments that the PMOI was involved in suppressing the Kurdish rebellion in Iraq. This plan was conducted under the supervision of Nasser Khajeh-Nouri, who was the regime's agent in the United States. He organized an interview for me and other agents with an Iranian radio station in Los Angeles to tell our story that PMOI suppressed the Kurdish people along with the Iraqi forces. Khajeh-Nouri consequently prepared a report under my name on this issue and sent it to US intelligence and government agencies as well as the United Nations. Consequently, a US non-governmental organization, the International Educational Development, prepared a report of their investigation on this issue refuting our allegations against the Mojahedin, which was published as a UN document on August 22, 1995.

In a similar move, Nasser Khajeh-Nouri once told me that he has received reliable information that PMOI is helping the Iraqi government to buy chemical weapons and other kinds of weapons of mass destruction. He asked me to expose the information and said we would then make it an international issue, by sending it to US government as well as European governments and international organizations. He said he would personally provide this information to US officials. To this end a public meeting was organized in June 1995, in Hamburg, Germany where I disclosed the information that had been given to me.

Along with thirteen other MOIS agents, Tafrishi went to see Professor Copithorne in January 1996 and claimed to have been tortured and imprisoned by the Mojahedin. This group held similar meetings with representatives of Amnesty International and Human Rights Watch. In late 2000, in a letter to Professor Copithorne, he wrote:

I am Jamshid Tafrishi and met with you in Geneva together with 13 other individuals, including two children, as former members of the People's Mojahedin Organization of Iran on January 16, 1996. I had written to you from Hamburg on the same subject a month prior to our meeting. The objective of our meeting was to accuse the Mojahedin of having prisons and committing torture, execution and violation of human rights on the eve of your anticipated visit to Iran and to request that you would reflect our information in your report.

After elaborating on the activities abroad against the PMOI in those years, Tafrishi wrote:

My last meeting with Intelligence Ministry officials in Tehran was in October 1998. The arrangement was that I set aside limitations on holding meetings abroad and go to Tehran. A travel document was provided to me by the regime's embassy in The Hague and I flew to Tehran on a direct flight. During the trip, I met Sanjari, Reza, Hossein and Pirnia. The meeting with Sanjari took place in Shiraz. The rest of my meetings were in Tehran in the Laleh Hotel. Owing to the secret nature of my ties with the Iranian regime, I was taken around in a vehicle with dark windshields. The objectives of these trips were to be briefed about more public support for the regime and activities against the Resistance outside Iran in tandem with other Intelligence Ministry agents. About one year after my last visit to Tehran, when the factional feuding within the regime heightened over the serial murders of Iranian dissidents in the country, I saw pictures of Saeed Emami and other perpetrators of the chain murders and realized what kind of criminals I had been collaborating with. That was the beginning of the process that finally led me to defect.[2]

Elaborate disinformation scheme

Another Iranian, Mahmoud Massoudi, wrote a letter in August 2002 to Ruud Lubbers, the UN High Commissioner for Refugees, and revealed the active links between the MOIS and agents who operate as 'ex-PMOI members' in such propaganda campaigns. The letter was published in a number of journals and posted on websites.

Massoudi wrote that in early 1994, he decided to leave the PMOI for personal reasons and asked to go to Europe to lead an ordinary life. He obtained political asylum in Germany and began to write articles in different newspapers as a dissident. This put him in contact with several MOIS agents and for seven years, Massoudi was in close touch with them. He wrote in his letter to the UN High Commissioner for Refugees:

My experience of the past seven years made it clear that the ruling religious dictatorship makes political and intelligence-gathering use of certain groups and individuals, who have identified themselves as political refugees and opponents of the mullahs' regime, in order to ensure its own survival and destroy its real opponents, who want to overthrow it. I therefore set out here some of my observations and reliable information, about which I am prepared to testify in any court of law:

1. I was informed in April 2002 that several individuals identifying themselves as 'former officials of the People's Mojahedin Organization of Iran' have come to Europe, including Germany, to obtain political asylum. I was then informed that on April 5, 2002, a meeting was held at the home of Bahman Rastgou in Cologne, Germany, with the participation of Karim Haghi, Hadi Shams-Haeri, Mehdi Khoshhal, Mohammad-Reza Haghi, Bahman Rastgou, and several of the new arrivals, including Mohammad-Hossein Sobhani and Farhad Javaheri-Yar. In the meeting, Sobhani, who is the senior agent over Javaheri-Yar, explained the plans

and aims of his team in coming to Germany and in this connection, they agreed on a division of labor. Sobhani and Javaheri-Yar told those present that they came from Iran and more agents would follow them.

2. Prior to the April 5 meeting, he had mentioned the Intelligence Ministry's forthcoming plan to bring individuals from Iran to Europe to Abol-Hassan Bani-Sadr, Mehdi Khan-Baba Tehrani, Bahman Niroumand, Mansour Bayatzadeh and several others so that they would assist the new arrivals from Iran and write letters of confirmation for them. These individuals promised to spare no effort.

3. Alireza Nourizadeh, an agent of the mullahs' Intelligence Ministry working under the cover of journalism, told me in a telephone conversation on May 8: 'There are new individuals who have come from the Mojahedin.' He mentioned Adham Tayyebi (a.k.a. Massoud Tayyebi) and said, 'They have come with documents to prove that the Mojahedin carried out espionage and operations for Iraq and intend to hold a big trial and prove that the Mojahedin are terrorists.'

My own experience and that of others who have defected from the Mojahedin and are leading their own lives in Europe showed clearly that these claims were not credible. I knew very well that the Islamic Republic had fabricated since a long time ago the stories of 'maltreatment' and 'imprisonment of innocent individuals' against their main opposition.

4. Nourizadeh emphasized that every support must be given to the Intelligence Ministry's agents being sent from Iran. He warmly welcomed an interview with Sobhani and asked me to do the interview for publication in the monthly *Rouzegar-e No*. Nourizadeh recently bought this monthly with the funds he received from the mullahs' regime. He told me that he would pay for all the expenses, including the trip to Doblen in Germany, where Sobhani is residing, so that I would make the interview. I went to Doblen on July 30, talked to Sobhani for eight hours, and recorded a 40-minute interview with him.

5. Sobhani's scenario was as follows: He was an official of 'the Mojahedin's Political Security Department' and had been 'imprisoned and tortured' by the Mojahedin because he was 'opposed to the organization's policies'. After years in solitary confinement, he was handed over to Iraq and then spent several years in Iraqi jails and was then 'extradited' to Iran and imprisoned by the Intelligence Ministry. But on the third day of arriving in Iran, he 'fled' the Intelligence Ministry's prison and came to Germany! Sobhani did not offer any explanation as to how he fled the Intelligence Ministry's prison and answered all my questions on this with a simple grin.

6. Sobhani claims that his 'mission' abroad is to fight against the

Mojahedin and the person of Mr. Massoud Rajavi and the most important thing, he says, is to attack Mr. Rajavi. He also said that he was responsible for organizing other 'Mojahedin defectors' who 'are escaping' from Iran.

7. After hours of discussion and numerous telephone conversations with Sobhani, it has become crystal clear to me that he is neither a political refugee, nor a defector seeking to lead an ordinary life. He is in fact a trained agent sent by the Intelligence Ministry with strong financial and communication backing and, as he put it, 'I have come outside Iran only for the purpose of fighting the Mojahedin and have no mission other than opposing them.'

8. On August 5, 2002, Sobhani faxed a ten-page statement to me with the joint signatures of Javaheri-Yar and Edward Termadoyan. On this typed statement, there were corrections in handwriting that belonged neither to Sobhani nor to Javaheri-Yar or Termadoyan. It was clear that they had received the typed text from outside Germany and the original sender was in the Intelligence Ministry in Tehran.

9. In this statement, Javaheri-Yar and Termadoyan were giving a scenario that was almost identical to Sobhani: they claimed that they were 'Mojahedin dissidents' who had been arrested by the Mojahedin and handed over to Iraq, which in turn handed them over to Iran and they then escaped from the Intelligence Ministry and came to Europe ... Precisely the same scenario was again repeated by another agent, Hamid-Reza Barahoun. Anyone least familiar with the notorious prisons in Iran knows very well that it is impossible to believe that so many political prisoners would have escaped one after the other in such a short time. Throughout the past 20 years, only a handful of political prisoners are known to have escaped from mullahs' jails. So how could these 'prisoners' escape one by one and quickly turn up in Europe, while thousands of Iranian refugees have been waiting to come to Europe from Iran's neighboring countries like Turkey, Pakistan, UAE and Azerbaijan?[3]

Murderous mission

The MOIS tried to use another infiltrator, Houshang Khosrowpour Bayat, to obtain information needed to plan terrorist attacks on the Mojahedin. Bayat was sent to Iraq in 1988 to join the NLA as an infiltrator. After a while, he informed NLA officials of all the plots devised by the MOIS. He eventually requested to be sent abroad in 1993 and went to the Netherlands, where he received political asylum.

In a letter published in the PMOI's weekly journal on 11 August 2002, Bayat described his recruitment by the MOIS and the plans to infiltrate and deliver blows to the PMOI and the NLA. He wrote:

After June 20, 1981, I lost contact with the PMOI due to the security situation. In March 1985, I was arrested and taken to Evin Prison. Fifteen agents were waiting for me where I worked. During interrogation sessions, I was offered my freedom in exchange for collaboration with the Intelligence Ministry. The MOIS suggested that I go abroad and request to join the NLA, which I did. They gave me three specific assignments: collecting information on bases, weapons, travel itineraries of officials, seeking out weak links, good targets for bombings, and locations of meetings where the PMOI leadership is present.

The PMOI had every right to deal with me, as do other forces, organizations, parties or partisans when confronted with a traitor. Yet, the PMOI displayed mercy and compassion. I saw in the Mojahedin and its leadership a democratic attitude. It was in this light that when after six years of being presence in the PMOI and the NLA, I requested to be sent abroad, they arranged my departure to the Netherlands in just three months. No one raised any voice of protest over my request. I again declare that I am willing to testify in any court or before any relevant body about the Intelligence Ministry's plots.

Notes

1. Remarks by Minister of Intelligence and Security, Hojjatol-Islam Ali Younessi, *Kayhan*, 29 June 2003.

2. Jamshid Tafrishi, *Plans and Conspiracies of the MOIS against the PMOI*, by NCRI's Counterterrorism Committee, Iran Ketab, 2001.

3. Mahmoud Massoudi, 'Letter to Ruud Lubbers', UNHCR, *Mojahed* weekly, issue 599, 22 August 2002.

12 | Masters of disinformation

Tell a lie that is big enough, and repeat it often enough, and the whole world will believe it. *Josef Goebbels*

'Psychological warfare is an indispensable part of our strategy. It is not a tactic in and of itself.'[1] The confidential memorandum came from the Islamic Culture and Communication Organization (ICCO), a key agency for export of fundamentalism and Islamic Revolution, and underscored the importance of psychological warfare against the Iranian Resistance.

The clerical regime has invested greatly in this strategy against the Iranian Resistance and set up an elaborate apparatus to implement it. The Ministry of Intelligence and Security (MOIS), the ICCO, the Foreign and Islamic Guidance ministries and the Islamic Revolutionary Guards Corps (IRGC) are all involved in psychological warfare against the PMOI. The clerical regime's propaganda campaign against its opponents was originally modelled, to a large degree, on the activities and modus operandi of the former Soviet KGB's disinformation department. Foreign instructors who trained Iranian operatives in 'psychological warfare' and propaganda techniques in the early 1980s were mainly from the Eastern bloc countries. Many Revolutionary Guards and Intelligence Ministry officers who rose to prominence in the latter half of the 1990s as journalists, editors or politicians, were among the first generation of trainees in these special courses.

Iran's convoluted propaganda machine conducts complex disinformation operations that may seem incidental or spontaneous to an unsuspecting mind: identical reports appear simultaneously in second- or third-rate European or American tabloids on alleged involvement of the PMOI in the suppression of Iraqi Kurds and Shiites; a few 'asylum-seekers' emerge from nowhere to claim that they were mistreated by the PMOI many years ago; state-run newspapers in Iran report that the (former) Iraqi regime is hiding its weapons of mass destruction in PMOI camps. In the absence of reliable information on how such propaganda is being disseminated by the clerical regime's agencies, one may rightly assume that both sides to this conflict have vested interests in making these claims and counter-claims. The mullahs' 'target audience' is sometimes affected by the propaganda and most of the time perplexed or confused. Either outcome is a win for the mullahs, for at least some shadow of doubt would be cast on their principal opposition group. Goebbels's infamous 'big lie' principle would seem to work for the mullahs.

The Resistance has responded to this propaganda blitz by relying on its extensive information-gathering network inside Iran to identify the agencies and officials involved in this psychological warfare and expose confidential documents and evidence relating to their activities. The Supreme National Security Council (SNSC), chaired by President Mohammad Khatami, is the highest authority that co-ordinates this campaign. The council's secretary, Hojjatol-Islam Hassan Rohani, is a confidant of ex-President Akbar Hashemi Rafsanjani, while Ali Rabii, a former MOIS deputy and a Khatami protégé, heads the SNSC's executive secretariat. Supreme Leader Khamenei approves the council's important decisions.

The mullahs' extensive propaganda against the PMOI began from the very first day they assumed power, but their 'psychological warfare' operations swung into action after the 1991 (Persian) Gulf War against Iraq. In those years, the mullahs tried to take advantage of the post-conflict mayhem in the region to finish off their main opponents, the PMOI. The MOIS sharply expanded its operations to achieve this objective. Tehran pumped up more anti-Mojahedin propaganda, while its hit squads stepped up the assassination of dissidents abroad. From 1990 to 1993, MOIS hit squads targeted prominent opposition figures in Geneva, Rome, Karachi, Istanbul, Paris, Berlin, Dubai, Oslo, Stockholm and Baghdad. At the same time, the MOIS recruited a number of PMOI defectors in Europe to enhance its anti-Mojahedin misinformation campaign.

The MOIS remained active against Iranian dissidents in Europe throughout the 1990s and was described in successive annual reports by the US State Department on global terrorism as 'the most active state sponsor of terrorism' in the world. A top Iranian official acknowledged that the MOIS had carried out 'hundreds of attacks' on the PMOI in Iraq alone while Saeed Emami was the MOIS deputy minister.

In March 1996, the German Federal Prosecutor issued an international arrest warrant for the Iranian Intelligence Minister Ali Fallahian for having ordered the assassination of four Iranian dissidents at the Mykonos, a Greek restaurant in Berlin, on 17 September 1992. In final statements in late November 1996, German prosecutors charged Iranian Supreme Leader Khamenei and Iranian President Rafsanjani with approving the operation. Guilty verdicts for four of the accused were announced in April 1997 and the court established that a Joint Committee for Special

Operations, made up of Khamenei, Rafsanjani, Intelligence Minister Ali Fallahian and Foreign Minister Ali-Akbar Velayati, was responsible for approving plans to assassinate Iranian dissidents abroad.

Iranian embassies were often the main hub of intelligence and terrorist activities against dissidents abroad. The international security organization, Global Security, reported:

One example of the coordinated efforts of Iranian intelligence is found in Iran's diplomatic mission in Bonn at Godesberger Allee 133–7, which is the headquarters of the Iranian intelligence services in Europe. Some 20 staff members work for the Ministry of Intelligence and Security, and representatives from other agencies also use the embassy's specially secured third floor, where six offices and a radio room are reserved for the agents. From the six-story building in the government district the services monitor the 100,000 Iranians living in Germany, harass undesirable opposition members, and attempt to procure technology in Germany for the production of nuclear, chemical, and biological weapons. In the German language area alone, there are as many as 100 firms allegedly under Iranian influence for the procurement of such sensitive technology. Other bases of operations include the consulates in Frankfurt and Hamburg, and the Imam-Ali Mosque in Hamburg, said to be the largest Muslim religious centre outside the Islamic world.

The next major change in the activities of the Iranian intelligence abroad came in the wake of the tragic events of 11 September 2001, and the war in Afghanistan. At the time, the SNSC decided to exploit the new political circumstances and focus its international efforts on the PMOI to persuade other governments, particularly the European Union countries, to designate the PMOI and the National Council of Resistance of Iran as terrorist organizations. Tehran was attempting to kill two birds with one stone: deliver a political blow to the Iranian Resistance and divert global attention from its terrorist record.

As a diplomatic offensive got under way to seek further restrictions on PMOI activities in other countries, the clerical regime embarked on a new misinformation campaign. The MOIS summoned a number of its agents to Turkey, the United Arab Emirates and Tehran to brief and instruct them to intensify their activities against the PMOI. MOIS agents Karim Haghi, Mohammad-Reza Haghi, Ahmad Shams-Haeri and Mehdi Khoshhal were instructed to pass a series of false reports on the PMOI to police and security services in France, Germany, the Netherlands and Scandinavian countries. The NCRI's Counterterrorism Committee exposed this plot in a statement on 29 April 2002.

The clerical regime also increased the number of publications and articles that sought to demonize the PMOI. To this end, the MOIS assembled a group of writers and analysts in Kayhan, the largest government-owned publishing house in Iran, run by Hossein Shariatmadari. Shariatmadari, a brigadier-general of the Revolutionary Guards and a close confidant of Khamenei, is a veteran interrogator, torturer and propagandist who has been a key player in the clerical regime's disinformation operations since the 1980s. Kayhan-based writers churned out a steady stream of propaganda materials against the PMOI and these were published in MOIS-sponsored journals abroad as articles written by ex-PMOI members. Haghi, Shams-Haeri, Khoshhal and Mohammad-Reza Eskandari were the agents whose names were most frequently used as the supposed authors of these writings.

In previous campaigns, MOIS disinformation officers paid much attention to details to cover up the fact, as much as possible, that anti-PMOI articles were actually being written in Iran, but in the rush to churn out as much propaganda as they could in recent months, the vocabulary in the articles has become strikingly similar to the language of the official press in Tehran. Now the articles refer to Khomeini as Imam Khomeini, describe the Mojahedin as the Monafeqin (the 'hypocrites') and the National Liberation Army as the Army of Hypocrites!

The MOIS has also sent thousands of anti-Mojahedin letters from Iran to parliamentarians and officials in Europe. The letters, with different signatures but often identical texts and handwriting, accuse the PMOI of terrorism and the murder of innocent civilians. They call on recipients to designate the PMOI a terrorist organization. In an article in Sweden's daily *Göteborg Posten*, Cecilia Malmström, a Swedish member of the European Parliament, unveiled one example of MOIS schemes to influence parliamentarians.[2]

The Islamic Culture and Communications Organization

Parallel agencies involved in the export of terrorism and fundamentalism sustained a number of blows in several countries, prompting the regime to reorganize and consolidate them. In early 1995, Khamenei brought those agencies active in the export of fundamentalism and anti-Mojahedin propaganda outside Iran under one unified organization: the Islamic Culture and Communications Organization, ICCO. He appointed Iraqi-born cleric Mohammad Ali Taskhiri as the head of the ICCO. Khamenei himself heads ICCO's Supreme Policy-making Council, which holds its meetings at his house.

The ICCO has five directorates – publications, communications, cultural logistics, research, administration and financial affairs – each of which has several subordinate departments. Cultural attachés in embassies abroad are linked to the ICCO's communications directorate. The ICCO has three sets of objectives:

1. anti-Mojahedin activities, including recruitment of operatives among deserters from the ranks of the Resistance, pursuance of psychological warfare, employing other opposition figures in anti-Mojahedin actions;
2. penetration of Iranian exile communities abroad through Farsi-language radio and other means, recruitment of agents and encouraging Iranians to return to Iran and infiltrating Iranian associations and groups;
3. exporting fundamentalism to other countries, including recruitment and organization of fundamentalist forces in Islamic nations, penetration of Muslim communities in Western countries for recruitment and incitement purposes, recruitment of Muslims, particularly Shiites, for terrorist hit squads.

During Khatami's presidency, the ICCO stepped up the scope of its activities. Khatami appointed three cabinet ministers to ICCO's Supreme Policy-making Council and increased the budget for this entity by 15 per cent.

Cultural attachés, who are trained intelligence agents, play an important role in the export of fundamentalism. Often they act as 'talent spotters', reaching out to fundamentalist groups in their countries of assignment and identifying individuals to recruit. New recruits will ultimately be sent to Iran via third countries for ideological indoctrination and terrorist training.

News fabrication as policy

In February 1999, the NCRI's Counterterrorism Committee published a book entitled, 'Documents on Plans and Conspiracies of the Islamic Culture and Communications Organization'. It contained previously unpublished and top-secret documents on the ICCO's modus operandi. Parts of the documents unveiled the clerical regime's policy of fabricating news reports. For instance, in autumn 1996, when the international community was alarmed over news reports on the presence of the Iranian regime's military forces in Iraqi Kurdistan, the Supreme National Security Council instructed the ICCO to put out false news reports claiming that the Iranians cited in Iraqi Kurdistan were PMOI members and not members of the mullahs' military!

An ICCO internal memorandum in September 1996 stated,

Turkish Foreign Minister Tansu Ciller said that there are reports of Iranian forces entering Iraqi Kurdistan. A Kurdish source told CNN, 'reports about the presence of Iranian forces in Iraq are not an allegation'. The reports on the presence of Iranian forces in Iraqi territory were deemed dangerous and steps were taken to divert the focus of these reports from Iran. A plan was devised to use the available information on the presence of Iranian forces in Iraqi Kurdistan and gradually introduce these forces as those of the Mojahedin. As such, it would appear that we have acknowledged the reports on the presence of forces of Iranian origin in Iraqi Kurdistan, but at the same time, we can attribute the negative aspect of this intervention to the Mojahedin.

To this end, in co-ordination with the official news agency, IRNA, and MOIS operatives in Europe and the United States, a news item was released in several stages:

News Item No. 1, 4 September 1996
Sources affiliated with the Patriotic Union of Iraqi Kurdistan said that the People's Mojahedin Organization of Iran has positioned its forces in strategic regions and bases near Hamilton Highway, close to the city of Sulaimaniya. These sources added that the Mojahedin plays an active role alongside the Iraqi army in suppressing the Kurdish people.

News Item No. 2, 4 September 1996
According to the latest reports from independent Kurdish sources in northern Iraq, forces of the People's Mojahedin Organization of Iran alongside forces of the Kurdish Democratic Party of Iraq, which enjoys Baghdad's support, are continuing their attacks against civilians and residential areas.

News Item No. 3, 7 September 1996
Sources affiliated with the Patriotic Union of Iraqi Kurdistan reported that KDP forces and militia units of the People's Mojahedin Organization of Iran, with support from the Iraqi army, are advancing towards Kuysanjaq. Based on the latest reports, these forces are positioned five kilometres from Degaleh region and 25 kilometres from Kuysanjaq. The KDP radio reported heavy fighting in the area.

News Item No. 4, 7 September 1996
Reliable sources from the city of Arbil report that security forces, Mokhaḃerat (intelligence), Estekhbarat (military intelligence), internal security and the People's Mojahedin Organization of Iran in Kurdish

attire are searching for Iraqi oppositionists in the city. After arresting them, they immediately transfer them to the city of Mosul.

News Item No. 5, IRNA, 8 September 1996

Mojahedin radio announced on Saturday that members of the PMOI grouplet staged a march in bases opposite the Iranian border. The radio said that the march commemorated the thirty-second anniversary of the founding of the People's Mojahedin Organization (the Monafeqin).

News Item No. 6, 8 September 1996

Following the extensive participation of the People's Mojahedin Organization of Iran in recent operations by the Iraqi army against the Kurds in the north, the organization's radio announced on Saturday that PMOI forces took part in a military manoeuvre to show their military might. The radio also reported a 32-gun salute. The organization invited its supporters to take advantage of the recent developments and join the PMOI bases from the western and southern borders.

The reports are typical of the way the clerical regime fabricates news and channels it through its own news agencies or other foreign news outlets influenced by it. News producers rarely put out totally fabricated dispatches. They distort real news stories such as replacing the news on the presence of the regime's forces in Iraqi Kurdistan with the presence of PMOI forces. In addition to its semi-official and official news outlets, the regime has bought the services of some journalists abroad. Through them, it publishes bogus reports in Western media outlets. Simultaneously, MOIS operatives abroad (such as Nasser Haji Nour in Washington, DC) relay these reports to Farsi-language news outlets to give it more coverage.

Harassment of dissidents' families

The MOIS routinely harasses and intimidates dissidents outside Iran by exerting pressure on their families inside the country. In most cases, the MOIS compels the families to contact their children abroad to urge them to discontinue their anti-regime activities and refrain from supporting the PMOI or the NCRI. In other cases, the MOIS has arrested families of exiled Iranians to force them to take a position against the Resistance or collaborate with the regime.

In one example in 1995, MOIS officials approached the parents of Mr Abbas Minachi, a veteran PMOI member, and claimed he had been imprisoned by the organization. In a statement that was distributed as a United Nations document at the Sub-commission for Prevention of Discrimination and Protection of Minorities at the time, Pax Christi wrote, 'The Intelligence Ministry and an Iranian diplomat in Paris contacted Mr. Abbas Minachi's family and told them that their son was imprisoned by the Mojahedin. By this, they made Mr. Minachi's parents write to Prof. Copithorne, Amnesty International and other human rights organizations and express their concern.'[3]

Ultimately, Mr Minachi came to Europe and contacted his father who was in the United States at the time, to assure him of his well-being. He also met Professor Copithorne in Geneva, unmasked the mullahs' ploys, and later wrote a letter to human rights organizations concerning the MOIS propaganda.

The United Nations Sub-commission for Prevention of Discrimination and Protection of Minorities issued a resolution on 16 August 1996, expressing profound concern over 'increasing harassment and persecution of families of Iranian exiles living under the Islamic Republic and pressures imposed by undercover government terrorists against Iranians residing abroad aiming to force them to cooperate with activities against dissidents in exile'.[4] The same year, the *Washington Times* wrote, 'The organized campaign concerning the exiles in Western Europe emanates from the Iranian Embassy in Bonn and is under the direction of a diplomat by the name of Vahidi Attain. Some 15,000 Iranian expatriates live in Germany ... The Iranian Parliament ratified legislation two years ago legalizing punitive actions of overseas dissidents "who conspire against Islam".'[5]

Annual reports by the German and Dutch security services, which appear in subsequent chapters, show that such activities are continuing.

In the first half of 2003, the MOIS forcibly assembled a number of PMOI families, especially elderly parents, outside the Swiss Embassy (US Interest Section), United Nations Development Office and Hotel Laleh, which is controlled by the Intelligence Ministry. These actions were intended to propagate the notion that PMOI members were being held in Iraq against their will and must be returned to Iran.

In the most recent case, on Wednesday 16 July 2003, the MOIS deceived the families of a number of Mojahedin and National Liberation Army combatants and took them to PMOI's central office in Baghdad to stage a demonstration against the organization. The MOIS had been working on this plan for several months. It set up a fake organization, the so-called 'Salvation Association', to help the families and promised them that they could see their children. The MOIS took the families to the border town of Mehran, where it briefed them. It then took them to Iraq, to the Al-Dhabi hotel in the Kadhamiya district of Baghdad.

There, MOIS agents told the families that the Mojahedin would not allow them to visit their children. On 16 July, the regime's agents handed the families placards bearing anti-Mojahedin slogans in Arabic and English and took them to the PMOI's central office in Baghdad. A camera crew from Iran's state-run television was filming the entire episode. Once informed by the PMOI representatives that they would welcome such visits, however, the families expressed their abhorrence at the regime for exploiting their feelings and said that all Iranians hated the mullahs and impatiently awaited their overthrow. The PMOI issued a statement the same day declaring its readiness to make the necessary arrangements for these families to meet their children. It also emphasized that the gates of PMOI camps were open to the families and that they could meet their relatives and children without any hindrance. Subsequently, the families stayed at Camp Ashraf for several days and met their relatives.

Cultural associations

Forming cultural associations to disseminate false propaganda against the Iranian Resistance is another MOIS tactic. These associations are purported not to be in contact with the regime and in fact even criticize it. One such association is the Damavand Cultural Association, which uses a Canadian address. Others are the Peyvand Association in the Netherlands and the Dena organization in Germany. Mahdis and Iran-Interlink websites are among other outlets set up by the MOIS to disseminate propaganda against the PMOI. All these associations and websites focus their propaganda against the PMOI while using the cover of independent or even anti-regime entities.

For example, the Iran-Interlink website, run by a British convert, Anne Khodabandeh (Singleton), is entirely controlled by MOIS. Prior to setting up Iran-Interlink, she travelled to Iran and stayed there for a month. Iran-Interlink is closely connected with the Intelligence Ministry's branches in the Netherlands and Germany. One of the website's information sources is the Dena organization in Germany. In introducing itself, the website states, 'our objective is to further expose the real nature of the Mojahedin and act as a pressure group ... This site has been formed as an outlet for families and persons the status of whose friends and acquaintances as disaffected members and cadres of the People's Mojahedin Organization in Iraq are unsettled and whose lives are in danger ...'

Infiltration and espionage

The clerical regime has long been engaged in attempts to infiltrate opposition organizations and exiles. It has been using this tactic in its psychological warfare against the Resistance and in intelligence-gathering for terrorist operations.

In late 1997, the counter-intelligence directorate of the National Liberation Army of Iran published the names of thirty-four MOIS agents who had been sent to infiltrate the NLA between 1992 and 1997. It also published the particulars and addresses of more than 150 MOIS officials and operatives and the addresses of more than sixty secret safe houses, hotels and locations used by the MOIS.[6] The directorate also revealed details on MOIS plans to 'assassinate commanders and combatants, poison drinking water and food, and collect intelligence on meetings'. The MOIS taught some of its spies to pretend to the PMOI that they had escaped from the regime's prisons.

In July 2002, the NLA counter-intelligence directorate also revealed the names and particulars of thirty-six more MOIS agents identified since the previous report.[7] In this 120-page report, the NLA counter-intelligence revealed the details of contact, payment and briefing of spies by the Intelligence Ministry in Iran before sending them abroad on assignment. The missions included, for example, intelligence-gathering, sabotage, writing pro-regime slogans in NLA bases, identifying potential collaborators within the organization and recruiting them, arresting or killing members of the Resistance inside Iran or near the border region and plans to assassinate and murder PMOI members through poisoning the water and food at their bases.

The report also gave the names of twenty-three PMOI members murdered by these infiltrators. They were Abdolreza Shatti Ahmadian, Behrouz Majd-Abadi, Ali Nouri, Loghman Haj Khanian, Abdollah Towhidi-far, Parviz Ahmadi, Farhad Tahmasbi, Jamal Ahani, Mahmoud Gholizadeh, Hadi Homayoun, Akbar Bagheri, Philip Yousefieh, Ramin Gholam Ghadaksaz, Ahmad Pahlevan Shandiz, Mehdi Baba'i, Issa Heidari, Abdollah Navid Hassanloui, Mahmoud Agah, Hossein Alamdari, Mohsen Arab-Mohammadi, Mehdi Baimani, Monireh Akbari and Mojgan Zahedi. Dozens more were trapped by infiltrators inside Iran and executed. Hundreds of others were captured.

Despite the gravity of the crimes committed by the mullahs' spies, the PMOI did not punish any of these agents. Instead, it informed international human rights organizations of the details of their actions and allowed them to return to Iran (see Chapter 7 for more details on the Resistance's amnesty policy).

In recent years, security services in different countries uncovered several cases of infiltration and espionage against Iranian refugees and dissidents in Europe, which led to the arrest of the MOIS agents. In the year 2000, a German court convicted an MOIS agent, Hamid Khorsand, of attempting to infiltrate the ranks of the supporters of the PMOI and the NCRI in order to collect information for terrorist purposes. The indictment issued by the federal prosecutor enumerated the methods used by Khorsand, including penetration of the pro-Mojahedin milieu of Iranian exiles, and many documents on espionage and his case officers in the MOIS. The indictment noted that the MOIS intended to deliver a blow to the PMOI through Khorsand's activities and paid him at least twice, each time a sum of DM 12,500. The indictment also said that Khorsand's first handler was an MOIS agent in the Iranian consulate in Berlin. After his expulsion in April 1997, in the aftermath of the Mykonos trial, a man named Seyyed became Khorsand's case officer and gave Khorsand instructions from Tehran.

In repeated telephone contacts, the MOIS repeatedly urged Khorsand to maintain closer ties with the PMOI and constantly criticized him for not doing enough. Khorsand stepped up his contacts with the NCRI office in Cologne to gather more intelligence.

Testimony by German security officers

In the course of the trial, two officers of the German Office to Protect the Constitution unveiled aspects of the activities of the Tehran regime against the PMOI and the NCRI. One officer said, for example, that Khorsand had been co-operating with the MOIS since 1995 and was specifically in contact with Kazem Darabi, who was involved in the killing of the Kurdish leaders at the Mykonos in Berlin in 1992. Noting that the regime was particularly keen on gathering intelligence on the PMOI, he told the court that a recorded conversation between an MOIS official in Tehran, Saeed, and Khorsand about Laila (Mahin Afshar, a PMOI official) showed that the MOIS was actively pursuing the activities of the opposition and the network of supporters. The officer added that since PMOI activities were public, Tehran was after identifying their officials. He also emphasized that German security services had learned from their experiences in the Mykonos killings that Iranian agents were not seeking information just for the sake of it, but that they sought to use it for terrorist operations against dissidents.

Another officer of the same department told the court that he was confident that Khorsand was an Iranian intelligence agent. He added that prior to the Mykonos trial, most MOIS agents were working out of the third floor of the Iranian embassy in Bonn. The officer said that the regime sends its agents to third countries such as Turkey and Malaysia to brief them. He said that the PMOI had been politically active for thirty years. While it was engaged in a military struggle against the regime inside Iran, outside the country it only carried out publicity activities aimed at exposing the Tehran regime. For instance, it held protests against visits by Iranian officials to Europe. The officer said that the MOIS was keenly interested in collecting information about such activities. It even sought to know how many bullhorns were used in such rallies to see how it could disrupt it. More importantly, it wanted to know who the organizers of such events were. Through Khorsand, the MOIS was trying to identify, put under surveillance and even assassinate a woman member of the PMOI named Laila, in a manner reminiscent of what happened in Turkey. There, the MOIS identified a woman, Zahra Rajabi, and assassinated her along with a colleague. The Intelligence Ministry devoted all its efforts to identifing the PMOI, while the latter conducted a political campaign against the Tehran regime in Europe. The German security official said the PMOI was the only active opposition group during the G-8 summit and at the Federal parliament. The Iranian government attempted to strike blows against it. The PMOI had extensive contacts with the media and provided them with interesting information. It even gave the names of the Iranian regime's spies to the media.

Murder of Christian priests

A glance at earlier examples of MOIS disinformation campaigns against the PMOI shows that it has been conducting such activities against the PMOI for a long time.

The leaders of the Assemblies of God churches in Iran, Bishop Haik Hovsepian-Mehr, Pastor Mehdi Dibaj and Bishop Tataos Michaelian, disappeared one after another and were mysteriously murdered in 1994. On 6 June 1994, Mehdi Dibaj was abducted on his way to Tehran's Mehrabad Airport. Shortly afterwards, his mutilated body, bearing multiple stab wounds, was found dumped in a remote park in Tehran. Pastor Dibaj had been imprisoned since 1986 and sentenced to death on charges of apostasy in a court in the northern Iranian city of Sari in December 1993. Extensive international pressure forced his release in January 1994. On 31 January 1994, the body of Bishop Haik Hovsepian-Mehr, the General Secretary of the Assemblies of God churches in Iran and chairman of the Council of Protestant Ministers, was found in a copse near Tehran. He disappeared three days after Mehdi Dibaj's release from prison. His body, riddled with stab wounds, was handed over to his family eleven days later. As the leader of the Assemblies of God's churches in Iran, he worked tirelessly to secure the release of Mehdi Dibaj from prison and was an unremitting advocate of religious freedom in Iran. MOIS agents murdered Bishop Tataos Michaelian in June 1994 in Tehran. He had replaced Hovsepian-Mehr as the leader of the Assemblies of God churches. He disappeared on 29 June 1994; the Intelligence Ministry delivered his body to his son on 2 July 1994.

At the time, the MOIS and the regime's officials lost no opportunity of accusing the Mojahedin of the murders. They even arranged a press conference in which three women, claiming to be PMOI members, confessed to the killings, which they said had been carried out on the orders of the Mojahedin. This ridiculous charade did not deceive anyone, however. Several prominent international bodies rejected the mullahs' claims as propaganda and explicitly or implicitly blamed the regime for the murders. Foreign Office Minister Jeremy Hanley of Britain wrote, in a letter on 4 December 1995, 'despite the fact that the trial was held in public, it is not possible to say that justice was done. We are concerned that certain aspects of the procedure did not conform to generally accepted international standards.'

In his 9 February 1996 report, Abdelfattah Amor, United Nations Special Rapporteur on Religious Tolerance, wrote, 'The Iranian government had apparently decided to execute those Protestant leaders in order not only to bring the Mojahedin organization into disrepute abroad by declaring it responsible for those crimes, but also, at the domestic level, partly to decapitate the Protestant community and force it to discontinue the conversion of Muslims.'

In the course of the escalation of factional feuding some years later, different government officials revealed that the entire episode had been the brainchild of Deputy Intelligence Minister Saeed Emami, a key figure in the serial murders of political dissidents in the fall of 1998. On 24 June 1999 the state-run *Hamshahri* daily wrote,

> A number of deputies representing religious minorities at the Islamic Assembly [Majlis], intend to call for the reopening of the file on the murder of three Christian clergymen killed a few years ago by three members of the Mojahedin. They said Saeed Emami's involvement in this affair prompted them to make such a call. During investigations into this case, Saeed Emami had arranged for a meeting between the three women and these Majlis deputies. As the Deputy Minister of Intelligence, Emami briefed the Majlis deputies.

The Interior Minister Abdollah Nouri wrote, on 30 October 1999, in the now-defunct *Khordad* daily: 'How is it that when those Christian clergymen were murdered and then their mutilated bodies were placed in a refrigerator, the killers' identities were not made public?' The same daily wrote two weeks later on 18 November:

> In what way were those who claimed in a television interview to be Mojahedin supporters and to have murdered the Christian priests connected to Saeed Emami, the number-two man in the Intelligence Ministry at the time? For what crime were the Iranian Christian clergymen kidnapped in 1994, and kept in a refrigerator after being mutilated? How did [these women] agree to be interviewed and what happened to them eventually?

Noting that the priests were murdered based on a religious decree, the daily added, 'Who issued the religious decree for these murders?'

A former Revolutionary Guards Commander, Akbar Ganji, now out of favour with the ruling faction, said in an interview with the *Arya* daily on 4 December: 'Murdering the clergymen and blaming it on the Mojahedin enabled the perpetrators to liquidate the Christian priests and further discredit the Mojahedin.'

Bombing of the holy shrine of Imam Reza

A powerful bomb rocked the holy shrine of Imam Reza, the revered eighth Shiite Imam, in the north-eastern city of Mashad on 20 June 1994. Scores of worshippers in the packed shrine were reportedly killed or wounded. Several hours later, the scenes of severed limbs and broken glass, broadcast on the state television, shocked viewers across the country.

Immediately after the news of the bombing broke out, Supreme Leader Ali Khamenei said on the state radio: 'The [Mojahedin], blind-hearted and treacherous as they are, have shown that they have no respect whatsoever for the holy family of the Prophet. Such a sacred and magnificent location and such a momentous occasion does not prevent them from displaying their vengeance and vicious enmity toward the Iranian nation.' The clerical regime tried to take advantage of this criminal act on the political and international level. Foreign Minister Ali Akbar Velayati summoned all foreign ambassadors to his ministry and demanded that their governments condemn the Mojahedin and the Iranian Resistance. Some time later, the mullahs claimed that the man who planted the bomb in Imam Reza's shrine had been wounded in a clash as he was trying to leave the country and had confessed that he was a member of the Mojahedin. Two days later, the mullahs announced that the man had died due to the severity of his wounds. Just before his death, the regime claimed, the man had been able to tell the authorities that he was a member of 'the Mojahedin' and ordered by them to plant the bomb! Hardly anyone inside or outside Iran took the clerics' fantastic stories seriously. This prompted the mullahs' propaganda organs to lash out at Western governments and international human rights agencies for not believing their propaganda. In a report of 16 July entitled 'The Most Unprecedented Western and Zionist News Censorship against Iran', the semi-official daily *Ressalat* wrote:

During the past three weeks, the official news agency, IRNA, has written more than 300 news stories, commentaries, etc. about the murder of two Christian priests, the bombing of Imam Reza's shrine ... and the Maki Mosque in Zahedan. In a co-ordinated fashion, the Western, Zionist media that are particularly sensitive to developments in Iran have remained silent about these terrorist actions and even backed the Mojahedin agents ...

Ultimately, during the revelations on the 1998 chain murders, the state-controlled media acknowledged that the bombing of Imam Reza's shrine, like the murder of the Christian priests, had been planned and carried out by the MOIS to tarnish the image of the Mojahedin. In a report on this matter on 20 November 1999, the daily *Khordad* wrote:

Is it not possible that those who plant bombs in public places to pressure the state officials to halt investigations into the case [of serial killings], may have masterminded the incidents of Feiz Mosque in Mashad ... and the bombing of the holy Shrine of Imam Reza a few years ago in order to defuse international pressures over the murder of the Christian clergymen? And was the linking of these three incidents not an attempt to undermine the notion that the murder of the Christian priests may have been an internal affair and to prevent any government official from being held responsible for the killings?

The murder of Christian leaders and the bombing of the holiest Shiite shrine in Iran are just two examples of the atrocities perpetrated by MOIS agents in their dirty war against the Mojahedin, but they reveal the shocking lengths to which the ruling theocrats are prepared to go to demonize their foes.

Notes

1. 'Islamic Culture and Communication Organization' (ICCO) documents, Chapter 3, Iran Ketab, February 1999.

2. *Göteborg Posten*, 19 January 2002.

3. United Nations documents at the Sub-commission of Prevention of Discrimination and Protection of Minorities, 22 August 1996, Appendix.

4. Resolution of 16 August 1996, United Nations documents at the Sub-commission of Prevention of Discrimination and Protection of Minorities, Appendix.

5. 'Iran's Visible Hand in Terrorism', *Washington Times*, 14 March 1996.

6. *Mojahed* weekly, no. 380, 2 March 1998.

7. *Mojahed* weekly, no. 592, 2 July 2002.

13 | In the service of ayatollahs

In a bid to discredit the PMOI's social and political activities, the Ministry of Intelligence and Security strives to demonize the Mojahedin in countries where the PMOI has a presence. *General Intelligence and Security Agency of the Netherlands, Annual Report, 2001*

The Ministry of Intelligence and Security (MOIS) is ranked by experts as one of the largest and most active intelligence agencies in the world, and yet it has been shrouded in so much mystery that apart from occasional revelations, little has ever been made public about its operations and functions. The notable exception to this came in 1998, when a series of gruesome murders of Iranian dissidents by MOIS hit squads led to the disclosure of a catalogue of crimes that had been committed by MOIS agents for more than a decade.

The clerical leaders blamed all the criminal activities of the MOIS on its Deputy Minister Saeed Emami, who was arrested and duly reported to have committed suicide in jail by drinking a hair remover potion. The bizarre account of Emami's death in prison while under round-the-clock supervision convinced no one and it was widely assumed that he had been murdered in order to prevent the leak of sensitive information about MOIS operations, which would have compromised the entire leadership of the Islamic Republic.[1]

The MOIS is no ordinary intelligence agency. It has been behind most of the 450 acts of terrorism the Iranian regime has sponsored around the world since the 1980s. It has a vast network of companies and offices around the world that act as fronts for its illegal operations. It conducts its espionage activities and surveillance operations against Iranian dissidents on every continent. It is involved in the illegal procurement of arms and weapons of mass destruction technology and materials. On the domestic scene, it is the principal agency responsible for dealing with opposition groups and dissidents. Its hit squads routinely abduct, torture and murder suspects at will, without any fear of accountability or punishment. In short, the MOIS is a murder machine.

Stalking the dissidents

The clandestine activities of MOIS outside Iran have long been reported by security agencies in numerous countries. The German security agency, the Office for the Protection of the Constitution, BfV, wrote in its 1997 annual report, 'One of the main tasks of the Iranian secret service is to keep an eye on Iranians living in Germany who oppose the regime.' Its top priority, according to the report, was to maintain surveillance on the People's Mojahedin and the National Council of Resistance.

The agency's 1999 annual report noted that the Iranian secret service was continuing the same pattern of activities:

The principal objective of the Iranian secret service continues to be the fight against Iranian oppositionists. The People's Mojahedin Organization of Iran (PMOI) and its political wing, the NCRI, are still the top target of the Intelligence Ministry's activities. To fight against the activities of the opposition in exile, the Ministry of Intelligence and Security (MOIS) has set up a series of cultural associations. These operate as a front for the MOIS and the Iranian regime. Other than this, the MOIS tries to publish various publications, some in the name of those who introduce themselves as ex-members of the PMOI, in order to persuade sympathizers to abandon the organization.

To undermine the organization, the MOIS even encourages PMOI supporters and other Iranians to visit their families in Iran. Those who accept the offer are approached by MOIS agents in Tehran, who will talk to them directly and sometimes offer bribes or intimidate them or their families in Iran to co-operate with the secret service and provide the ministry with all their information.

The BfV noted in its annual report in 2000:

The Iranian opposition in exile in Germany is at the core of surveillance activities by the MOIS. Various organizations and groups ... are systematically under the surveillance and scrutiny of this service, but the principal target is the most active opposition group, the PMOI and its political wing the NCRI, which is active world-wide. The MOIS has apparently concentrated its efforts on neutralizing opposition groups and their political activities. To this end, the MOIS conducts and finances a propaganda campaign against the NCRI, and even makes use of former opponents of the Iranian regime.

The German security agency's report also noted that on 24 July 2001, an Iranian residing in Germany was arrested in Offenbach and charged with working as an agent of the Iranian secret service. The agent had been spying on Iranian dissidents in Frankfurt.

The BfV's annual report for 2002 noted that 'the priority target of the Iranian intelligence service VEVAK (Ministry for Intelligence and Security) in 2002 was the Iranian opposition groups within the Iranian community in Germany, which numbers more than 100,000 persons'. The report pointed out that, as in the past, the PMOI and the NCRI remain 'the special focus' of the MOIS in Germany. The report noted:

By recruiting active or former members of these organizations, VEVAK seeks to gain information on their anti-regime activities, their structures and leadership cadres. Furthermore, it seeks to weaken their position by intervening in various ways and by focused counter-propaganda.

Intelligence officers as well as staff members committed to co-operate at the diplomatic and consular missions of Iran in Germany are involved, on an undiminished scale, in intelligence-gathering activities. They are trying to recruit informants and exploit them as sources, or give logistic support to operations controlled by their Tehran headquarters.

Personal meetings of these agents and VEVAK's agent handlers as a rule take place in Iran or in third countries.

Dutch Security Agency

The National Intelligence and Security Agency of the Netherlands (Binnenlandse Veiligheidsdienst or BVD, which has since changed its name to AIVD or the General Intelligence and Security Agency) noted in its 1998 annual report: 'We continue to observe that Iranian secret service organizations are active in the Netherlands. Iranian agents are determined to recruit members of opposition groups in order to destabilize their organizations. Their special focus is on present and past members of the People's Mojahedin. The Iranian secret service uses intimidation to obtain Iranians' co-operation.' The BVD observed that 'the control of the Iranian secret services has been shifted to inside Iran. Contacts are increasingly being made directly from Tehran and/or by secret service officers who introduce themselves as, for example, businessmen.'

A year later, the BVD reported:

Iranian officials continue to treat opposition groups with severity. An important assignment of the Iranian secret services is to track and enlist opposition members abroad, especially past and present members of the Mujaheddin-e Khalq (PMOI). The PMOI, the main Iranian opposition organization, has representatives in the Netherlands ... In the West, the PMOI's activities are limited to organizing demonstrations and providing written and oral information on Iran.

The BVD's annual report for the year 2000 noted:

Iranian officials act harshly against opposition groups. Most of their attention is directed at ex-supporters of the PMOI. The Iranian secret service administers its tasks not only under the usual cover of diplomatic activities, but also increasingly from inside Iran. In this respect, they use secret service officers and expatriates. These agents' assignment is to disrupt and harm the Iranian opposition's activities.

The BVD's 2001 report showed that the Iranian regime's campaign to demonize the PMOI in the West was on the rise:

The Ministry of Intelligence and Security (MOIS) has the task of tracking and identifying persons who have contacts with opposition groups abroad. Supporters of the principal opposition group, the Mujaheddin-e Khalq, are the subject of greatest attention by the Iranian secret service. The MOIS tries to collect as much information on this organization as possible through 'ex-members'. MOIS agents are instructed to propagate disinformation about PMOI and its members. In this way, they attempt to undermine the organization and, in a bid to discredit the PMOI's social and political activities, the MOIS strives to demonize the Mojahedin in countries where the PMOI has a presence.

Police investigations

As MOIS agents stepped up their activities in several European nations, police authorities in these countries interviewed many of them and warned them about their ties with the MOIS. Karim Haghi, one of these agents, wrote in a statement under the name of a society called 'Peyvand' (an MOIS front in the Netherlands):

On Tuesday, 1 February 2000, an agent of the Dutch secret service arrived at Karim Haghi's residence in Elst and, after initial talks, started reading names from a list which included Messrs Bani-Sadr, Alireza Nourizadeh, Bahman Niroomand, Nasser Khajeh-Nouri, Parviz Yaghoobi, Mehdi Khanbaba Tehrani, Mehdi Khoshhal, Asghar Barzoo, Bahman Rastgoo, Jaafar Baghalnejad, Hassan Khalaj, Aabed Haj Esmaili, Hadi Shams Haeri, Ghassem (Mohammad Tofigh Assadi), Hassan Alijani, Karim Haghi and Mrs Nadereh Afshari ...

The secret agent said there were more names on the list, but he could not pronounce them and that was why he stopped there. He said: 'All of you are in contact with the Iranian regime and have formed a large network ... You must tell us who else is in contact with the Iranian regime ... We have enough information about your ties with the regime and know that your publication is being financed by the Iranian regime.

We also know that Mr Shams Haeri is in touch with the regime and his contact with the Ministry of Intelligence is his brother. He has travelled to Singapore to meet his MOIS contacts. Mr Parviz Yaghoobi, who lives in France, is also in touch with the Iranian regime ... We want the Netherlands calm and peaceful and do not like to have demonstrations and fighting here. It is best for you to abandon this sort of work at once and go after a normal life and think of your children's future.'

On the same day another secret agent was present at the parking lot near the workplace of Mrs Roya Roodsaz, Karim Haghi's wife, and when she was about to get into her car, he introduced himself and told her that he intended to talk to her. He talked about Haghi's activities and where the funds for the Peyvand publication were coming from. The secret agent told her that Karim and his friends have formed a large network and all of them are in touch with the Iranian regime. Karim has once travelled to Cyprus in this regard.

At the same time, two police cars followed another friend who had taken Mr Haj Esmaili to the train station. When Haj Esmaili got on the train, a person approached him and asked similar questions.

On the same day, six persons in groups of two approached Mehdi Khoshhal, Bahman Rastgoo and Mrs Nadereh Afshari in three German cities, Cologne, Wiesbaden and Hanover, and asked about the contacts and the circulation of the Peyvand publication, how it was financed, etc. In the first week of February, Messrs Shams Haeri, Mohammad Reza Eskandari and his wife Tahereh Khorrami were subjected to questioning (by the Dutch security service). On 9 February, two Dutch secret agents contacted Alireza Mohseni in the Netherlands and asked him what he knew about the names listed above and his contacts with Fereydoon Gilani.[2]

The Counter-terrorism Committee of the National Council of Resistance of Iran issued a statement on 15 February, noting that 'in recent weeks, police and security agencies in a number of countries, including the Netherlands, Germany, Britain, Sweden, Norway and Canada, have called on a number of MOIS agents and warned them about their activities'. The statement added:

As the agents of the mullahs' secret service have reported to their superiors in various embassies as well as to the headquarters in Tehran, police have undeniable evidence like photographs and tapes of conversations of these agents with their handlers in the Ministry of Intelligence. Police authorities have detailed information on the secret trips of these agents to Iran and other neighbouring countries, and in some cases to the Far East, such as Malaysia and Singapore, in order to meet their handlers and officials of the Intelligence Ministry. Likewise, they are aware of trips by a number of these agents to Europe and America in recent months and also know about the money paid to them by the Iranian secret service. In some cases, police are aware of even the amount of weekly or monthly payments to these agents.

In addition, police and intelligence organizations have been informed that the mullahs' Intelligence Ministry has given instructions to such agents as to how to respond to calls from the police and other official agencies and how to defend themselves under the pretext of 'democratic rights'. Police in the Netherlands have been aware of Karim Haghi's ties with the Intelligence Ministry since 1994, as well as his trips to Cyprus and Malaysia and meetings with representatives of the mullahs' Intelligence Ministry.

According to the Dutch security service, the Ministry of Intelligence and Security has been using Karim Haghi to set up a network of its agents in several European countries. Police have numerous photographs of Karim Haghi with official and recognized elements of the MOIS. Distribution of a journal called *Peyvand*, produced by Haghi and fully financed by the MOIS, is in line with the Intelligence Ministry's efforts to create the network. Police have a list of names of Iranians receiving regular payment from the MOIS for their involvement in the journal.

Haghi, while posing as a political refugee, has been using an Iranian passport with the first name Mahmood, with German visa, for his travels. The Ministry of Intelligence in many instances uses Karim Haghi's wife, Roya Roodsaz, for contacting him. Haghi sends his wife to Tehran to deliver 'sensitive reports' and to take 'special instruction' from his contacts. One of his contacts in the ministry is an interrogator-torturer called Nasseri. He is one of the two who, after the arrest of Hamid Khorsand[3] were ordered to arrange his release at any cost.

Police know that Ahmad Shams-Haeri, through a close relative in Iran, is in touch with the Ministry of Intelligence. He was sent to Singapore to visit a representative of the ministry and is considered one of the active members of the network.

Police are also aware of a trip by Haj Esmaili to Singapore to meet MOIS officials and receive money from them. Haj Esmaili's co-operation with MOIS agents and Iranian embassies in Britain and the Netherlands is well known to security agencies. He has received thousands of dollars from the MOIS on several occasions. He went to the Netherlands some time ago and stayed in Haghi's home. Hassan Alijani went to the Netherlands from the United States at the same time and they held joint meetings with other MOIS agents.

In Germany too, the security police approached Ali Akbar (Bahman) Rastgoo, Mehdi Khoshhal and Nadereh Afshari, and told them of their knowledge of the details of their ties with the Ministry of Intelligence. They questioned Rastgoo about the funds he received from the MOIS for his contribution to the *Peyvand* publication.

To protect and boost the sagging morale of its exposed agents, who were shocked and terrified when they realized that police and security agencies in Europe were aware of their MOIS ties, the Intelligence Ministry gave them the following instructions:

- Increase your contacts with each other and exchange your experiences in dealing with police and the type of questions they ask, so that when police approach anyone, he/she would know what questions to expect.
- Spread everywhere that this is a plot by the Mojahedin and that they are trying to halt your activities.
- Spread the rumour among Iranians that this move by police is an international conspiracy to muzzle you.

Different levels of service

Those who are actively in the service of the mullahs' propaganda and espionage campaign against Iranian dissidents and the PMOI abroad can be divided into four categories, according to their background and their effectiveness. The common denominator is that they are now working for the MOIS.

The first group consists of those who have been agents of the MOIS or the Revolutionary Guards' Qods Force and were sent to Iraq on a specific assignment to infiltrate the Mojahedin and the National Liberation Army of Iran. Many of these agents have been arrested and later released by the PMOI after the completion of investigation into their cases; they returned whence they came. After these agents returned to Iran, the MOIS dispatched some of them on new missions abroad. This time they introduced themselves as former members of the Mojahedin who had been subjected to torture and persecution and then forced back to Iran. They now claim to have fled Iran and are applying for asylum in other countries. They claim that they are being threatened by both the Iranian regime and the Mojahedin.

The second group are those who were at one time within the ranks of the Resistance and left the Resistance for personal reasons. A very small percentage of these persons were then recruited by the Intelligence Ministry. To put things into perspective, one must note that the PMOI, during the four decades of struggle against two dictatorships in Iran, has had hundreds of thousands of members and active supporters. According to officials of the clerical regime, half a million persons were recruited by the Mojahedin Organization in Iran in the early 1980s. In the course of such a struggle where 120,000 have been executed, it is natural that some individuals would opt out because, for any number of reasons, they cannot find the motivation or the strength to continue along this demanding path.

Over the years many people have left the ranks of the Resistance to lead an ordinary life. The vast majority of these people remained supportive of the Resistance movement and continue to back it. Many of them have reacted to the Intelligence Ministry's propaganda against the Mojahedin and have even published books in response to false information spread against the Mojahedin, in particular on the alleged mistreatment of former members, but some of them were recruited to the MOIS through threats or enticement.

In a book entitled *Iran: State of Terror*, Lord Eric Avebury wrote on the results of an extensive investigation he personally conducted into the allegations made by such individuals:

> Another method [used by the Iranian intelligence service] is using the small number of defectors who had at one stage cooperated with opposition organizations and individuals. These persons, due to their low or non-existent motivation to continue the struggle and maintain their principles, allowed themselves to be bought by the regime at a later stage. Such people have so far provided the regime's terrorists in Europe with the most extensive intelligence and political services. In addition to providing information on the assassination targets to the regime, they prepare the political grounds for the murders of the dissidents by spreading propaganda against the individuals or organizations they had previously cooperated with, defaming them and accusing them of being worse than the ruling regime.[4]

Mullah Dorri Najafabadi, Khatami's first Minister of Intelligence, said on this issue: 'The Intelligence Ministry provides support for Mojahedin defectors.'[5]

The third group are those who have never been in the Mojahedin organization. For example, a man by the name of Bahman Rastgou, residing in Germany, has been serving the MOIS as 'a former member of the Mojahedin', but he has never been even an active supporter of the Mojahedin.

MOIS 'recycles' exposed agents

Mohammad-Hossein Sobhani was sent on a mission in the 1980s by the Intelligence Ministry to infiltrate the Mojahedin. Today, Sobhani is one of several Intelligence Ministry agents who turned up in Europe within a short period in spring 2002, all using a similar scenario to apply for political asylum. Sobhani, now in Germany, claims that he was 'a senior member of the Mojahedin', jailed for several years after he criticized the strategy and ideology of the organization. He claims that he was sent to Iraqi jails and later exchanged for Iraqi POWs and handed over to the Iranian regime. Once in Iran, he says, he was able to escape from an Iranian prison and find his way to Europe.

Those with even a scant knowledge of prisons in Iran know very well that in the past two decades the number of political prisoners who have managed to escape has not exceeded a handful. In light of this, how feasible does it look that within a period of two months several political prisoners, specially the ones who according to themselves have been handed over by the Mojahedin to Iraqi authorities and by the Iraqis to the Iranian regime, have been able to escape from top-security prisons? Their credibility is not enhanced when one considers the fact that once in Europe, they utter not a word of criticism against the mullahs' regime and attack only the Iranian Resistance and the PMOI.

The Counter-terrorism Committee of the National Council of Resistance of Iran issued a statement on 30 April declaring:

> Mohammad Hossein Sobhani, who three years ago, after his ties with the Iranian regime were exposed, fled the PMOI bases only to be arrested by Iraqi police, and who finally made his way to Iran legally, has recently been sent to Germany by the Ministry of Intelligence. He has established relations with other agents of the MOIS and has been told to pretend that he was a prisoner of the regime who has fled the mullahs' tyranny by some sort of sophisticated scheme and has secretly made his way to Germany!

On 11 June 2002, a month and half later, an Internet site used as a front by the Intelligence Ministry posted an interview with Sobhani to claim that although he was returned to Iran from Iraq on 21 January 2002, he escaped following a clash and a shoot-out in Tehran, fled Iran and came to Europe in March 2002. But what is the reality? A report by the Counter-intelligence Directorate of the NLA, published in the PMOI's weekly journal, *Mojahed*, on 2 July 2002, disclosed:

> Mohammad Hossein Sobhani was a member of the mullahs' army who

was assigned in February 1983 to infiltrate the Mojahedin in Kurdistan. He was first deployed in logistics bases and from February 1990 to autumn 1991 was a member of a protection team for transportation. But suspicions over his case persisted and he never gained the trust of PMOI officials. In 1986, his commander, Fereydoun Varmazyari, became so suspicious of Sobhani's behaviour that he had Sobhani disarmed. In the conspiracy to assassinate Mr Massoud Rajavi in 1992, Sobhani's falsified records and his ties to the Intelligence Ministry were unveiled. Thorough investigations into the assassination attempt and the heavy bombing of a PMOI camp only seventeen days later led to the discovery of suspicious links between Mohammad Hossein Sobhani and his brother, Ja'afar Sobhani, an Intelligence Ministry agent seconded to the Education Ministry, and another Revolutionary Guards official in Evin Prison.

In 1999, Sobhani ran away from the NLA to cross the border into Iran, but was arrested by the Iraqi authorities and subsequently sent to Iran through a legal process in 2002. A few weeks later, the Intelligence Ministry sent him to Europe on a new assignment. Two senior officials of the Intelligence Ministry by the names of Haj Gholami and Haj Saeed were responsible for the debriefing and preparation of Sobhani and his companions, who included Ardeshir Parhizkari, Farhad Javaheri Yar and Edouard Termadoyan, for their new assignment. Another MOIS agent in the group, Ramin Darami, described the events in a letter addressed to 'dear brother Haj Saeed' on 20 February 2002:

After we entered Iran through legal channels, we were sent to the Marmar Hotel in Tehran and were given a high-level reception. While we were in the Marmar Hotel, the head of our team was brother Mohammad Hossein Sobhani and others in our group were Ali Qashqavi and Taleb Jalilian. Our brothers from the Intelligence (Ministry) paid us daily visits and resolved any problems we had and during this period I spoke to Haj Mahmoud ... My stay in the hotel lasted ten days ... During the period we stayed in the Marmar Hotel, your proposed plans were reviewed several times by brother Mohammad Hossein Sobhani within our team and we were briefed on that.[6]

'Dissident' exposed as MOIS agent

Karim Haghi introduces himself as 'the former head of personal protection of Maryam Rajavi and now a political refugee in the Netherlands' and claims that he was a 'member of the People's Mojahedin for fifteen years'.[7] Haghi has never been 'the head of personal protection of Mrs Rajavi' or a 'member of the Mojahedin for 15 years'. Haghi was in the NLA, like thousands of other combatants and, like all the others, performed sentry and guard duties on a rotational basis. During the bombings of Iraq in 1991, he said that for physical reasons he could no longer remain in the NLA and asked to be transferred to Baghdad to lead an ordinary life, a request that was granted. In January 1993, Haghi and his wife and child were sent to France, with their expenses for the trip and stay in France paid in full by the PMOI. Within a few months more than 67,000 French francs were paid to him by the Mojahedin, but after a few months he decided to go to the Netherlands and apply for asylum in that country. After May 1993, he had no contacts with the Mojahedin.

In 1994, Haghi was recruited by the MOIS and from 1995 on, he was in regular contact with Maqsoudi, an MOIS handler working under diplomatic cover in the Iranian consulate in the Netherlands. It was then that, three years after leaving Iraq, Haghi suddenly 'remembered' that he had been imprisoned and tortured by the Mojahedin during the years he had been in Iraq. The MOIS made Haghi the ringleader of its espionage network in the Netherlands. The network was set up around a journal called Peyvand, which had been launched by the Intelligence Ministry against the PMOI. Haghi receives money and other facilities directly from the Intelligence Ministry and is in contact with other known agents of the Intelligence Ministry in Europe.

On the instructions of his MOIS handlers, Haghi has raised a series of false allegations against the PMOI in the Netherlands, once accusing PMOI supporters of breaking into his home and committing theft. The Dutch Ministers of Justice and Interior, asked during a debate in a parliamentary committee about allegations of PMOI wrongdoing in the Netherlands, gave this joint response:

> The Mojahedin are known in the Netherlands as an organization that organizes peaceful demonstrations. It is also apparent that they collect contributions in the streets under an affiliated charity called SIM. In that respect, there has been some conflict on the way the collectors deal with the people to raise contributions. But there is no record or document indicating that Mojahedin have been involved in smuggling people or committing any other serious illegal acts of a criminal nature.[8]

In his revelations, Jamshid Tafrishi, a former MOIS agent who defected after ten years, said:

> In April 1996, Karim Haghi met with Saeed Emami in Singapore and Peyvand publications was used as a cover to receive money for members

of the network. After releasing the first issue of *Peyvand* in July 1997, Amir Hossein Taqavi (director general of MOIS for Europe and in charge of the office for special operations who directly guided the terrorist operations abroad) contacted me and asked for my views on the publication.[9]

Karim Haghi was one of the organizers of the Intelligence Ministry's seminar on 18 April 2003 against the Mojahedin in Paris. During Mrs Rajavi's detention in Paris, he was involved in a co-ordinated campaign trying to fill the empty judicial file with false propaganda against the Mojahedin. He told the French daily *La Croix*: 'Having Mrs Rajavi in jail gives us hope to live in Europe!'

Getting away with murder

Some of the Intelligence Ministry agents now being used in the propaganda campaign against the PMOI have committed murder or other serious crimes against PMOI members. Qassem Salehi, for example, is one of the individuals used by the Intelligence Ministry in Tehran to meet with journalists and foreign visitors and pose as a former member of the Mojahedin. He was an MOIS agent who was sent on a specific mission to assassinate Resistance officials. He entered Iraq via the Qasr-e Shirin border post in January 1998 with the help of the Intelligence Ministry. On 13 June 1999, he shot dead, from behind, PMOI member Mahmoud Agah in a bus terminal in Abadan. He wounded two other members of the Mojahedin and several innocent passengers and then went to the Intelligence Department. In subsequent investigations, it was revealed that in 1992 he had murdered someone and that the MOIS had given him a chance to evade execution if he agreed to be hired by them as a professional killer. He accepted, and after a six-year service in Iran, was sent on a murderous mission against the PMOI.[10]

Ali Qashqavi is another such case. Born in 1969 in Babol, northern Iran, he went to Iraq through Turkey in 1993 and joined the NLA. He was later discovered to have been a member of Hezbollah since 1986. He admitted that he had been briefed on his assignment to infiltrate the PMOI by Haji Rezapour and Qorbanali Sadeqi at Babol Intelligence Department in mid-1993. He was pardoned in May 1998 and later returned to Iran, where the Intelligence Ministry is using him to intimidate the families of PMOI members.[11]

Abbas Sadeqi Nejad was an army lieutenant when he received his instructions to infiltrate the PMOI on 25 April 1991. He was given the assignment in a meeting in his native Malayer, in western Iran, attended by the intelligence commander of the Revolutionary Guards, the representative of Supreme Leader Khamenei in Malayer and several other senior officials. His mission was to carry out a suicide attack against the Mojahedin leadership, but he was uncovered by the NLA's counter-intelligence. He was detained for three months and then released by the NLA to pursue his life in Iran, but he insisted on remaining. He wrote:

I was assigned by Ali-Mohammad Panji from the Revolutionary Guards Corps on 25 April 1991. In the meeting where I was assigned, Gholam Akbari, head of the intelligence, Manouchehr Abedi, the Supreme Leader's representative in Malayer, Ali Fazelian, Friday prayers leader at the time, Mansour Omid, Revolutionary Guards Corps deputy and Reza Esmail-Pour, in charge of the Guards Corps supply in extraterritorial operations, were present. My assignment was to carry out a suicide attack against the leadership of the People's Mojahedin Organization using hand grenades or TNT, which had to be procured locally. To avoid any leak, I was supposed to go for it on my own and plan for necessary supplies and the operation on the scene. The location for the operation was to be one of the general meetings.

On 17 April 2001, Sadeqi Nejad received a coded letter together with a message from his wife from Iran. In June 2002, he stole a vehicle, some money and equipment and fled to Iran through the Jalawla region. He has also been used by the MOIS since his return to make propaganda against the Mojahedin.

Adham Tayyebi, another MOIS agent, tried to murder a Mojahedin member, Hamid Arbab, as he made his getaway to Iran in December 2001. After stealing a car and a weapon, he went to Iraqi Kurdistan and, with the help of Intelligence Ministry agents in that area, went to Iran. He went to Tehran via Baneh and Saqez. The Intelligence Ministry dispatched him to Europe after he was debriefed and received instructions on his new mission. Tayyebi is now introducing himself as 'the head of production, and programme presenter of the Resistance's satellite broadcasting service', while the fact is that he played the role of an actor in TV comedy programmes during the time he was in the border region in a PMOI base.

The MOIS agents mentioned in this chapter are but a few of the many being used by the Iranian regime in a variety of ways, either in its propaganda campaign to smear the PMOI and the NCRI or to facilitate or conduct its terrorist plots. It must be noted, however, that the freedom of action enjoyed by the Intelligence Ministry's spies, terrorists and agents against the Iranian Resistance and refugees in Europe is a direct consequence of a misguided policy that places trade and short-term interests ahead of political and ethical principles. While MOIS agents roam freely in these countries, the masterminds and perpetrators of the murders of dozens of Iranian dissidents on European soil have yet to face justice.

Notes

1. For a full treatment of the 'serial political murders' and the role of the MOIS, see Lord Avebury's 'Fatal Writ: An Account of Murders and Cover-ups', British Committee on Iran Freedom, 2000.

2. Statement by the publishers of *Peyvand*, cited in *Mojahed* weekly, no. 481, 22 February 2000.

3. Hamid Khorsand is one of the spies who infiltrated into the network of Mojahedin supporters in Germany and was identified and arrested. After a long trial in Berlin, he was sentenced to eighteen months' imprisonment.

4. Lord Avebury, *Iran: State of Terror*, London: Parliamentary Human Rights Group, 1996.

5. Islamic Republic News Agency (IRNA), interview with Hojjatol-Islam Dorri Najafabadi, Minister of Intelligence and Security, 4 December 1998.

6. Ramin Darami, letter to 'Haj Saeed', *Mojahed*, no. 597, 8 August 2002.

7. French television, FR3, interview with Karim Haghi, 1 July 2003.

8. Minutes of proceedings, House of Representatives of the Netherlands, Tweede Kamer der Staten-Generaal, no. 1436, 1998–99.

9. Jamshid Tafrishi, 'Intelligence Ministry's Plans and Conspiracies', Iran Ketab, 2001.

10. Report by the Counter-intelligence Directorate of the NLA on the discovery of plots by infiltrators of the MOIS, *Mojahed*, no. 592, 2 July 2002.

11. Ibid.

14 | On cults and cult of personality

In a typical 'cult' diatribe against the Mojahedin, the state-owned Tehran daily *Hamshahri* wrote, on 28 February 2002, 'In its military camps, the PMOI uses unique methods to indoctrinate supporters. Means of brainwashing with the use of force and weapons are prevalent in these bases. In general, the organization is the cult of one person, its leader, [Massoud] Rajavi.'

The use of the term 'cult' against a resistance movement may be justified, if a scientific and impartial study of the movement confirms the accusation, but those who are behind the propaganda to depict the PMOI as a cult are interested neither in objectivity nor precision. They seek to demonize the Iranian Resistance by stigmatizing it with a word that immediately conjures up an extremely negative meaning in most people's minds. In *The Kingdom of Cults*, Walter Martin cites one of the many definitions of a cult as 'a small, evil religious group which engages in brainwashing and other mind-control techniques'. The term cult evokes such strong reactions that in May 1998, the Associated Press sent a memorandum to its editors, instructing them not to use the term because it had acquired a 'pejorative aura'. *Christianity Today* – the largest Evangelical magazine in the USA – recommended to its members in February 1990 that Christians should avoid using the word.

In testimony about 'cults', Professor William Taft Stuart said,

the term cult is an inherently prejudicial one, especially as it is understood in the ordinary American English that we all speak. Specifically the term 'cult' carries a variety of negative connotations that are fundamentally prejudgmental in character. As a result, the term is singularly ill-suited to achieving what I would think would be the required dispassion and even-handedness [in] an inquiry that should stay above the fray of highly charged, often hostile, even shrill prejudgment that frequently amounts to persecution.

Professor Taft noted that 'the interests of fair-play and due-process' require that inquiries into such issues 'be based not on hearsay, anecdotes, and impassioned alarms, but on careful, even-handed scholarship'.[1]

What is a cult?

The term 'cult' is derived from the Latin noun *cultus*, which is related to the verb *colere*, which means 'to worship or give reference to a deity'. The Oxford Dictionary (1971) defines 'cult' as a 'particular form or system of religious worship; especially in reference to its external rites and ceremonies'. The Miriam Webster Dictionary offers a broader definition: 'A religion regarded as unorthodox or spurious ... a usually small group of people characterized by great devotion to a person, idea, object, movement, or work'.

The works and debates of social psychologists and sociologists in the United States and Europe in the past four decades show that when it comes to the question of defining a cult, the main issue is to distinguish between a cult, a sect and a religion. No conventional political or social party or movement, irrespective of its ideology or size, falls within this ambit of assessment. Today, such movements are essentially described as 'new religious movements', as opposed to being called 'cults'. Even at the turn of the twentieth century, distinguished German sociologists Max Weber and Ernest Troeltsch, when offering a sociological definition for cult, distinguished between religion, denomination and cult. They contrasted 'Church' (i.e., established religion) with both 'sect' – a schismatic group that is in tense, critically judgemental relations with the (parent) religion, although intentionally remaining within the pale of acceptability, a kind of loyal opposition – and with 'cult', where the movement – in its and/or its parent church's definition – goes beyond what at least the parent church, and perhaps even the new religion itself, would consider acceptably orthodox in the old order.

The main attributes of a cult

Researchers have offered different attributes and criteria for identifying a cult, depending on one's perspective. Some of the most important attributes of a cult about which there is consensus are as follows:

- being introverted and isolated from the outside world;
- limited size and geographical spread;
- lack of leadership structure and accountability mechanism;
- secret beliefs;
- purporting that the 'leader' has superhuman powers or is infallible;
- brainwashing and techniques to control the mind;
- employing deceptive or coercive means to recruit; and
- in many cases propagating misogynistic thinking.

Relying on these sociological criteria or any definition of a cult to accuse the PMOI of being one is absurd and pursues toxic political objectives.

A long-standing, extensive political movement

Friend and foe concur that the People's Mojahedin Organization of Iran is the largest political organization in Iran's history. Since its inception, nearly forty years ago, the organization has defined itself as a democratic, nationalist and anti-fundamentalist Muslim organization that espoused a clear and transparent strategy, political programme and objectives. It quickly became an important opposition group at the time of the Shah, whose regime executed all PMOI founders and many of its members. In the past two decades, the clerical regime has executed 120,000 of its members and activists, and imprisoned and tortured hundreds of thousands more. In 1988, Khomeini issued a fatwa, later revealed by his deposed successor Ayatollah Hossein-Ali Montazeri, which called for the massacre of all PMOI political prisoners. In a matter of several months, 30,000 Mojahedin were executed in Iran's prisons.

Last year, the PMOI organized more than a thousand demonstrations and protests in Iran and at least twenty major demonstrations in Europe and North America in which tens of thousands of Iranians took part. A pro-Khatami daily, Akhbar Eqtesad, wrote, 'The number of viewers of Mojahedin's television program is greater than the circulation of newspapers published by the 23 May [pro-Khatami] coalition.'[2]

In a research paper in 1997, Dr Kelton Rhodes of the University of Southern California stated that the most important difference between a cult and a political party or movement is its 'ultimate goal'. In a cult, that goal is entirely introverted. Cult expert Margaret Thaler Singer, who teaches at the University of California, Berkeley, wrote in her book, *Cults in Our Midst* (San Francisco, 1996), that the energy and focus of parties and political parties is directed at the environment outside their own organization and with the objective of improving the lives of people who are not their own members. On the other hand, the energy and focus of a cult is entirely internally directed, with no interest in the outside world. She described a cult as a closed circle that serves only itself and not wider goals beyond the cult.

A deeply rooted popular movement

A common attribute of cults is their limited size and lack of deep roots in society. The PMOI enjoys extensive popular support and has deep social roots in Iran, attributable to its four decades of extensive political and social activity against two dictatorships in Iran. No cult can organize political rallies and meetings attended by hundreds of thousands of people, as the PMOI did in Tehran and other Iranian cities prior to the reign of absolute repression and summary executions by the mullahs.

In the first post-revolutionary presidential election in Iran, the PMOI Secretary General Massoud Rajavi was endorsed by all anti-clerical opposition forces, and ethnic and religious groups such as the Kurds, Christians, Zoroastrians and Jews, as their presidential candidate. But Khomeini issued a fatwa, barring Rajavi from running in the election because the PMOI did not vote for the regime's constitution, based on *velayat-e faqih* and the mullahs' absolute rule.

The mullahs' deep-seated fear of the PMOI and the broader Resistance movement is a reflection of their insecurity, for they are acutely aware of their own unpopularity and the Resistance's mass following. The clerical regime's own official survey showed that 94 per cent of Iranians oppose clerical rule.[3] This phenomenon explains the hysterical reaction that the Iranian regime shows to anything that highlights the broad appeal not only of the PMOI, but also that of the Resistance movement as a whole. When the Tehran-based daily *Asia* created a sensation by publishing on the front page of its 4 July issue a picture of Maryam Rajavi being greeted by her supporters at Auvers-sur-Oise, officials banned the paper and arrested the editor in chief, the executive editor and at least seven of their colleagues and relatives, including the editor's seventeen-year-old son, piling up a frightening array of bogus charges against them. The clerical authorities' sole aim was to 'teach a lesson' to other editors and journalists and make sure no one would repeat such a 'mistake'.

An open movement with vast international support

To survive, a cult must by definition be introverted and reclusive. The PMOI, on the contrary, has the most extensive contacts with Iranian society and with the international community. For more than two decades, the PMOI has been a member of a 550-member political coalition, the National Council of Resistance of Iran, which represents a spectrum of different, even conflicting, views and ideologies, from liberals to free-market supporters, socialists and Marxists. Acting as the Resistance's parliament, it is the highest authority for adopting the plans and programmes of the Resistance.

The PMOI is a component of a broader resistance movement that is present or has offices in 200 cities around the world and enjoys widespread contacts with political parties and the media in more than thirty countries. Majorities in the United States Congress, British House of Commons and parliaments in Italy, Belgium and Luxembourg as well as thousands of other parliamentarians and political personalities, support the Iranian Resistance. The offices of the movement, whether in Iraq or elsewhere, have always been open to foreign visitors, journalists, political figures and United Nations representatives. Hundreds of foreign journalists have for years visited the movement's bases along the Iran–Iraq frontier and engaged freely with its members and activists.

Formal leadership structure and accountability

A cult does not have a formal, openly announced and institutionalized leadership structure. Generally speaking, it is a one-man show. The PMOI, in contrast, has a collective leadership structure and has been completely transparent and open in telling the Iranian people and the world at large how its leadership is elected and who its members are. In the past sixteen years, despite the repression prevailing in Iran and threats of mullahs' terrorism, the PMOI has held, according to its constitution, the bi-annual congress of its members and officials in the presence of foreign journalists and guests. It has elected five secretaries general through the direct vote of all its members. Members of the PMOI's leadership councils, who are all elected to their posts and lead the organization's different departments, are not only criticized and held accountable by lower-ranking members in congresses, but are also in regular departmental meetings. So institutionalized is the collective decision-making process in the PMOI that all those involved would testify that in the past two decades, not a single decision on important matters has been taken by an individual. PMOI members take part in more decision-making meetings than do members of any other opposition movements to dictatorships in the contemporary world.

Despite the obvious security risks involved for an organization fighting a brutal religious tyranny, moreover, the PMOI has consistently announced the names of its officials at all times.

Rejection of reactionary interpretations of leadership

A distinct feature of the PMOI's ideology has been its emphasis on collective leadership and the fallibility of its leaders, who can be openly criticized for their errors. This viewpoint is diametrically opposed to Khomeini's, who maintained that the Supreme Leader, the *vali-e faqih*, is God's representative on earth and consequently infallible.

The PMOI was the only major Iranian political organization that did not vote for the new regime's constitution in 1980, because it viewed the principle of *velayat-e faqih* (literally 'guardianship of the jurisprudent', resulting in unlimited powers in the hands of the Supreme Leader, who is by definition a Shiite cleric) as reactionary and undemocratic. For this reason, Khomeini vetoed Massoud Rajavi's candidacy in the presidential election.

The PMOI has always stressed that the leadership of a political and social movement is not and cannot be infallible. The organization's books talk candidly about mistakes committed at the highest level of the leadership at various stages of the struggle both against the Shah and the mullahs' dictatorship. In the organization's congresses, the Leadership Council presents its record warts and all for the scrutiny and criticism of the other officials and the rank and file of the organization. This tradition is a carry-over from the days when Massoud Rajavi was the Secretary General.

PMOI composition and diversity

A look at the composition of PMOI members, their scientific background, educational level, birthplace and other particulars shows clearly that the movement's members come from all across Iran and from all social groupings. They are of various educational levels and ages. These attributes are a world apart from the usual composition of a cult. PMOI members include eighteen-year-old women and men as well as those in their seventies. Most members come from the urban areas, while others have joined from the rural regions. Before joining the movement, they were students, teachers, professors, workers, engineers, physicians, architects, army officers, artists, computer scientists, entrepreneurs and holders of a variety of other jobs, bringing to the organization a diversity that enriches its relationships and enhances its strengths.

Committed to transparency

The PMOI is profoundly committed to transparency and openness. It is engaged in a struggle against a regime the international community regards as 'the most active state sponsor of terrorism in the world', which carried out 450 terrorist attacks in the past two decades and killed or wounded hundreds of the Resistance's activists outside Iran. Despite such security risks, and contrary to prevailing practice among organizations involved in a war of liberation, the PMOI has always announced the names of its officials.

The Resistance's media outlets provide detailed reports on the activities of the PMOI to the public. It has never engaged in secretive deals, never conducted clandestine diplomacy, and has never had skeletons hidden in its closet. Extraordinary for a large political entity this may be, but it is a record that more than two decades of struggle against the mullahs' regime readily prove. When the Resistance decided that it must promote peace in the devastating Iran–Iraq war, it announced its decision openly and Massoud Rajavi held a meeting with Iraq's foreign minister in Paris, appearing with him in front of journalists. When he met Iraq's president in Baghdad in 1986, again it was a public meeting and Rajavi did not mince his words when he wanted to remind his Iraqi interlocutors that PMOI forces fought the Iraqi army when it invaded Iran in 1980. Through public statements and press releases, the Resistance has also presented the public in Iran and around the world with facts dealing with accusations and allegations against it. The Iranian Resistance has always published in great detail its political programmes, ideological views and strategic positions, more so than any other liberation movement.

Women's status in the Resistance

Sociologists have highlighted misogynistic thinking and the abuse of women's rights as a common attribute of cults. In this respect, the PMOI and the Iranian Resistance are unique, not only in the Middle East but also around the world. Women are active in all levels of the Resistance, including its leadership. They comprise more than half the members of the Parliament-in-exile, the National Council of Resistance of Iran. This is particularly outstanding, because the mullahs' misogynistic regime has reduced women to second-class citizens and violated their most basic human rights.

The most educated liberation army

International journalists, diplomats and UN representatives who have visited PMOI bases in Iraq have noted that the movement's members are essentially graduates of Western universities or intellectuals, who have joined the movement to liberate their country from the clutches of the ruling theocratic state. Sociologists and cult experts often cite paranoia, nervous breakdown, indecisiveness, rigid mindset and poor judgement as commonly found traits among cult members. The hundreds of journalists and numerous diplomats and dignitaries who have visited Resistance camps or been in contact with PMOI officials over the years have not reported any such behavioural anomalies. On the contrary, outsiders' descriptions of PMOI members often revolve around such characteristics as self-confidence, determination, calmness, hospitality and creativity. These attributes have been put to the test repeatedly in the different arenas of the struggle against the clerical regime. Without such members, the Resistance could not possibly have survived, let alone grown, in the face of a most brutal dictatorship, a tyranny so terrorizing that many governments, meek or mighty, have tried to mollify it, either in the hope of being spared from its terrorism or of obtaining trade benefits.

Coercive recruitment and treatment of members

Two decades of bloody suppression sanctioned by Khomeini's fatwa, which declared the lives and properties of PMOI members and sympathizers fair game, saw 120,000 members and sympathizers executed. Thus, those who take the risks – directly, to their lives – to join the PMOI are fully aware of the personal costs that such an action might entail. No one can join such a well-known organization through coercion or ignorance. Indeed, the democratic modus operandi within the PMOI is primarily attributable to the fact that PMOI members in and out of Iran have joined the fight against the mullahs' dictatorship of their own free will. This exercise of free will remains with them throughout their struggle in the ranks of the Resistance. No one can be forced to fight against a ruthless dictatorship against his/her will. In their reports, dozens of journalists who have interviewed PMOI members in Iran or along the Iran–Iraq frontier or in different countries around the world have noted this fact. Meanwhile, the PMOI has always said that while joining the organization is difficult, leaving its ranks is relatively easy. The presence of hundreds of former PMOI activists, transferred with the organization's money and resources to Europe from the Iran–Iraq border region once they said they could no longer tolerate the difficulties of the struggle, is a testament to this fact. The vast majority of these former activists have continued to lead ordinary lives.

The 'mind doctor'

Amid public expressions of abhorrence over the arrest of Mrs Maryam Rajavi and a number of refugees in France, Ehsan Naraghi said that Saddam Hussein had been 'the guru of the cult' of the Mojahedin and their 'great defender.'[4] Naraghi was, in fact, one of the first 'intellectual collaborators' of the mullahs' security services to suggest the use of 'cult' as a label to attack the Mojahedin. This happened in Tehran's notorious Evin Prison back in the 1980s.

Political prisoners lucky enough to escape from the clerical regime's torture centres have testified that since the early 1980s, the clerical regime has used the services of several collaborating intellectuals in a bid to break the resistance of political prisoners who would not succumb to brutal physical torture. The objective was to convince the prisoners that the PMOI was 'deviant' and 'deceptive' and that its leadership recruited members through 'brainwashing' and 'mind control.' Ehsan Naraghi was one of the collaborators who became known as Evin Prison's 'mind doctors'.

During the Shah's regime, Naraghi was for some time a communist Tudeh Party activist.[5] After the Tudeh Party's demise in the wake of the 1953 coup, he joined many other party cadres who switched overnight from Stalinist communism to avowed monarchism and collaborated with the Shah's secret police, SAVAK. While Naraghi wrote a book after the 1979 revolution titled *From Palace to Prison*, he has been silent on a far more interesting transformation, namely from an extreme-left organizer in Geneva University to KGB-dominated Tudeh Party activist in Iran and then 'From the Tudeh Party to the Shah's SAVAK'.

Naraghi became one of the active figures in intellectual and cultural matters in the Shah's court and a confidant of the Prime Minister Amir-Abbas Hoveida. In post-revolutionary times, he quickly offered his services to the mullahs. By holding debates with defiant political prisoners, Naraghi tried to break their morale. He had close ties to religious judges, torturers and interrogators such as the notorious hanging judge Mohammadi Gilani, currently President of the Supreme Court, chief interrogator Hossein Shariatmadari, currently editor-in-chief of the daily *Kayhan*, his deputy Hassan Bakhshafar, and one of the founders of the Intelligence Ministry, Saeed Hajjarian, who adopted the pseudonym Saeed Mozaffari while he worked as a torturer and interrogator in Evin Prison in the 1980s.

Political prisoners in Evin knew full well that Ehsan Naraghi and like-minded friends complemented the work of the mullahs' henchmen in the prisons with many, such as Shariatmadari, using both tactics. For this reason, prisoners despised Naraghi and other 'brains' behind the torturers' 'brawn'. Even the public, accustomed to daily executions and repression in every corner of every town, scoffed at such propaganda and expressed outrage towards them. Naraghi's loyal services to the mullahs in Evin Prison earned the clerics' trust and, seeing the need for such anti-PMOI propaganda outside Iran, the clerical regime sent him abroad to join the propaganda campaign. Interestingly, in a 12 November 1999 interview with the 'Voice of America' television station, Naraghi emphasized that torture in Iran 'could be justified a hundred per cent' and that 'one could not absolutely say that torture is a bad thing'. In a 6 May 1994 interview with the daily *Kayhan*, Naraghi endorsed

Khomeini's fatwa to murder Salman Rushdie: 'When I heard the news about the fatwa, I was overcome with joy, because in Rushdie's book I saw blasphemy and impudence.'

Fifteen-year 'impasse'

Another PMOI-basher who incidentally shares Mr Naraghi's Tudeh Party background is Ervand Abrahamian. After almost a decade-long silence on the issue of the PMOI, Abrahamian joined the fray again in the summer of 2003, as the international community began to focus once again on the clerical regime's fundamentalist and terrorist designs in Iraq and on its vigorous pursuit of weapons of mass destruction, and amid public outrage over France's clamp-down on Iranian refugees and the NCRI. Abrahamian told the *New York Times*, 'No one can criticize Rajavi ... [Self-criticism sessions are] all done on tape, so they have records of what you say. If there's a sign of resistance, you're considered not revolutionary enough, and you need more ideological training. Either people break away or succumb.' He told the *Washington Post* that the Mojahedin 'had degenerated into a tightknit cult dedicated to studying the thought of Massoud Rajavi'.

There is no ambiguity about Abrahamian's new mandate after his decade-long silence on the PMOI. The Iranian Resistance had exposed the mullahs' role in terrorism, fundamentalism and weapons of mass destruction. Such activities dismay certain circles in the United States, who see their interests rooted in maintaining the status quo in Iran. In response, they launched a well-orchestrated campaign to prevent the USA from adopting a realistic policy *vis-à-vis* the 'most active state sponsor of terrorism', which is on the verge of acquiring nuclear weapons.

The leitmotif of this campaign was to demonize the PMOI by using a discredited label, namely 'cult'. This would, in turn, open the way for doing business with the religious dictatorship in Iran. In these interviews, however, Abrahamian has not explained how his prediction fifteen years ago, about the PMOI's 'demise', turned out to be wrong. In the aftermath of the Irangate fiasco, which included Mojahedin-bashing to 'facilitate' rapprochement with Tehran,[6] Abrahamian published a book, *The Iranian Mojahedin*, in which he described the PMOI for the first time as a 'cult'. *The Iranian Mojahedin* is a curious book. In the first ten of the book's eleven chapters, the reader learns about a Mojahedin organization that has become the strongest opposition force to the mullahs' regime. 'Today they are among the most active groups in opposition to Khomeini ... a group who may yet emerge as a force in post-Khomeini Iran,' the reader is told. Then all of a sudden, the final chapter comes as a complete break with previous passages and an organization with deep and extensive roots in Iranian society suddenly turns into an 'inward-looking sect' and, a few lines later, into a 'cult'. In 1988, Abrahamian's edict was that the 'Mojahedin became increasingly a world unto itself' and no longer able to influence events in Iran. History has proven him wrong, and his prediction of the Mojahedin's demise turned out to be wishful thinking. He had lost sight of the fact that before him, the ruling mullahs, from Khomeini to Khamenei and Rafsanjani, had declared hundreds of times that the PMOI was finished and destroyed, only to see the organization grow and pose a continuing threat to their rule.

For years after writing his book, Abrahamian did not, publicly, make any comments about the PMOI, believing that his mission had ended. But the Irangate holdovers in Washington, who vigorously promote appeasement as the best policy option on Iran, again used Abrahamian in the propaganda blitz about moderation after Khatami became president in May 1997. He put up a vociferous defence of Khatami. In an interview with Radio Azadi, Abrahamian said, 'What gives the Islamic Republic a great deal of legitimacy is a republican definition of the system. By a republican system, I mean the fact that there is an environment for elections, participation, representation and an elected president who was elected with 80 per cent of the vote in 1997.'

Most recently, despite government-sponsored surveys that indicated that a vast majority of Iranians demand regime change, Abrahamian told ABC News, 'The vast majority of Iranians do not seek a regime change; a vocal minority does not reflect the sentiments of society's grass roots.'

If the PMOI, as Abrahamian has claimed, had reached an impasse fifteen years ago, what is all the fuss all about now?

Cult of personality

'Cult of personality', 'inward-looking sect', 'leader worship' and other similar allegations against the Iranian Resistance are not based on any careful and impartial investigation. They smack of a new McCarthyism, which has no objective other than character assassination of the leaders of the Iranian Resistance. The public still remembers the McCarthy era in the late 1940s and early 1950s. Howard Zinn's book, *A People's History of the United States* (New York, Harper Row: 1980), describes what this weird period of American history was like:

Speaking to a Republican Women's Club in Wheeling, West Virginia, in early 1950, Senator Joseph McCarthy held up some papers and shouted,

'I have here in my hand a list of 205 – a list of names that were made known to the Secretary of State as being members of the Communist Party and who nevertheless are still working and shaping policy in the State Department.'

The next day, speaking in Salt Lake City, McCarthy claimed he had a list of fifty-seven (the number kept changing) such communists in the State Department. Shortly afterward, he appeared on the floor of the Senate with photostatic copies of about a hundred dossiers from State Department loyalty files. The dossiers were three years old, and most of the people were no longer with the State Department, but McCarthy read from them anyway, inventing, adding, and changing as he read. In one case, he changed the dossier's description of 'liberal' to 'communistically inclined', in another from 'active fellow traveler' to 'active communist', and so on. Under pressure from Senator McCarthy's propaganda campaign, the State Department issued directives to remove books by authors suspected of being communists from its overseas libraries. One of those removed was *The Selected Works of Thomas Jefferson*, author of America's Declaration of Independence.

Slanders and smear campaigns are no strangers to the treacherous world of politics, but this does not make them any less immoral or, at times, criminal. General Charles de Gaulle, France's most famous president and the leader of the Resistance during the Nazi occupation, was slandered so often that in 1958, when he ran for president, he said that although he had fought for France's liberty, some people accused him of being a dictator.

When it comes to the question of the cult of personality, how does one distinguish between a cult of personality and a political leader's genuine popularity?

Soviet leader Nikita Khrushchev's confidential address to the twentieth congress of the Communist Party of the Soviet Union, on 25 February 1956, continues to be the most reverberating document history has produced on the 'cult of personality'. Citing Lenin, Marx and other Marxist icons, Khrushchev condemned some of the methods that took shape during Stalin's reign as a cult of personality and demanded that they be eliminated. After half a century, one is jolted by reading about atrocities that Khrushchev described as the consequences of such a cult. For example, he referred to the purging and execution of a large number of members and officials of the Communist Party in the 1930s: 'Many party activists who were branded in 1937–38 as "enemies" were actually never enemies, spies, wreckers, etc., but were always honest communists

... and often, no longer able to bear barbaric tortures, they charged themselves with all kinds of grave and unlikely crimes.'

In the book *Ambiguities of Domination*, author Lisa Wedeen writes that the Syrian regime devoted 'a substantial proportion of its meager resources to the ubiquitous celebration of Asad' and promoted such titles for him as 'the premier pharmacist' of the country and suggested that he was immortal. She notes that his cult of personality reinforced Asad's power by 'demonstrating that his regime can compel people to say the ridiculous and to avow the absurd'.[7]

Similar examples could be found in other Third World countries. Extravagant and expensive birthday celebrations, personal fortunes and the huge gap between a leader's lifestyle and those of his followers have specific consequences and repercussions of which the public is all too aware.

As far as the Iranian Resistance is concerned, Maryam and Massoud Rajavi enjoy huge support and great respect among Iranians, not as a couple, but as two distinguished figures in Iran's recent history. With a background of unrelenting struggle against the Shah and Khomeini, the support for them goes far beyond PMOI and NCRI sympathizers. Their foes, the clerical regime's leaders, have made it clear that they would spare no effort to undermine this movement and strike at its leadership. The movement's leaders have been singled out for the most vicious vilification campaign by the religious dictatorship.

What is the truth?

There is nothing in the conduct of this movement that would resemble cult-like behaviour towards its political leaders. In this movement, all important decisions are taken collectively. Collective leadership and long-established elected posts, such as the Secretary General, Leadership Council and the organization's bi-annual Congress are guarantees of a democratic process and healthy decision-making.

In this movement, no birthday celebration is held for any leader; indeed, no one even knows the dates! In the movement, members' elevation has always been based on their own merits and efficiency. The plagues of other organizations or large-scale institutions, such as nepotism, favouritism or elitism, have no place in the People's Mojahedin Organization. The children of the movement's leaders, who are among the rank and file, do not receive any privileges or special favours. Compared with those of other movements, the leaders of this movement have taken far greater risks and paid a far heavier personal price than others in the organization. One of Maryam Rajavi's sisters, Narges, was executed by the Shah. Her other sister, Massoumeh, pregnant at the time, was murdered under torture along with her husband. During a raid on their home in Tehran on 8 February 1982, Massoud Rajavi's first wife, Ashraf, was killed along with Moussa Khiabaní, Rajavi's deputy. The same night, the infamous Butcher of Evin, Assadollah Lajevardi, held the Rajavis' infant child, Mostafa, over the bullet-riddled body of his mother, Ashraf, in front of television cameras and vowed to make a 'good Hezbollahi' out of the infant. Massoud's older brother, Professor Kazemi Rajavi, was assassinated in April 1990 in Geneva. His sister Moiré and her husband, Asghar Kazemi, were among political prisoners massacred in 1988. His elderly parents were repeatedly arrested and savagely treated, to the point where both died under constant pressure and harassment.

The talk of 'cult of personality' about Maryam Rajavi, a woman at the helm of a popular Resistance against a religious fascism whose most distinct feature is misogyny, is simply absurd. Massoud Rajavi's nearly four decades of struggle against the monarchic and religious dictatorships explains his enormous popularity. Having spent seven years in the Shah's prisons as the symbol of defiance against torture, Rajavi was first to reject the newly established clerical dictatorship and challenged Khomeini's policy of suppression and export of terrorism. While Khomeini issued a fatwa to veto Massoud Rajavi's candidacy in the first presidential election, hundreds of thousands took part in meetings he addressed in Tehran, Tabriz (north-west Iran) and Rasht (northern Iran).

At the time, *Le Monde's* special envoy, Eric Rouleau, who later became France's ambassador to Tunisia and Turkey, wrote on 1 March 1980 from Tehran: 'One of the most important events not to be missed in Tehran is the courses on comparative philosophy, taught every Friday afternoon by Mr Massoud Rajavi. Some 10,000 people present their admission cards to listen for three hours to the lectures by the leader of the People's Mojahedin on Sharif University's lawn.' He added: 'The courses are published in paperback and sold by the hundreds of thousands of copies.'

Yet Rajavi's important role in the democratic movement never resulted in the decision-making process departing from the realm of relevant organs, collective procedure and formal and announced rules. In a statement on 12 December 1994, the NCRI stressed: 'The NCRI's modus operandi and decision-making process are conducted in accordance with democratic guidelines and regulations that have been formally announced. Throughout the thirteen years since the NCRI's foundation, its president has unfailingly adhered to these guidelines and regulations.'

Since 1989, Massoud Rajavi has had no executive responsibilities in the PMOI. His role in safeguarding the principles of the Mojahedin as a Muslim, democratic, nationalist and progressive organization in the 1970s, in the face of a communist coup, and more importantly, against Khomeini's all-out assault to destroy the PMOI, have made him a historical leader for the Mojahedin. With the formation of the National Council of Resistance of Iran, most of Mr Rajavi's efforts have been devoted to the council. His patient, democratic manner of managing the NCRI's affairs has been instrumental in the council's expansion and resilience, and has earned him the trust of NCRI's diverse membership. Mohammad Hossein Naghdi, an Iranian diplomat, joined the council in 1982. He was assassinated by the regime's terrorists in 1993 in Rome. Mr Naghdi said of Massoud Rajavi in a December 1992 interview: 'We in the council are hesitant to highlight the role of individuals, but compliments aside, I really think that in the world of politics, Mr Rajavi must, more than anyone, be credited for the rise of the NCRI and the Iranian Resistance.'[8]

Dr Manouchehr Hezarkhani, a distinguished Iranian writer and chairman of the NCRI's Committee on Culture and Arts, commented on the procedures of NCRI's meetings:

When we arrive at the meetings, we do not share the same views ... When we meet in session, sometimes we have serious arguments about certain matters, about political solutions. It is generally well understood that the point is to hold such meetings, where differences can be talked about and a consensus reached, but the individual capable of chairing such meetings and keeping the delicate balance of co-operation between different groups, none of whom is a career politician, is gifted with the art of leadership ... We have this leadership, and I think that to a large extent, it irons out the bumps.[9]

Whenever the interests of the Iranian people and democracy have been at stake, political considerations or concerns about his personal prestige have never prevented Massoud Rajavi from taking a decision. The PMOI's peace campaign in the Iran–Iraq war, launched in 1983 at the height of Khomeini's jingoistic fever, generated venomous propaganda by the regime and its internal and external allies. It was one of many examples of risks that few are willing to take.

Mr Rajavi has always stressed that the NCRI and the PMOI are not 'writings on the wall' as far as the Resistance movement is concerned. 'If at any time, any group or alternative is found to be better equipped to overthrow the regime and guarantee Iran's independence, democracy and popular sovereignty, we will definitely and wholeheartedly support it, even if it is opposed to our way of thinking,' he said.

At one of the most sensitive junctures of Iran's history, Khomeini sought to revive an Ottoman-like Islamic caliphate by taking advantage of special circumstances and usurping both temporal and spiritual power. Massoud Rajavi launched all-out resistance against him. For this reason, he no longer belongs to a specific group; Massoud Rajavi is a national leader, following in the footsteps of previous Iranian leaders, from Sattar-Khan[10] to Mirza Kuchak-Khan[11] to Dr Mossadeq.

Sabre-rattling, manipulative tactics and baseless slanders aside, those who are pursuing a premeditated propaganda scheme against the PMOI by accusing it of being a 'cult' and promoting a 'cult of personality' have in reality targeted the PMOI as an organization with many institutions and political and social roots in Iranian society. The PMOI has been active for nearly forty years in the struggle against two dictatorships and paid the heaviest possible price, notably in the form of 120,000 martyrs to the cause of Iran's freedom. In that time, it has developed deep roots in Iranian society and emerged from under the harshest repression in Iran's entire history stronger and more resilient. The PMOI is the only major Iranian political party – whether in power or in opposition – that has not suffered from any split since the 1979 anti-monarchic revolution. Despite its vast dimensions and geographical spread in Iran and across five continents, as well as its struggle against a regime that is dubbed the godfather of international terrorism, the PMOI has remained intact and cohesive as an organization.

Such cohesiveness could not have been maintained without a profoundly democratic set of internal relationships and without a justice-seeking ideal, which has inspired the forces that have joined it in the movement against the medieval dictatorship ruling Iran. Indeed, since the start of the twentieth century, no liberation movement has been the target of so much conspiracy and propaganda. The clerical leaders have given top priority to their war against the Iranian Resistance. To this end, they have allocated tremendous political, diplomatic, military, intelligence, propaganda and economic resources and petro-dollars to this fight. Besides the crackdown and terror, as well as psychological warfare directly used against the Resistance, the regime uses its economic and political lever as well as terrorist threats to compel other governments to act against the PMOI.

A historic judgement

Mrs Danielle Mitterrand, former French first lady, president of France Liberté foundation and a renowned human rights campaigner in France, addressed this issue at a Paris news conference on 23 June 2003:

I heard a journalist describe the Mojahedin as a cult today and this I find completely false and I want to deal with it because it can give the public a wrong impression of this organization.

I want to remind people of my own generation that during the Vichy government, which was allied with the Nazi occupiers, we had an armed resistance and a political resistance in this country. But our political resistance that had an armed branch, was it a cult? If the office of our resistance movement in London was raided and money that was destined to be used for the resistance were found, could they claim that this money was to be used against the internal security of Britain?

I believe we have to be very careful in using terms that can mislead the public. If someone believes in the war on injustice and oppression and would even go as far as self-immolation, should one call him or her a fanatic? I have known people in our own resistance movement who took cyanide pills so as not to be captured alive, so as to protest and say that this Nazi regime is not acceptable, so as not to fall into the hands of henchmen. Words are important. Some newspapers have said that there is a cult of personality around Maryam Rajavi. Today I am seventy-eight years old. When I was nineteen, I was a courier in the resistance against fascism. I can assure you that General de Gaulle was our idol. No matter how much people criticized him, he was for us the face of our resistance. This was wartime France and what happened later was another story. But I want words to be used in their correct context and when I heard the word 'cult' being used about the Mojahedin, I felt I had to speak out.

The People's Mojahedin Organization of Iran was founded in 1965 to resist the Shah's tyranny. They took part in the Iranian revolution and were later banned by the Islamic republic. They took refuge in France in 1981 and we welcomed them ... They have never committed acts of terrorism in France or anywhere else. We must not equate their resistance to terrorism. We must recognize that they handed their weapons to the Americans. They thus showed their readiness even to struggle against the Iranian regime which suppresses them through a means other than arms. They are supporting the student movement in Iran and why should we protest? We must compare the Mojahedin's resistance in Iran with other resistance movements against tyranny and dictatorship. Their strategy is theirs to adopt, but they have never committed terrorism anywhere. We must respect what they consider to be an appropriate means of fighting a fascist and fanatical regime in their country.

Notes

1. 'Anthropological Perspectives on New Religious Movements on Campus', William Taft Stuart, PhD, Department of Anthropology, University of Maryland-College Park, 15 June 1999.

2. Emadoddin Baghi, *Akhbar Eqtesad*, 24 May 1999.

3. Thomas Freidman, *New York Times*, 23 June 2002.

4. 'La détention de Maryam Radjavi pourrait durcir les protestations des Modjahedines', AFP, 22 June 2003.

5. Ehsan Naraghi, interview with *Hamshahri*, 4 July 2002.

6. Attacking the PMOI was, according to the Tower Commission Report, p. 360, published by the *New York Times*, one of the mullahs' essential demands during secret Irangate negotiations.

7. Lisa Wedeen, *Ambiguities of Domination: Politics, Rhetoric, and Symbols in Contemporary Syria*, Chicago, IL: Chicago University Press, 1999.

8. Mohammad Hossein Naghdi, News Bulletin of the Union of Moslem Students' Associations, 25 December 1992.

9. Ibid.

10. Sattar-Khan (1868–1914), national hero and great general of the Iranian Constitutional Revolution.

11. Mirza Kuchek-Khan (1880–1921), national hero and leader of the Jangal Uprising in northern Iran against British domination.

15 | Inside the PMOI

For more than a decade prior to the US-led war in Iraq in March 2003, the leitmotif of the anti-PMOI propaganda from Tehran was the accusation that the Mojahedin mistreated, abused, even tortured or executed 'dissidents' within its ranks. The psychological warfare zealots at the Ministry of Intelligence and Security came up with a motley variety of such allegations, but they all pursued one principal objective. In Tehran, they talked about 'turning the tables on the Mojahedin' on the issue of human rights.

The cold calculation behind the clerical regime's strategy was that if it could use fabricated testimonies by former members or supporters of the Mojahedin to level credible accusations of human rights violations against the PMOI, it would discredit the principal source of revelations of human rights violations and the most active advocate of human rights in Iran in the international arena. Consequently, the Islamic Republic would be able to evade the international community's spotlight on its own violations of human rights.

For a regime that has been condemned on forty-nine occasions by the United Nations General Assembly and the Commission on Human Rights for its grave and systematic violations of human rights, this was a vital war that had to be won. In recent years, the Iranian regime has spent huge sums of money and devoted enormous resources to this effort. It is interesting to note, however, that the continuous stream of written and oral propaganda against the PMOI on this particular issue, namely accusations of human rights abuses in its camps in Iraq, came to an abrupt end after the US-led war in Iraq. With the United States and its allies occupying Iraq and being present in PMOI and NLA camps, it became obvious that the mullahs' previous propaganda could no longer deceive anyone. If there had been the slightest hint of violations of human rights in NLA and PMOI camps, as the mullahs' regime alleged, the Americans would have been the first to see and report them. Moreover, if anyone in these camps had been maltreated and held against his or her wishes, he or she would have used the arrival of the Americans and their allies to leave. No such thing has happened. Like their other outrageous propaganda, such as claims that the PMOI was hiding Saddam Hussein's weapons of mass destruction, the fabricated allegations of human rights abuses by the PMOI have been proven wrong by the turn of events. The mullahs' propaganda chiefs are acutely aware that these lies can no longer find an audience, which is why they have stopped them.

While events of the past few months have put these lies to rest, however, it is important to review the way the mullahs' regime conducted this particular propaganda campaign. A glance at revelations made by MOIS defectors and admissions by intelligence agents sent to infiltrate the PMOI show how much energy and money the mullahs' regime had devoted to this aspect of its propaganda campaign against the Resistance movement. In his memoirs, MOIS defector Jamshid Tafrishi wrote:

> Khajeh Nouri [the Intelligence Ministry's agents in the USA] told us, 'You should tell [UN Special Representative for human rights in Iran Maurice] Copithorne that you are opposed to the regime and have been in its jails, but that you are also opposed to the PMOI. When you did not want to cooperate with it, you were imprisoned and subjected to psychological torture.'
>
> I told him that we knew that the Mojahedin had no prisoners and had not subjected anyone to psychological torture, so how could we make Copithorne believe it? To which Khajeh Nouri replied nonchalantly, 'When you all say with one voice that the organization has jails and that you have been harassed and persecuted, then Copithorne will have no alternative but to believe you.'

Tafrishi quoted Khajeh Nouri as saying: 'With these testimonies, we will achieve three things. First, you will make Copithorne believe that you are opponents of the regime. Second, you gain credibility by disgracing the Mojahedin. And third, you will be recognized and trusted by international organizations as democratic forces opposed both to the Iranian regime and the organization.'

MOIS agents posing as ex-members of the Mojahedin have on many occasions approached human rights organizations to claim that the organization had imprisoned and tortured them and even accused the Mojahedin of executing dissidents. The fact is that the Mojahedin organization has never imprisoned anyone from within its ranks. Nor has it ever carried out an execution. Not even a single member of the Revolutionary Guards or enemy infiltrators, some of whom had murdered several Mojahedin members before being arrested, was executed. Detailed reports by the Counter-intelligence Directorate of the National Liberation Army of Iran[1] have named seventy infiltrators of the mullahs' regime and also twenty-three members of the Mojahedin who were assassinated by them. The reports also noted that hundreds of Mojahedin members and supporters inside Iran have been arrested and executed as a result of the activities of these infiltrators. Some of the infiltrators, according to their own admission, were involved in the torture of Mojahedin members in Iranian jails and some took part in terrorist operations against the Mojahedin in other countries. There is no doubt that these spies and terrorists would have received heavy sentences if they were tried justly anywhere in the world. But the PMOI simply expelled them at the end of its investigations and they were sent back where they had come from. In the vast majority of cases, that meant Iran.

A brief look at the record of some of the MOIS agents who were sent to penetrate the ranks of the Mojahedin and commit criminal acts, including mass murder, shows that the Iranian regime stops at nothing in its bid to deal a crushing blow to its main opponents.

Daryoush Chatr Abgoun, born in 1951 in Kermanshah

He was working for the intelligence department in the western city of Kermanshah. In February 2002, he was sent on a mission to Iraq to infiltrate the Mojahedin and assassinate its members. He received his final briefings on this assignment from MOIS officials at two of Tehran's most prestigious hotels, the Esteqlal and the Laleh. They told him that he would receive a monthly salary of $200 paid into his account and would get additional bonus for every 'hit'. He was to flee back to Iran across the land border once he had carried out the assassinations.

Mehdi Hamidfar, born in 1979 in Kermanshah

He was sent to infiltrate the NLA in November 1998. Hamidfar had been recruited by the Intelligence Ministry in Kermanshah. He was trained in sabotage and terrorist operations in the Revolutionary Guards' training garrison in Kermanshah. To cover his tracks, he spent six months in the Kurdish region with other Iranian political groups. Once in the NLA, he planned to flee to Iran after throwing a hand grenade into a gathering of combatants.

Mokhtar Dizgouni, born in 1959 in Abadan

He assassinated Hossein Alamdari, a member of the Mojahedin, at the border region on 24 November 1999, and then fled to Iran and reported to the intelligence department in Abadan.

Qassem Salehi Fargani, born in 1968 in Masjed-Soleiman

The Intelligence Ministry sent Salehi to Iraq via the Qasr-e Shirin border crossing in January 1998. Once in the NLA, he opened fire from behind and killed Mahmoud Agah, a member of the Mojahedin, in

Abadan. He also wounded two others and a number of innocent passengers in the city's bus terminal. After these murders, he reported to the city's intelligence department. Qassem Salehi had been convicted of a murder in 1992 and sentenced to death. MOIS agents looking for professional killers spotted him in jail and he was recruited by the Intelligence Ministry to avoid execution. Ironically, he is now being shown to foreign journalists in Iran as a person who had been subjected to harassment and persecution by the Mojahedin.

Farhad Adeli, born in 1975 in Khoramabad
He left Iran through the southern border region with Iraq in January 2000 and joined the NLA. He had been working for the military counter-intelligence in Mashad since 1999 and his superiors proposed him as a potential infiltrator. He was sent to Tehran to be trained by the counter-intelligence organization on various subjects such as espionage techniques, interrogation and counter-interrogation, observation and description, surveillance, hand guns and sub-machine guns, and making bombs with TNT and C4 explosives. His mission was to assassinate Massoud Rajavi, the leader of the Iranian Resistance. He received special training for this at a safe house belonging to the Intelligence Ministry in Tehran. He was promised $5 million for every member of the Mojahedin he could bring back alive and $3 million for each assassination. After completing his training, Adeli was sent to Ahwaz by the Intelligence Ministry and from there he went to Iraq.

Alireza Fatahian, born in 1970 in Islamabad
He was sent to Iraq in July 2001. He had been working for the Intelligence Ministry since 1992 and was officially recruited in 1997. His main duty was to take part in ambushes to capture or kill Mojahedin supporters and he was responsible for the arrest of many individuals. He also recruited informants for the intelligence department in Islamabad. Once it was decided to send him on a mission to penetrate the Mojahedin, he was taken to the Laleh Hotel in Tehran and trained by senior MOIS operatives. His assignment included a plan to mass murder Mojahedin members through poisoning their food and water.

Ali Qashqavi, born in 1969 in Babol
He went to Iraq through Turkey and joined the NLA in 1993. It was later revealed that he had been a member of Hezbollah in Iran since 1986. He admitted that he had been briefed by two MOIS officials, Haji Rezapour and Qorbanali Sadeqi, in April 1993 to penetrate the PMOI and assassinate its leaders.

Mahmoud Motavari from Abadan

Motavari had been an MOIS agent for a long time. After penetrating the NLA, he was able to turn in two Mojahedin supporters, Mohsen Arab Mohammadi and Saeed Shah Qaleh, to the intelligence department in Ahwaz on 14 April 2000. MOIS interrogators killed Mohsen Arab Mohammadi under torture.

A report by the Directorate of Counter-intelligence of the NLA on the uncovering of MOIS plans to infiltrate the NLA was published in the Mojahedin's weekly journal on 2 July 2002. The report released the names and particulars of thirty-six infiltrators. On the fate of these agents, the report said:

> Undoubtedly, if it was not for prevention of the leader of the Resistance, the Mojahedin would have punished the mercenaries of the Intelligence Ministry in a just manner and in accordance with the practice and tradition of all the liberation and nationalist movements in dealing with treason and capital crimes. Any competent court anywhere in the world would have handed down heavy punishment to these criminals. But the Mojahedin is proud of its own tradition: it has not punished even a single enemy agent outside Iranian territory and the agents have been released eventually to return home. For a movement that has lost 120,000 of its members and supporters to executions, terrorist attacks and criminal acts of infiltrators, this has not been an easy decision. Many international human rights organizations are aware of the plots by the mullahs' Intelligence Ministry and the crimes committed by the infiltrators and how they were treated by the Mojahedin.

It is equally true that the Intelligence Ministry and its exposed and unexposed agents all know very clearly that there is no torture or maltreatment by the Mojahedin for an infiltrator who is under investigation. This has certainly emboldened them even further.

Despite all this, releasing these agents and refraining from punishing them is a matter of great pride for a resistance that is and strives to be completely different from the ruling clerical regime in every respect. For this reason, the Mojahedin's approach has been humane and devoid of any vengeance: the PMOI has not only avoided punishment of the criminal agents, but has given them the opportunity to arrange their lawful return to Iran. In addition, expenses of all those who intended to return to their families in Iran without going though the normal procedures (for security or other reasons) were met fully by the Mojahedin and all necessary means provided.

Treatment of prisoners of war

A total of 2,650 members of the Revolutionary Guards and other military or security agencies of the clerical regime have been captured in combat operations by the National Liberation Army of Iran and the PMOI. Every single prisoner was registered with the International Committee of the Red Cross in accordance with internationally recognized rules of war. In official letters, the ICRC has recognized the PMOI/NLA's humane treatment of detained Iranian soldiers and free access for ICRC delegates to hold private interviews with the detainees.

All the officers, soldiers and Revolutionary Guards' agents taken prisoner were later released on the orders of Massoud Rajavi, the NLA commander in chief, even though many of them had killed members of the Mojahedin or the NLA. This was in sharp contrast to the brutal treatment of captured members and supporters of the Mojahedin in the mullahs' jails in Iran. The ICRC was fully aware of the release of these prisoners and indeed supervised many of these cases.

Contrary to the mullahs' propaganda, the Mojahedin and the NCRI have nothing to hide and have always shared information about their internal relations with anyone interested with the utmost transparency, and would welcome any investigation into these relations with complete openness. The Iranian Resistance has repeatedly invited Amnesty International and Professor Maurice Copithorne, Special Representative of the UN Human Rights Commission, to visit Mojahedin bases in Iraq. One of the latest offers was made in a letter by Mr Massoud Rajavi, leader of the Iranian Resistance, addressed to the General Secretary of Amnesty International on 26 June 2002: 'As we have repeatedly informed Amnesty International in the past two decades, I reiterate that the Iranian Resistance would welcome your representatives in all its offices, headquarters and camps, including those in the Iran–Iraq border region, without any preconditions.'[2]

In my capacity as chairman of the Foreign Affairs Committee of the National Council of Resistance of Iran, I wrote to Amnesty International to inform it of the willingness of the Resistance's leadership to allow Amnesty International to post permanent observers or representatives in Mojahedin bases in Iraq.[3]

A sobering comparison

Treason, espionage and particularly attempts to infiltrate with the intention of sabotage and murder, are considered major crimes in almost every country. In many countries, capital punishment is handed down to those found guilty of such crimes. It is well known that in liberation movements engaged in armed resistance against a repressive state, the harshest punishments are reserved for treason and attempts to infiltrate the movement by spies.

In Europe, some countries which had abolished capital punishment prior to the Second World War reinstated it after the war so as to be able to execute those who had committed treason against the anti-Nazi resistance. This phenomenon is not restricted to any movement, revolution or country. The history of contemporary resistance movements and major revolutions is replete with individuals and groups who, motivated by fear, greed or other appeals, defected or betrayed their ideals. In *The Patriotic Traitors*, David Littlejohn wrote:

> [The Dutch collaborator] Anton Adraan Mussert was brought to trial at The Hague in November 1945 on a charge of high treason ... On 7th May 1946, just a year after the final liberation of his country, Mussert was executed by a firing squad at Scheveningen where, under the occupation, many resistance fighters had met a similar fate.
> The Dutch had abolished the death penalty in 1873, but had to reintroduce it to deal with extreme cases of collaboration. In all 138 death sentences were pronounced, although only 36 were actually carried out.[4]

Littlejohn writes that for similar treason cases in Norway 'thirty death sentences were passed, although only twenty-five were actually carried out. Not all of those condemned to death were prominent N.S. officials, some were little-known informers or secret torturers of resistance men. Henry Rinnan, found guilty of thirteen killings, was executed.'

In France, Pierre Lavale, a collaborator of the Vichy regime under whose rule many patriotic Frenchmen were arrested and executed, was himself sentenced to death. Lavale was executed in Mourdoux. 'Almost 40,000 Frenchmen received prison terms; between 700 to 800 were executed.'

Historically, treason and wartime desertion have been punished by death. In the American Revolution and the Civil War, many collaborators were court-martialled and sentenced to death, sent into exile, or exchanged for POWs. Rose Greenhow, a socially prominent widow in the North, had given valuable information to Jefferson Davis and the southerners about the North's military plans. She was arrested by Allen Pinkerton, Abraham Lincoln's Chief of the Secret Service, and eventually released in a prisoner exchange. Another celebrated female traitor was Belle Boyd, a young Virginian who carried secret intelligence through Union lines for General Stonewall Jackson dozens of times. She was finally arrested and released in a prisoner exchange.

On 17 July 1862, an act of Congress prescribed a $10,000 fine and punishment of five years with hard labour to execution for anyone convicted of insurrection, conspiracy or treason against the government. US Army regulations, as stated in the Military Laws of the United States, read:

> All officers and soldiers who, having received pay, or having been duly enlisted in the service of the United States, shall be convicted of having deserted the same, shall suffer death, or such other punishment as by a court-martial shall be inflicted ... Whatsoever officer or soldier shall be convicted of having advised or persuaded any other officer or soldier to desert the service of the United States, shall suffer such punishment as shall be inflicted upon him by the sentence of a court-martial ... Whosoever shall be convicted of holding correspondence with, to giving intelligence to, the enemy, either directly or indirectly, shall suffer death, or such other punishment as shall be ordered by the sentence of a court-martial.

It is indeed difficult to find a movement in history whose original members remained steadfast to the end, without weariness, weakness, surrender, differences of opinion, despair or even treason. Just as abandoning the cause to join the counter-revolution does not reflect the enemy's ability to instil fear, it also does not blemish the legitimacy of a resistance or revolution. History is not written by traitors, but by dedicated individuals who sacrifice their personal interests and privileges, and stand firm on their principles.

The late French President François Mitterrand, who was a member of the French Resistance during the Second World War, was once asked: 'Were you not a member of a network which committed a murder before examination?' Mitterrand replied:

> Before examination, no. Sometimes we did so for security reasons. Execution of the head of Gestapo in Clairmont-Ferrant on December 2, 1943, was for this reason. He threatened our movement, deprived us of security and forced us to react this way. The head of the counter-insurgency campaign in Clairmont-Ferrant, the Germans and the Vichy government treated members of the Resistance as terrorists. A Frenchman by the name of Henri Morlin was in the Francist Legion [Marcel Boucard movement, one of the fascist leaders before the war, a hard-line supporter of co-operation with Germans who was executed after the liberation]. He was a senior commander who later served the Gestapo. Jean Munie took up the mission to execute Morlin and killed him in a

garage in Clairmont-Ferrant. Munie immediately went to seek refuge at my father's home in Jarnak and my father welcomed him without knowing about him or even asking him any questions. After this there were cases where I myself exceptionally called for execution but their fate struck before I acted.[5]

The way the French Resistance operated has been typical of almost all liberation or guerrilla movements, but the PMOI and the NLA have worked hard to set a new precedent, one that would refuse execution and imprisonment even for infiltrators who have committed murder.

The NLA is made up entirely of volunteers. When joining the army, all applicants pledge in writing that they will remain with the NLA until the downfall of the mullahs' regime and respect the regulations of the army. On the basis of this pledge, the NLA bears no responsibility towards those who leave its ranks for any reason. In addition to this, the Mojahedin and the NLA need to make sure that the intelligence, security and protection regulations are observed, as they are at war with a brutal enemy that stops at nothing to destroy them. Compared with regulations enforced by other armies around the world, the NLA's rules are lenient and flexible. Even so, the NLA has not to date enforced these regulations. Those who have violated their written commitments and wanted to leave the ranks of the army because they could not tolerate the circumstances have been allowed to do so without any problem. The PMOI has gone even further and has sent hundreds of these people to the countries of their choice and paid all their travel expenses. The office of the United Nations High Commissioner for Refugees in Iraq was fully aware that in the 1990s, the PMOI arranged the resettlement in Europe of hundreds of former Resistance activists in Al-Tash refugee camp in Iraq who could not continue to remain within the ranks of the movement.

There is no doubt that the open-door policy of the PMOI and the NLA has entailed great risks for members and activists. The air strikes against NLA bases and other terrorist attacks by the mullahs' regime have been carried out on the basis of information provided by defectors to the mullahs' regime. Despite the risks and the dangers, however, the movement has continued to pursue the same open-door, open-exit policy. A mere comparison of the Resistance movement's track record and rules with those prevalent in the most democratic countries with regard to army defectors makes it evident that the Mojahedin and the NLA have exercised the utmost flexibility in this regard, even though they have paid a heavy price, which sometimes has meant the lives of NLA combatants and the leaking of sensitive information to the enemy.

Transparency and accountability

A glance at the correspondence and minutes of meetings at the archives of the Foreign Affairs Committee of the National Council of Resistance and other Resistance institutions which deal with human rights organizations and international bodies clearly shows that the Resistance has exercised complete transparency and full accountability on any issue related to its internal relations. Since the 1990s, hundreds of letters, reports and documents have been submitted to these organizations by the Resistance and the movement's journals have published hundreds of articles and reports on this issue. In addition, several books have been published in response to the allegations made against the Iranian Resistance by the clerical regime.

In my response to a question by Amnesty International on an article in a London-based Farsi-language newspaper accusing the Mojahedin of torture, imprisonment and execution of 'dissident' members, I wrote a letter to Amnesty on 6 August 1996:

> In my letter of July 31, 1991 [to Mr Ian Martin, then AI Secretary General], and in Mr. Rajavi's letters of September 30 and November 20, 1991, invitations were extended to Amnesty International to visit the Iranian Resistance's bases.
>
> In a letter by Mr. Behzad Saffari to Ms. June Ray on February 17, 1994, we repeated our invitation in response to similar questions.
>
> In my letter of February 12, 1996, to [Amnesty International], on behalf of the NCR President, I again extended another invitation for an Amnesty International delegation to visit our bases and to conduct an independent investigation.
>
> Besides these five written invitations that I presently recall, our representatives have repeated this invitation in several meetings with AI officials.
>
> If the intention is to monitor the behavior of Mojahedin/NLA or to train their members in the area of human rights, what would be better than visiting the bases? When I spoke to the NCRI president after the receipt of Mr. Berger's letter on December 21, he insisted that once again the invitation to Amnesty International should be repeated and added that AI can even post a permanent observer and representation in any or all of these bases.

In another letter to Amnesty International concerning the release of more than 2,600 POWs, I wrote:

> On different occasions, Mr. Rajavi issued orders for the release of all the Revolutionary Guards and other agents taken prisoner in clashes with

the Mojahedin and the National Liberation Army of Iran. They have been released to the last man and they subsequently returned to Iran. The International Committee of the Red Cross either supervised these arrangements or received precise reports on them. The last of such series of releases was that of six members of the Revolutionary Guards captured during the Iranian regime's offensive against the Iranian Resistance's bases in Iraq [in April 1991]. The six had been visited regularly by Red Cross delegates, who met them without witness, until they were released in March 1994 and handed over to the ICRC ... They were not tried in any court. They did not receive any sentences, although some of them had been involved in the murder of NLA members. The ICRC oversaw their release and is aware of all the details.

The National Liberation Army is a resistance army that complies fully with the Geneva Conventions, which apply to resistance armies, too. The NLA has never violated the Geneva Conventions, neither in combat and operations nor in the treatment of POWs.

I added in my letter that if Amnesty International's representatives came to visit NLA/PMOI bases in Iraq and found anyone willing to leave with them, there would be no interference by the NLA or the PMOI. I wrote:

We urge Amnesty International to use its international influence to provide us with the visas or *laissez passez* from Western countries so that we can offer them to anyone who might want to leave the NLA in future. As you are aware, it has become increasingly difficult to obtain visas and travel documents in Europe and the U.S. and Turkey does not accept such cases, either, and deports the applicants to Iran.

It is quite evident that with life being harsh on the arid deserts of the Iran–Iraq border region, where one is away from one's home and family, there would always be people who may feel they want to leave. It must always be noted that in light of the severe suppression inside Iran, there are always many people who escape arrest, torture and execution at the hands of the mullahs by crossing the border to reach the Mojahedin, and request either to join the NLA or to receive support and assistance to go to Europe. They include army deserters, Kurdish families and women with children, the sick, and war disabled, who do not want to go to the refugee camps in Iraq, where the conditions have become intolerable as a result of the sanctions. We would appreciate any humanitarian aid in this regard from Amnesty International. Regrettably, in the past 15 years, international human rights organizations have seldom helped us in such cases.

Open-door policy

The gates of the Iranian Resistance's bases are open to all but the agents of the mullahs' regime. In response to the clerical regime's false propaganda on imprisonment and torture of its former members or holding Iraqi weapons of mass destruction, the PMOI has repeatedly challenged the Iranian regime to prove its claims in any way it can. The PMOI has even agreed to accept a delegation of representatives of the human rights organizations, lawyers and jurists along with representatives of the Iranian regime to visit the Resistance's bases in Iraq to investigate these allegations.

The mullahs' regime, however, knows a visit by any international fact-finding mission would only prove the falsehood of its claims against the Mojahedin, which is why it has stonewalled and never accepted such offers.

As I mentioned at the beginning of this chapter, the fabricated story of imprisonment and torture of dissident Mojahedin belongs to the past. Following the downfall of the Iraqi regime and the US occupation of Iraq, there is no room for such lies, and the mullahs know this very well, which is why they are switching to other tactics in their psychological war on the PMOI.

Notes

1. Two reports by the Counter-intelligence Directorate of the National Liberation Army of Iran, *Mojahed*, no. 380, 1 March 1998 and no. 592, 2 July 2002.

2. Letter by Massoud Rajavi, President of the National Council of Resistance of Iran, to Mrs Irene Khan, the General Secretary of Amnesty International, 26 June 2002.

3. Letter by Mohammad Mohaddessin to Mrs June Ray, Middle East Programme Director, Amnesty International, 5 August 1996.

4. David Littlejohn, *Patriotic Traitors: History of Collaboration in German Occupied Europe, 1940–45*, London: Heinemann, 1972.

5. François Mitterrand and Georges-Marc Benamou, *Mémoires Interrompus*, Paris: Editions Odile Jacob, 1996.

16 | Controversy over celibacy

The subjection of women to men being a universal custom, any
departure from it quite naturally appears unnatural. *John Stuart Mill*[1]

'Since 1991, forced divorces were introduced in the organization. All
couples separated and marriage was banned. Then came the turn for
the only thing that kept the couples together: their children. They were
separated from their parents because the latter had to focus only on
their organizational activities.'[2]

These lines are typical of the family-centred allegations that have been
repeated, with a variety of flowery details, since the early 1990s in the
clerical regime's media and official pronouncements. The purpose is two-
fold. Inside Iran, the clerical regime seeks to enforce the notion that the
Resistance is opposed to family relations and values and that, if the current regime were to fall, the PMOI would abolish families, conjuring up
images that would make Pol Pot's chilling record pale in comparison.

More importantly, the regime seeks to convince Western nations
that PMOI members are without emotions, affection, rigid and ruthless,
thereby strengthening the myth that the PMOI is a reclusive cult. We say
more importantly, because inside Iran, Iranians in general are reluctant
to accept the mullahs' propaganda at face value; a quarter-century of
daily doses of 'mullahspeak' has taught them better. Moreover, a large
section of society has had first-hand experience with PMOI members
and sympathizers in neighbourhoods, schools, universities, offices and
factories and there are millions of families who have had a member
imprisoned or executed. They are even less likely than the average
Iranian to believe the mullahs' false propaganda. For all these reasons,
the mullahs' misinformation campaign against the PMOI is essentially
geared for external consumption

Even so, it would take a propaganda feat of Goebbelsian magnitude
to depict a well-established, freedom-fighters' resistance movement as a
sadistic and violent cult whose members would rather live a life fraught
with the threat of jail, torture and execution, rather than have a happy,
peaceful, prosperous family with children. To make their propaganda
work, the mullahs' spin masters have tried deceptively to confuse two
issues: the PMOI's views on family life and the rights and benefits that
families in a future democratic Iran must enjoy, and the requirements

of a tortuous, two-decades-long struggle against this repressive and ruthless regime, which left PMOI members with no choice but to forsake family life in Iraq, of their own free will.

The Iranian Resistance's views on the future Iran are spelled out in the programmes of the National Council of Resistance of Iran, the Resistance's parliament, including the plan adopted in 1983 on freedoms and rights of women, in the Charter of Fundamental Freedoms announced in 1995 by the Resistance's President-elect Maryam Rajavi, and in many other resolutions and declarations. All of them underlined the sanctity of the personal and private lives of individuals, condemned any breach of those rights and promoted equal rights for women. The NCRI's plan stipulated: 'Absolute freedom in choice of spouse and marriage, which can take place only with the consent of both parties and must be registered with legal (lay) authorities; marriage prior to the attainment of legal age is prohibited, any form of compulsion or coercion of the wife is prohibited.'[3] The Charter of Fundamental Freedoms underscored 'the right to freely choose the spouse, to marry, equal rights to divorce'.[4]

After their release from the Shah's prisons in 1979, those PMOI members who were celibate married. Thousands of married couples joined the ranks of the organization. Those in a position to know would testify that bonds of affection and compassion within Mojahedin families were very strong, with divorce a rare event. The names of thousands of couples appear in the list of names of 20,000 executed PMOI members.

That today Iranian freedom-fighters have forsaken family life, owing to the inevitable necessity of fighting the medieval clerical dictatorship outside their country, does not reflect any change in the views of the PMOI and the Iranian Resistance on family matters and values. After all, Mahatma Gandhi opted for celibacy during the struggle for India's independence.

After Khomeini's death in 1989, the Rafsanjani–Khamenei duo took over the helm of the clerical state and imposed, through conspiracy and terrorism, an extremely complex political and security situation on the Iranian Resistance. The PMOI's forty- to fifty-member Executive Committee decided voluntarily to give up family life until the overthrow of the religious dictatorship and the PMOI's return to Iran. The decision was kept confidential and no one was asked to do the same. A year later, however, Iraq invaded Kuwait and the Persian Gulf War broke out. The PMOI came face to face with a situation in Iraq that made family life for its members impossible. Consequently, all those who still wanted to continue their family lives inevitably left the front lines and relocated to other countries.

Abandoning family life

No one in his or her right mind would accept for a moment the notion that by coercing volunteers in the ranks of a nationwide resistance movement to divorce and abandon their children, one could compel them to put a 'greater focus on organizational activity' as some PMOI detractors have suggested. Moreover, it has always been a matter of ethical and political principle for the PMOI not to interfere in the family affairs of anyone.

The many journalists who visited PMOI and NLA bases and centres from 1986 – when the PMOI first went to Iraq – until 1991 – when the Kuwaiti war began – recognized that the PMOI had set up many schools and day care centres for the children of the combatants. A significant number of the organization's cadres, previously teachers and schoolmasters in Iran or elsewhere, taught at these centres. PMOI couples lived in separate, detached homes inside or outside the bases, including apartments in Baghdad or other Iraqi cities.

The 1991 Persian Gulf War, the heaviest bombings in recent history, the most crippling economic sanctions and the resultant insecurity in Iraq changed the situation dramatically. Unlike in the past, a secure 'behind-the-lines' for families and children no longer existed. Tehran's terrorists carried out more than 150 operations in Iraq against the PMOI after the war. They considered any home, car or person affiliated with the Mojahedin a target of opportunity. These included the homes of families of slain Mojahedin in Baghdad and residential quarters of couples. Mullahs' hitmen attacked several apartments and civilian buses in and around Baghdad with RPGS or remote-controlled bombs that left much damage. The clerical regime's repeated attacks on PMOI camps and centres in Iraq made family life extremely difficult and on many occasions entailed military and security risks, particularly for women and children. As the Tehran regime stepped up its meddling in Iraqi territory, providing security for residential complexes became far more difficult, if not impossible. The new environment posed a major question: could this situation continue despite the obvious risks to people's lives? The harsh realities of life in Iraq left few alternatives, particularly since the PMOI was not in its own social milieu, where it would have been able to resolve these problems by relying on supporters and the public at large.

Besides the heavy bombings in Iraq during the 1991 war, many parts of Iraqi territory, especially PMOI bases, came under attack by the Revolutionary Guards and operatives sent from Iran. These attacks not only continued during March and April 1991, after Iraq's defeat in Kuwait, but went on for the next twelve years, causing many deaths and injuries among the PMOI and innocent Iraqi civilians.

The Tehran regime bombed PMOI bases in April 1992, June 1992 and September 1997; launched dozens of mortars, mini-katyushas and 320-mm 'superguns' and 500-kg missiles. These included mortar attacks in November 1993 and September 1994, as well as Scud missile attacks in November 1994 and June 1999. The regime also attacked the homes of elderly mothers of PMOI martyrs with RPGS. In April 2001, Tehran launched seventy-seven surface-to-surface missiles in simultaneous attacks on seven PMOI camps along the Iran–Iraq frontier. Altogether, the clerical regime carried out 150 terrorist operations on PMOI camps and combatants from 1993 until the fall of the Iraqi regime in April 2003. The risks of maintaining family life in such circumstances were simply too much as far as the security of PMOI's personnel was concerned.

In short, everywhere in Iraq turned into the frontline for the PMOI. It became necessary, after 1991, to notify anyone wanting to join the PMOI in Iraq of the austere circumstances there, particularly with regard to the security situation. Volunteers were told, before leaving for Iraq, that if they could not tolerate such conditions they should not go to Iraq and that it would be more effective to wage their campaign against the clerical regime in the framework of Resistance support groups outside or inside Iran.

The 'celibacy' lifestyle in PMOI's camps in Iraq after the war was not unique to the movement. Even an institution such as the International Committee of the Red Cross (ICRC) traditionally uses unmarried members for long-haul missions in trouble spots around the world. The United Nations has set up a five-grade security system in countries such as Iraq to determine threat level to its personnel. In Iraq before the recent war, UN employees were not allowed to bring their families to the country due to security concerns.

Tehran's assessment

In its public propaganda, the clerical regime always tried to exploit the sanctity of the family in society and popular sensitivity on the subject of family values to depict the PMOI and their supporters as opposed to family life and devoid of affection. Privately, however, the mullahs know better.

In 1988, one of the regime's suppressive organs, the Central Komiteh, admitted in an internal report to Khomeini that revolutionary emancipation of women had in fact strengthened and expanded the Resistance movement, and served as a major attraction for Iranian women. One passage of the report read: 'The Mojahedin's internal revolution has become a means of proving the organization's advocacy of equal rights for women and men ... and it has resulted in more women being attracted and loyal to the organization.' Elsewhere it wrote: 'The PMOI has used appealing methods, mixed them with practical application and examples, and achieved its objectives.'

Children

During the 1991 Persian Gulf War, Baghdad and other parts of Iraq were being heavily bombed and PMOI's camps were unsafe for children. It was at that time that parents sought to relocate their children outside Iraq. Some of them sent the children to relatives in Iran; others sent them abroad, to Europe and America. These parents put everything in writing so that in case of martyrdom in the course of the struggle, the status of their children would be clear. Many Iranian families in and out of Iran also asked if they might act as guardians for these innocent children.

The PMOI, at the request of parents, put the lives of some of its members on the line and spent huge amounts of money taking the children out of Iraq safely so that they could get on with their normal lives and education. In a letter in 1996 to Professor Maurice Danby Copithorne, the United Nations Human Rights Commission's Special Representative on Iran, Christoph Meertens, a well-known German lawyer and the guardian for many of these children in Cologne, wrote: 'In our view, the People's Mojahedin's sense of responsibility towards their children is a good example, particularly in light of the well-known fact that an exiled organization has limited social and financial resources.'

In trying to demonize the PMOI, the clerical regime has completely distorted the facts on a noble undertaking by men and women who have sacrificed their family lives for the sake of liberating their fettered nation and 70 million oppressed Iranians. It has tried to portray PMOI members as lacking any willpower, as having been forced to divorce their spouses and abandon their children. It has made the bewildering claim that the PMOI leadership believed such coercion would further focus the rank and file on organizational activities. Anyone knows, however, that such coercion could never work in a resistance movement based on its members' voluntary commitment and endeavour to advance its cause. Any use of coercion would lead only to anguish, anxiety and vengeance among them and would consequently backfire.

Source of allegations

Iranians in and out of Iran have admired PMOI members for forgoing their families and children to liberate their compatriots and their homeland, seeing their actions as an unprecedented and noble sacrifice. Those men and women who made this decision can testify as to the reasons why they chose to do this. One has to wonder, then, how were these allegations about forced divorces and separation of children disseminated, and by whom?

The source is Iran's Ministry of Intelligence and Security (MOIS). It has used the services of several individuals who lost the resolve to continue a struggle that was growing more difficult by the day. When these people left the ranks of the Resistance, they sought to take along their wives forcibly, as if they owned them, but their wives refused to submit to their wishes. These individuals later sold their services to the Intelligence Ministry and churned out astounding lies about forced divorces and the separation of children from the parents.

Inverting the truth

Karim Haghi has been an MOIS agent for more than ten years. For some time now, he has been shedding crocodile tears for couples 'forced' to divorce and children 'forcefully separated' from their parents.

During the 1991 Persian Gulf War and and the ensuing hardships caused by sanctions, Haghi and his wife, Mohtaram Baba'i, could no longer tolerate the difficulties of struggle. They, however, stayed with the PMOI and received more accommodations and amenities than any NLA combatant or commander. They were ultimately relocated to Europe in January 1993 at the expense of the PMOI. Some time later, they chose to settle in the Netherlands, where they applied for and received political asylum.

In a letter in November 1992 to the PMOI, Mohtaram Baba'i confirmed this:

> After the bombing raid on Ashraf Camp, the PMOI transferred me, my husband and our child to Jalalzadeh building in the heart of Baghdad for greater protection. During this period, in addition to all the accommodations that all combatants and members of the PMOI received, we were given special treatment and extra accommodations. We were also provided with an exclusive apartment, a car to commute in Baghdad, and a monthly allowance of 1,000 dinars.

After settling in the Netherlands, however, Haghi was recruited by the MOIS in April 1995, through Mansour Maqsoudi, an under-cover intelligence officer in charge of espionage operations in the Netherlands. He provided valuable information to facilitate Tehran's terrorist attacks on NLA bases and combatants.

Three years after leaving the ranks of the Resistance, Haghi suddenly remembered that the PMOI had imprisoned and tortured him. When his wife committed suicide in spring 1995, he claimed that she had died due to the physical and psychological trauma suffered at the hands of the PMOI in Iraq. This was, of course, completely false. Haghi's wife committed suicide because of his abusive behaviour in the home and promiscuity outside it. The Dutch police have a copy of the suicide note left by Haghi's wife, in which she referred to his violent and abusive conduct and illicit relationships as the reason why she committed suicide.

Secret agent rebuffed

A well-known agent of the MOIS, Ahmad Shams-Haeri has been one of the main proponents of the allegations about forced divorces and the separation of children from their parents in the past ten years.

In 1991, Shams-Haeri left the PMOI and went to Altash refugee camp in Ramadi. He demanded that his wife, Mahin Nazari, accompany him. In a letter published at the time in the PMOI publication, *Mojahed*, Shams-Haeri wrote: 'Bring my wife to me in Ramadi. According to religious law, I have the right to divorce, not the woman.' Even after the PMOI asked Ms Nazari to go to Ramadi with her husband, in the interests of keeping the husband and wife together, she refused to do so.

The couple's children, Amir and Nosrat, had earlier been sent to Germany at the request of both parents. Once in Ramadi, however, Shams-Haeri demanded that the children be returned to Iraq to live with him in Altash refugee camp. While the interests of the children would not have been served by transferring them from Germany to a refugee camp with minimum living accommodations and security, Shams-Haeri insisted that they be returned. After using the two innocent children to make propaganda against the Mojahedin, however, he abandoned them near a PMOI office in Baghdad. Several hours later, the children (aged seven and eleven at the time) found their way to the PMOI office with the help of local people. In a note given to the children, Shams-Haeri had written, 'The children belong to their mother and the organization must pay for their expenses.' This was after he had taken away the children's clothes and other belongings. The PMOI, at the request of Ms Nazari, sent the children back to Germany to go on with their normal lives.

Shams-Haeri subsequently went to Europe and alleged again that the PMOI had taken away his children. In a lawsuit against the PMOI and Ms Nazari, he claimed that she had brainwashed the children. He also wrote several articles that were published in the Iranian regime's newspapers and distributed by its embassies in Europe and Arab countries.

After investigating the case and talking to the children, a court in Cologne ruled, on 7 June 1994, that Shams-Haeri was unfit to look after and keep the children, and awarded custody to their mother. In explaining his decision, the judge wrote:

> These children have been living in Cologne since early 1992 along with other Iranian children. They belong to a group of Iranian refugee children who were brought to Germany without their parents after the outbreak of the [Persian] Gulf War by a humanitarian organization.
>
> After hearing the parents, the children and the Youth Department, the court is convinced that the children's welfare is better secured with the mother than anyone else. At the outset, the two children clearly stated in a hearing that they want to stay with their mother in the future. After the separation of the family, the mother, unlike the father, has tried to establish regular contact with the children since 1993. The Youth Department notes that in the last ten years, some sort of alienation has affected the children and their parents. The court investigation shows that the mother is doing her utmost to reduce this problem. The father's request to appoint someone other than the mother to take care of the children cannot be accepted under these circumstances. The parent's right to custody takes precedence over other persons'. The danger of brainwashing and unilateral exertion of influence on the children appears to be greater with the father than with the mother. An example is the sudden appearance of the father at his son's school. The children's mother gives the impression that she does not see the welfare of her children solely through political indoctrination. All things considered, giving the mother custody is the best option as far as the welfare of the children is concerned.

In its April 1994 report to the court, the Youth Department in Cologne wrote that Shams-Haeri 'is suspected of collaborating with the Iranian regime' and that he 'had tried to impose a particular political viewpoint on his sons'. The official of the Youth Department added in the same report, 'I have so far been unable to identify [any] deliberate form of indoctrination by the Mojahedin, which the father accuses them of.'

Following the court's ruling, Shams-Haeri described the court as a 'pawn of Rajavi', alleging that its decision was arranged by Mr Rajavi to destroy his family and achieve the legal separation of his children from him. But this claim can hardly be credible, not least because one cannot imagine how a German court could be 'told' what to do (and in particular by a foreign political organization); in any event, it was Shams-Haeri himself who brought the proceedings in the first place.

Shams-Haeri met with UN Special Representative Professor Maurice Copithorne in January 1996, along with thirteen other agents of the regime, and repeated the same false allegations. At around the same time, Ms Nazari also met with Professor Copithorne and told him what had really happened.

In his letter to Professor Copithorne, Mr Meertens referred to Shams-Haeri's political agenda against the PMOI:

> One of the people affiliated with the disinformation system of the ruling regime in Tehran is an Iranian national called Ahmad Shams-Haeri, who filed suit against his wife who has separated from him, Ms Mahin Nazari, for the guardianship of their two children, Amir and Nosrat ... Mr Shams-Haeri is by no means concerned about his children, nor is he worried about their welfare or more difficult living conditions after settling as refugees in Germany. As far as Mr Haeri is concerned, he is not at all concerned about his children. His objective is to influence the children for political propaganda. The suspicion is strengthened even more in the mind of the writer since he abuses his own children to that end. The validity of the accusations by Mr Shams-Haeri was proven false in the court hearing that ended. We hope the same will happen in your case so that he would not be able to build his façade of lies and slander.

An agent reveals his story

Heidar Baba'i also attempted, at the behest of the MOIS, to make a similar case against the PMOI. In a letter to Professor Copithorne on 7 January 2001, he unveiled the MOIS scheme and apologized to the PMOI. He wrote:

> I, Heidar Baba'i, came to see you on 16 January 1996, along with my children, Hamed and Hemad. My mission, and that of a number of other MOIS operatives, was to accuse the PMOI of torture, execution, imprisonment and human rights abuses.
>
> I was not aware of the depth of this conspiracy. But because I had children, I was quite suitable for such a plot. We were told to raise bogus allegations against the PMOI, such as forced divorces, killing Iraqi Kurds, separating children from parents, torture, imprisonment and execution of dissident members, to convince you to condemn the PMOI in your

annual human rights report. We were instructed to make wild accusations to demonize the PMOI and garner your sympathy. Karim Haghi was told to complain about the use of torture by the PMOI. I was told to make a case about my children to influence you. The masterminds of this dirty plot were using my small children as pawns for their sinister schemes.

Although I have parted ways with these agents long ago, I am not at peace with my conscience for my role in this MOIS plot against the PMOI. This is why I decided to expose this scheme to redeem myself and apologize to the combatants of Iran's freedom. I would like to meet you to personally inform you of the behind-the-scenes plots in this case.

A mother's letter

Five years before Baba'i wrote that letter, his ex-wife and the mother of his children, Nasrin Younessi, wrote an open letter, published in a Farsi-language weekly, *Iran Zamin*, on 5 February 1996. She unveiled the bogus nature of the letters written in the name of her children. Referring to her decision to divorce Heidar Baba'i, and revealing why she had rejected the advice by the PMOI to keep her marriage, she wrote:

They have quoted my child as saying that 'the PMOI separated a two-month-old infant from her mother, while he was desperately in need of being breast-fed'. He was also quoted as saying that 'as far as he could remember, her mother was kind and affectionate' but the PMOI 'forced his mother to live away from her child'.

Obviously, this letter could not have been written by a fourteen-year-old. He is neither a member of a political party, nor at the age that would enable him to take such a position. The statement attributed to my son, Hamed, says 'in the winter of 1981, I was born in one of the dungeons of the Islamic Republic and remained in jail with my mother until 1987, or sought refuge in different Iranian cities'.

This is totally false and an attempt by the regime to overshadow the real and countless atrocities perpetrated by the clerical regime against PMOI prisoners and martyrs. There is no truth to the claim that he was born in a dungeon. I was arrested in early September 1981 in Kermanshah and imprisoned for about three months. I gave birth to Hamed outside prison and under normal circumstances.

The letter by Mr Meertens, cited earlier in this chapter, sheds light on the efforts undertaken by the PMOI on behalf of these innocent children and renders hollow the claims about their forcible separation from their parents. It reads in part:

In 1991, our Iranian clients sought the assistance of our law firm which specializes in family and refugee affairs. The legal assistance was sought for a group of 100 Iranian children, who, due to the Gulf War, had moved with the assistance of human rights organizations from the Iran–Iraq border strip and sought refuge in the Republic of Germany. We later found out that the People's Mojahedin Organization had relocated a few hundred of their children and youths from their centres, namely at Ashraf base camp on the Iran–Iraq border which were no longer safe, to Western European countries. According to information we have received, Iran repeatedly attacked this base by missiles and fighter jets, during the Gulf War and particularly after the end of the war between the allied forces and Iraq ... We later realized that a number of children have lost their parents either due to executions in Iran or in operations of the National Liberation Army ... The parents of a number of other children are in the National Liberation Army or in the organization's political bureaux abroad, and are therefore not in a position to take back the custody of their own children. It is clear to us that the parents and relatives of these children are followed and murdered even in exile, e.g., in Pakistan and Iran, by the agents of the Ministry of Intelligence of Tehran's ruling regime. Therefore, the reason why some of these parents are not able to take back the guardianship of their children because of their political involvement is somewhat understandable ... In our view, the People's Mojahedin's sense of responsibility towards their children is a good example, particularly in light of the well-known fact that an exiled organization has limited social and financial resources.

Women in the Iranian Resistance

In the difficult and dangerous circumstances endured by the PMOI and the broader resistance movement in the past seventeen years in Iraq, which adversely affected family life, women have been doubly victimized by the hardships of family life. Family relationships, particularly with regard to children, have further burdened women and hindered their ability to assume greater and higher responsibility in leadership and management positions in the movement. Given the complex political and regional circumstances in Iraq, it would have been natural for women to be marginalized or, in the best-case scenario, perform behind-the-lines duties.

That, of course, did not happen. On the contrary, by providing ever greater opportunities for women, the PMOI succeeded in elevating its political, military and social capabilities through their liberation and empowerment. This was achieved only because men and women in the PMOI, and in the Iranian Resistance as a whole, were prepared to pay the heaviest possible personal price. In response to the mullahs' propaganda claiming that PMOI members were forced to divorce their wives or husbands, one should simply ask: how could anyone make such a great sacrifice in the path of the liberation of the Iranian people through blind obedience?

A closer look at the role of women in the ranks of the Iranian Resistance clearly shows that the mullahs' propaganda holds no water. Not only do women enjoy equal rights in the Resistance, but they have overturned the male-dominated value system by taking on key positions of leadership and management. Women account for more than half the members of the National Council of Resistance of Iran, the Resistance's parliament-in-exile, and all of the Mojahedin's Leadership Council.

To achieve this objective, the Iranian Resistance has travelled a long, arduous path. In 1984, three years after the nationwide Resistance against the Khomeini regime began, Resistance leader Massoud Rajavi raised the question as to why women had not risen beyond the level of department directors, three tiers below the leadership body, within the People's Mojahedin, the Resistance's principal organization, despite the fact that they had taken on wide-ranging responsibilities in the struggle against the mullahs' regime. The PMOI leadership decided that, for a movement fighting the misogynous mullahs, such discrimination between men and women could not be tolerated.

The issue was debated for months at the various levels of the organization. Women had fought courageously and in large numbers. In sacrifice, resistance and risk-taking, they were leading the way, but in one sphere, leadership, the advance was slow and unimpressive. Mrs Maryam Rajavi, as a leading woman in the Resistance movement and a former secretary-general of the PMOI, played a major role in charting the path to the unprecedented participation and prominence of women in the Resistance. She described her experience in those gruelling years:

> While women in the Resistance movement were among the best educated, many with university degrees, they were still marginalized. Technical jobs were purely for men. Political work also seemed impractical, because apparently nobody took women seriously.
>
> Men would assume those responsibilities and women, after listing a range of problems, automatically inclined towards marginal jobs or jobs considered one hundred per cent fit for females. This was their spontaneous inclination. Whatever the job or the profession, women's problems in our movement at that time could be summarized in one phrase: fear

of taking on responsibility. The progress of the Resistance movement, however, depended on women's fully accepting responsibility. We could not walk on one leg. We needed a revolution to break through these taboos and discover new conviction in women.[5]

A gender revolution

That revolution came with the introduction of women into the movement's leadership in 1985, when Maryam Rajavi was elected as the PMOI's co-leader. The issue had been hotly debated within a broad forum in the movement. Some believed that the solution must come from below, with women's increased participation in executive affairs. Others agreed that the way to redress the existing imbalance was through a bold, new step: having women at the helm. Maryam Rajavi describes the sea-change:

None of us anticipated what actually happened. This change – a woman in the leadership – brought about a major internal revolution in our movement. For women, it acted like a springboard. The organization's annual report for that year indicated that the percentage of women in the central council rose from 15 to 34 per cent, more than double.

The impasse on women accepting responsibility had been overcome, and it was just the beginning. This leap forward and the new atmosphere it brought to the organization allowed us to carry on a revolution in outlook, for we did not intend to stop there. The movement's primary goals, democracy and growth, had become entwined with this drive to emancipate women. We were a movement which believed, body and soul, that any progress and development depended on the women's movement. We were determined to walk the walk: total rejection of the male-dominated culture. This required a revolution in our thinking. As women gradually occupied key positions at the top and in command, their male subordinates felt as if their world was shrinking. It was difficult for them to believe in the women, and their hidden resistance revealed itself in a lack of interest in their responsibilities. Most difficult for the women was their problem, from time immemorial, of not believing in themselves.

It took me several years and thousands of hours of discussions, in small and large groups, to convince these women and men – none of whom ever denied that in theory men and women were equal – to enter this new world in practice.

Gradually, our movement began to see the fruits of its labour in practical terms, and went forward, step by step. In addition to my everyday

interaction, I regularly convened meetings to examine individual problems. These meetings were followed up by the officials in charge of each
section or department. Three years later, the number of women in the
leadership rose to about 50 per cent.

We organized our movement in a way that allowed women into all of
the sections, departments and fields traditionally reserved for men, giving
them access to that expertise. Women began to move up the ladder of
responsibility in every area of management and politics.

One of the precious achievements of this era was the new, fresh relationship among the women themselves. Before all else, these women had
to feel a sense of solidarity in their endeavours. Such relationships could
become a reality only when these women really believed in one another:
women leading other women – mutual acceptance of this relationship.
This marked the beginning of a mature relationship between them.

Had our women not gone through this process, they could not have
taken the subsequent actions required of a pioneering generation. It
was, of course, a tortuous path. Some said it felt as if they had lived an
entire lifetime. It was also very difficult for the men. Today, however,
we have an energetic generation which has experienced something very
important and new in the world. Now, that generation is ready to share
its accomplishments with the emancipation movement, in the effort to
uproot discrimination and gender-based apartheid.[6]

These changes have greatly impressed outside observers who have
been able to see them at first hand. After gaining insight into the status
of women in the PMOI, Egyptian writer and intellectual Mona Helmi
wrote:

Throughout the seven days that I intimately stayed with the Mojahedin, I saw women who, despite the difficult circumstances of being
in exile, are adorned with tenacity, courage and the most dignified
forms of struggle. I also met men who live under constant daily
danger from their enemy, the Iranian regime. Despite this, a highly
developed spirit of real liberation and a deep faith in peace, justice
and freedom are present in their lives. They believe in the separation of church and state and they respect freedom of opinion and
religions, and the performing of religious rituals and rites. They
recognize all minority rights (for instance the rights of the Kurds).
With regard to women, there is complete equality between men
and women. Women are entitled to take on all leadership positions,
functions and posts. A woman can travel without needing to get
someone else's permission. She is a human being who enjoys her full

potential, dignity and respect. She can choose her lifestyle, marriage, work and the way she dresses. In the future Iran, the door is open to all freethinkers, ranging from scientists to artists. The parliament of the Iranian Resistance reflects this democratic spirit in its present composition, because it has 572 members, 52 per cent of whom are women. All organizations, regardless of the number of their members, have one vote. This parliament has presented a unique model of its genuine belief in the status of women by electing a woman, Mrs Maryam Rajavi, as president. This choice proves that this parliament does not intend to bury the capabilities of women under the veil of religious or social thought and crush women's energies at the expense of work, rebellion and change.[7]

In a story from Camp Ashraf entitled 'Mullahs, Look! Women, Armed and Dangerous', Douglas Jehl of the New York Times wrote on 30 December 1996:

Mrs Tahmasbi, and most other top officers are women, whose standard issue attire includes khaki head scarves and modestly cut tunics that would be acceptable even on a Tehran street. But who exercise an authority unimaginable at home. Soldiers live communally, even into their 30s and 40s, bunking as many as 20 to a sex-segregated room. Since 1991, the married couples among them have put their marriage on ice: their children have been sent abroad, and those who once lived as husbands and wives now live chastely as brothers and sisters.

To anybody who might have tried to manage a mixed army anywhere in the world, the 'chastity' to which the New York Times journalist refers is more a necessity in the code of conduct than any intrinsic moral value. Even if you could forget that all this is going on in the Middle East, the complexities of having a properly functioning and active mixed army are immense, with problems ranging from sexual discrimination to serious shortcomings for women.

Prospects for the future

The status of women in the Iranian Resistance is the best guarantee that democracy will be institutionalized and preserved in the post-theocratic Iran. In most resistance movements, women were marginalized after victory, despite their active role during the movement. But in the PMOI and the broader resistance movement, women have achieved indispensable positions of leadership and management. Moreover, the

National Council of Resistance of Iran has adopted a concrete plan to guarantee the equality of men and women in tomorrow's free Iran. All members of the Resistance are committed to this programme.

In what was a historic breakthrough for women's rights in Iran, Mrs Rajavi declared a sixteen-article Charter of Fundamental Freedoms for Future Iran in 1995, which pledged to guarantee rights and freedoms that Iranian women have for long yearned to achieve. These were:

- The right to elect and be elected in all elections, and the right to suffrage in all referenda.
- The right to employment and freedom of choice in profession, and the right to hold any public or government position, office or profession, including presidency and judgeship in all judicial bodies.
- The right to free political and social activity and travel without the permission of another person.
- The right to freely choose clothing and covering.
- The right to use, without discrimination, all instructional, educational, athletic and artistic resources, and the right to participate in all athletic competitions and artistic activities.
- Recognition of women's associations and support for their voluntary formation throughout the country.
- Consideration of special privileges in various social, administrative, and cultural fields to abolish inequality and the dual oppression of women.
- Equal pay for equal work, prohibition of discrimination in hiring and during employment.
- The right to salary and special accommodations during pregnancy, childbirth, and care of infants.
- Absolute freedom of choice regarding spouse and marriage, which can take place only with the consent of both parties.
- Equal right to divorce; women and men are equal in presenting grounds for divorce.
- Support for widowed and divorced women and for children in their custody; care will be provided through the National Social Welfare System.
- Elimination of legal inequalities with regard to testimony, guardianship, custody and inheritance.
- In family life, any form of compulsion or coercion of the wife is prohibited.
- Polygamy is prohibited.
- Prohibition of all forms of sexual exploitation of women on any pretext.

The provisions of this charter stand in sharp contrast to the gender apartheid and exploitation of women that form the Islamic fundamentalists' viewpoint on the question of women. This contrast is indeed the sharpest line of demarcation that sets apart the progressive, democratic vision of Islam from that of fanatics and obscurantists.

Notes

1. John Stuart Mill, *The Subjection of Women*, London: Longmans, Green and Co., 1909.

2. French television, FR3, interview with Karim Haghi, 1 July 2003.

3. Declaration of the NCRI on the Freedoms and Rights of Iranian Women, 17 April 1987.

4. Charter for Fundamental Freedoms for Future Iran, Maryam Rajavi, 16 June 1995.

5. Maryam Rajavi, 'Women, Fundamentalism and Islam', *Iran Zamin*, 8 April 1996.

6. Ibid.

7. Mona Helmi, 'Revolution Makes People Beautiful', *October* Magazine, 14 April 1996.

Conclusion

Iran at the dawn of 2004 is a country on the brink. Clashes between anti-government demonstrators and security forces have become daily occurrences, with chants of 'Khatami, resign' and 'Referendum, now' gaining prominence. Labour unrest in Iran's petrochemical industries confronted the ruling clerics with the ominous prospects of widespread strikes in other sectors of the economy spreading to the long-suppressed workers in the crucial oil industry. A resolution adopted by the United Nations General Assembly in December 2003 strongly condemned the continuing street executions, torture, arbitrary arrests, suppression of women and discrimination against ethnic and religious minorities.

The international community put Tehran on notice over its nuclear weapons project, as the International Atomic Energy Agency's governing board adopted a consensus resolution warning the mullahs that any further violation of their international non-proliferation commitments would be referred to the UN Security Council for possible sanctions. On the terrorism front, newspapers in Turkey and Saudi Arabia cited 'strong suspicions' harboured by intelligence agencies in both countries as to the involvement of the Iranian regime in bloody terrorist attacks in Istanbul and Riyadh. Iran as an Islamic fundamentalist theocracy continued to be regarded, justifiably, as the 'most active state sponsor of terrorism'.

With most observers predicting a massive boycott of the parliamentary elections in February 2004 – a repeat of voters' apathy during the municipal elections in February 2003 – factional strife continued to plague the clerical regime. The dominant Khamenei faction, aware of the massive disillusionment of Iranians with Khatami's hollow promises of change and reform, is confident of re-establishing control over the Majlis and, by 2005, regaining the presidency. For the clerical elite that holds the reins of real power in Iran, the Khatami era was a necessary breathing space to take the regime out of the perilous quagmire of the mid-1990s. They tolerated this bifurcation of power as a 'safety valve' that would take the steam out of the built-up popular discontent with years of clerical misrule, while attracting much-needed foreign support for the Tehran regime. Even though the net result of the past seven years has been an overall weakening of the theocratic state, the ayatollahs now feel they have a fighting chance of weathering the political storms at home and abroad that inevitably lie ahead.

The most important shot in the arm for the mullahs' faltering regime was the turn of events in 'post-conflict' neighbouring Iraq. Originally apprehensive of having US divisions on their eastern and western flanks after the fall of the Iraqi regime, the ayatollahs' confidence appeared to rise in direct proportion to the growing list of American casualties on the Mesopotamian plains. Khamenei and his cohorts feel their strategy of quietly building up clandestine armed cells in Iraq under the supervision of the Revolutionary Guards' elite Qods (Jerusalem) Force, while ostensibly pursuing a political strategy, has met with success. By December, they had grown confident enough for a political gambit, openly calling on Iraqi Shiites to defy the 'American invaders'. Khamenei said in a message addressed to the 'God-fearing and zealous people of Iraq' on 2 December:

> The beastly, arrogant invaders have shown that they have no respect either for the lives of innocent people, or for the sanctity of their religion. They seek to rule only through intimidation and the use of bayonets. The stupid, arrogant American politicians think foolishly that bullets and fire can force the faithful and zealous people of Iraq to surrender and be brought to their knees. It is precisely this wrong understanding and imperial outlook that will, God willing, bring this invading, plundering and oppressive regime to ruin and destruction in the not-too-distant future.[1]

On the same day, ex-president and powerbroker Rafsanjani told a visiting member of the Iraqi Governing Council that 'the elimination of Saddam was a historical opportunity for the region' and added: 'If a popular government demanded by a majority of Iraqis is not formed, the future of Iraq and the region will be jeopardized in an irreparable way.' He said the 'only way to save Iraq' would be to 'hold free elections and draw up a constitution based on the vote of the people'. Otherwise, Rafsanjani warned, 'Neither the Americans nor any other foreign country would be able to manage Iraq.'[2]

The Iranian ayatollahs' advocacy of free elections and popular government in Iraq might have been seen as a noble goal, if their extensive meddling in Iraq's internal affairs were not known and if they would not so vehemently oppose the same prescription being applied in their own country. When the mullahs in Tehran repeatedly turn down calls for free elections and a referendum to determine the future of the Islamic

Republic, their championing the cause of grassroots democracy in neighbouring Iraq is seen as hypocrisy. Within the cloisters of power in Tehran, the mullahs talk of Iraq as a 'ripe' apple that will ultimately fall in their lap, be it through a creeping coup or a violent showdown.

With the spectre of Iraq sinking deeper into crisis, with most authoritative experts now agreeing that the Iranian nuclear programme could reach the point of no return in the near future, with the clerical regime increasingly turning to the export of terrorism and fundamentalism to shore up its power at home and abroad, and with domestic unrest in Iran on the rise, Western governments face a tough challenge in shaping their policy towards Iran. The old policy of business as usual with Iran in the name of 'supporting the moderates within the regime' is discredited and ineffective. Appeasement has clearly worked to the advantage of the most brutal and violent factions of the theocratic state. But is there a viable alternative to the policy of engagement?

There is. It is clear, even from the Iranian government's own opinion polls, that a large portion of the Iranian people believe that real change will be brought about only when the mullahs' regime is removed from power. The international community, and the West in particular, must support any mechanism that would allow the voice of this overwhelming majority to be heard and heeded.

There is growing support inside and outside Iran for the call by Mrs Maryam Rajavi, President-elect of the Iranian Resistance, for a national referendum, under United Nations supervision, to determine the future of the current regime. She called such a referendum 'a question of destiny for all sectors of Iranian society and people from all classes and groupings. This referendum would solve the issues that have arisen as a result of mullahs' illegitimate rule and offer a final recourse to peacefully change the regime of religious tyranny.'[3]

The Iranian Resistance has pledged that it would accept the result of such a plebiscite unquestioningly. Iranians of all political persuasion are rallying around the referendum call to seek a peaceful regime change, if that were to prove possible. Governments around the world must back the Iranian people's demand and put pressure on the Iranian regime to accept such a referendum. If the clerical rulers of Iran continue to thumb their nose at the world and reject calls to give the Iranian people a real chance to express their wishes, they will not only demonstrate the complete illegitimacy of their rule, but will also reveal the hypocrisy of their call for democracy in Iraq. The civilized world has every interest to give this option a chance.

Notes

1. Islamic Republic News Agency (IRNA), 'The Supreme Leader's Message on the Massacre of Muslims in Samarra', 2 December 2003.

2. Islamic Republic News Agency (IRNA), Ayatollah Hashemi Rafsanjani's meeting with Ahmad Chalabi of the Iraqi Governing Council, 2 December 2003.

3. Message of Maryam Rajavi on a referendum for regime change in Iran, statement issued by the Secretariat of the National Council of Resistance of Iran, 17 October 2003.

Index

253; psychological warfare against, 177–8, 185, 187, 193–208, 252; refrains from punishing hostile agents, 245; refusal of execution for infiltrators, 249; rejection of Khomeini's constitution, 53; resettlement of former Resistance activists, 249; Simay-e Moghavemat TV programme, 172; terrorist attacks against, 83, 123, 255; US opinion mobilized against, 129; US State Department report on, 54–5; US view of, 137–8; view of Islam, 70–1; Washington office shut down, 145 see also weapons of mass destruction, allegedly stored by PMOI

Perkins, David, 144

personality cult accusation against People's Mojahedin, 223–40

Peshawar, 15–16

Peyvand Association, 201

Peyvand journal, 214, 215, 219–20

Peyvand society, 212–13

Pinkerton, Allen, 247

Pipes, Daniel, 5, 17, 88

pluralism, 45, 75–6

Poland, James M., 96

polygamy, prohibition of, 268

Pompidou, Georges, 49

Pour-Eshraq, Massoumeh, killing of, 136

Powell, Colin, 106, 134, 143; letter from Mohammad Mohaddessin, 131–2

Priest, Donna, 149

prisoners of war: release of, 250–1; treatment of, 246

psychological warfare against PMOI see People's Mojahedin, psychological warfare against

Al-Qaeda, 24, 106, 144, 161; alleged connections to PMOI, 129

Qaleh, Saeed Shah, 245

Qannadi, Mohammad, 40

Qashqavi, Ali, 218, 220, 244

Qassemlou, Abdol Rahman, 178

Qobbeh, Morteza, 186

Qods Force, 128, 153, 155, 215, 272

Qom, 162

Quran, 12–13, 46, 62–77 passim, 151;

Sura 3: Al-e Imran, 64; verses declared outdated, 65

Rabii, Ali, 194

Rafiqdust, Hajj Mohsen, 34, 114

Rafsanjani, Ali-Akbar Hashemi, 26, 47, 49, 110, 113, 118–19, 121, 128, 137, 146, 152, 153, 157, 194, 195, 254, 272

Rajabi, Zahra, killing of, 98, 204

Rajavi, Ashraf, killing of, 236

Rajavi, Kazem, killing of, 48, 98, 236

Rajavi, Maryam, 73–4, 81–2, 84, 164, 166, 173, 218, 226, 235, 236, 239, 254, 264–5, 265–7, 268, 273; imprisoned in France, 164, 220, 230

Rajavi, Massoud, 45–6, 47, 48, 50, 54, 55, 69–70, 76, 81, 83, 93, 95, 111, 115, 130, 178, 179, 181, 191, 218, 223, 226, 232, 235, 236, 246, 250, 260, 264; courses in philosophy, 236; expulsion from France, 113–14; goes to Iraq, 114–15; imprisonment of, 48; Khomeini fatwa against, 226, 228, 236; no executive responsibilities in PMOI, 236; released from prison, 51; speech on relations with Iraq, 17, 170; visit to Paris, 52

Rajavi, Moiré, 236

Rajavi, Mostafa, 236

Ramandeh nuclear site, 37–8

Ramazan Garrison, 158

rape, 73

Rashed, Abu Ahmad, 154, 160

Rastgoo, Ali Akbar (Bahman), 189, 212, 213, 215, 216

Ratzinger, Cardinal Joseph, 85

Ray, June, 250

Reagan, Ronald, 115

referendum, calls for, 271, 273

reign of terror, 59

religious totalitarianism, 71–3

Revolutionary Guards, 21–2, 28, 37, 41, 54, 55, 58, 59, 88, 89, 109, 110, 114, 118, 121, 128, 136, 152, 154, 155, 157, 158, 160, 171, 174, 193, 215, 221, 243, 246, 250, 272; attacks on NLA in Iraq, 153; attacks on PMOI, 122, 167, 255

Rezaii, Mohsen, 119, 133–4

Rezapour, Haji, 220, 244

Rhodes, Kelton, 225

Rice, Condoleezza, 134, 161